disabled child, his comments are also filled with fatherly care. I have no doubt that his thoughts will minister to many who wrestle with loved ones with mental illness, reminding them that absolutely no one is beyond the reach of our sovereign God."
—**Peter Y. Lee**, Associate Professor of Old Testament, Reformed Theological Seminary, Washington DC

"*It Has Not Yet Appeared What We Shall Be* is a powerful study of the image of God and also of the practical impact that our beliefs hold for our treatment of those who are mentally broken. This carefully researched and well-written book will move, disturb, challenge and bless readers. I am privileged to know George and Donna Hammond, to have met Rebecca, and now to have read this book. I commend the study of these pages to professors, pastors, and students, and urge the consideration of its argument upon those engaged in the care of the cognitively disabled."
—**Chad Van Dixhoorn**, Chancellor's Professor of Historical Theology, Reformed Theological Seminary, Washington DC

AF074496

It Has Not Yet Appeared What We Shall Be

Reformed Academic Dissertations

A Series

Series Editor

John J. Hughes

"Parents of children with severe disabilities face a sobering truth: I will not be able to 'fix' my child, and, in all likelihood, I will not see him or her 'grow up,' marry, and have a life of his or her own. It is common, sadly, for such a despairing situation to yield wreckage. But out of just such a burden, Dr. Hammond has given us a vital window into the heart of God for the broken, and wisdom for the ongoing question of what it means to be made *imago Dei*. Dr. Hammond's work is a gift born out of much affliction of soul and mind. I for one am grateful for it. In an age when the secular discussion of 'personhood' runs parallel to the theological discussion of *imago Dei*, Dr. Hammond gives us a careful, clear, and theologically detailed treatment of this vital doctrine for our day. May God use this resource to help the church respond in a manner that honors God and His image present in all people, no matter how disabled they might be."
—**Michael S. Beates**, Dean of Students, The Geneva School, Winter Park, Florida

"Are severely challenged people nevertheless made in the image of God, or has their disability barred them from this unique class? After reading this study, you will have no doubts. The *imago* does not depend on being healthy, agile, brilliant or without limitations, but on God's kind act of creation. This book is a gem, for it defends the traditional view of who we are in the face of the relevant theological and scientific issues. Dr. Hammond's presentation of the disabled child is heartbreaking, at first, but then deeply heart re-making. Parents, but also church leaders, as well as the average person should find much encouragement in this study. It is unique, powerful, biblically sound, and practical. I am not aware of anything quite like it."
—**William Edgar**, Professor of Apologetics, Westminster Theological Seminary

"I read this new book with great interest since I myself have a niece who has severe cognitive disabilities. This book has risen out of the crucible of personal experience and serious, sustained engagement

with the biblical text and secondary literature. Hammond challenges many commonly held *shibboleths* about the *Imago Dei*. Although I may not be persuaded by all of the book's formulations, this is a book that deserves a careful read and will be of great benefit to our thinking about the *Imago Dei* and also to families and churches who seek to love and care for those with severe cognitive disabilities."
—**Bryan D. Estelle,** Professor of Old Testament, Westminster Seminary California

"Are those with severe cognitive disabilities God's image bearers? Prompted by the author's own deeply personal quest, the historical and theological reflection he provides, solidly grounded in Scripture, shows convincingly that the image of God does not reside in any one or more capacities or functions that mark human beings but is simply (and profoundly) what *all* human beings *are* and so are to be valued as such. Addressed as well are the important and practical implications this conclusion carries including how the church is to deal with the cognitively disabled in its midst so that they are not neglected but cherished and cared for appropriately—all the more important at a time when 'quality of life' and value ethics views are increasingly undermining Scripture's understanding of what a human person is."
—**Richard B. Gaffin Jr.**, Professor of Biblical and Systematic Theology, Emeritus, Westminster Theological Seminary

"The doctrine of the *imago Dei* has suffered inattention and often misrepresentation by the church. Such negligence has caused many to misunderstand the fundamental nature of humanity, that being image bearers of God. Nowhere is this better illustrated than with the mentally disabled, who historically have been viewed as not bearing that divine image. Nothing could be further from the truth. In his book, *It Has Not Yet Appeared What We Shall Be*, not only does Dr. Hammond articulate the biblical truth of the *imago Dei* with biblical and theological acumen, he also writes with pastoral sensitivity and wisdom. As he has personal experience with a mentally

It Has Not Yet Appeared What We Shall Be

*A Reconsideration of the Imago Dei
in Light of Those with Severe
Cognitive Disabilities*

George C. Hammond

P U B L I S H I N G
P.O. BOX 817 • PHILLIPSBURG • NEW JERSEY 08865-0817

© 2017 by George C. Hammond

All rights reserved. No part of this book may be reproduced, stored in a retrieval system, or transmitted in any form or by any means—electronic, mechanical, photocopy, recording, or otherwise—except for brief quotations for the purpose of review or comment, without the prior permission of the publisher, P&R Publishing Company, P.O. Box 817, Phillipsburg, New Jersey 08865–0817.

It Has Not Yet Appeared What We Shall Be: A Reconsideration of the Imago Dei *in Light of Those with Severe Cognitive Disabilities*. George C. Hammond, M.Div., D.Min. Submitted to Gordon-Conwell Theological Seminary, South Hamilton, MA, 2014, for the D.Min. degree. Supervisor: David Curry.

Printed in the United States of America

ISBN 978-1-62995-313-7 (pbk)
ISBN 978-1-62995-314-4 (ePub)
ISBN 978-1-62995-315-1 (Mobi)

For my daughter Rebecca who has taught me about
what it means to be made as the image of God, and for my wife
Donna who has so often been her interpreter to me.

Contents

Series Introduction   ix

Foreword by Peter A. Lillback   xi

Preface   xvii

Acknowledgments   xix

Introduction   xxi

Abbreviations   xxiii

Prologue   xxv

1. The Problem and Its Setting   1
   Introduction
   The Imago Dei: A Brief Historical Overview
   *Societal and Ecclesiastical Acceptance of Those with Disabilities:
       A Historical Overview*
   *The Disability Rights Movement: The Divide Between Physical
       and Cognitive*
   The Church's More Recent Response to Those with Disabilities
   Resource Allocation, "Persons," and Hierarchy of Value
   The Contours of This Study
   Justification for a Reconsideration of the Doctrine of the Imago Dei

2. Literature Review   49
   A Survey of Modern Approaches to the Imago Dei
   A Survey of the Theology of Disabilities Literature

Contents

A Brief Consideration of the Historical Adam Debate and Its Consequences
Conclusions

3. Exegesis of Pertinent Passages   133
   Old Testament
   Bridge Texts: Genesis 9:6 and James 3:9
   New Testament
   Conclusion

4. A Reconsideration of the *Imago Dei*   162
   The Imago Dei in Creation
   The Imago Dei in the Fall
   The Imago Dei in Redemption
   Cognitive Disability and the Imago Dei: Can it be Restored ad Imago Christi?
   Sola Gratia

5. Implications and Practical Applications   213
   A Word to Seminary Professors
   A Word to Pastors
   A Word to Parishes

Epilogue   231

Appendix 1: Survey   233

Appendix 2: Raw Data   235

Appendix 3: Survey Analysis   240

Appendix 4: Herman Bavinck's *Reformed Dogmatics*   265

Bibliography   272

Index of Scripture   287

Index of Subjects and Names   293

Series Introduction

P&R Publishing has a long and distinguished history of publishing carefully selected, high-value theological books in the Reformed tradition. Many theological books begin as dissertations, but many dissertations are worthy of publication in their own right. Realizing this, P&R has launched the Reformed Academic Dissertation (RAD) program to publish top-tier dissertations (Ph.D., Th.D., D.Min., and Th.M.) that advance biblical and theological scholarship by making distinctive contributions in the areas of theology, ethics, biblical studies, apologetics, and counseling.

Dissertations in the RAD series are *curated*, which means that they are carefully selected, on the basis of strong recommendations by the authors' supervisors and examiners and by our internal readers, to be part of our collection. Each selected dissertation will provide clear, fresh, and engaging insights about significant theological issues.

A number of theological institutions have partnered with us to recommend dissertations that they believe worthy of publication in the RAD series. Not only does this provide increased visibility for participating institutions, it also makes outstanding dissertations available to a broad range of readers, while helping to introduce promising authors to the publishing world.

We look forward to seeing the RAD program grow into a large collection of curated dissertations that will help to advance Reformed scholarship and learning.

John J. Hughes
Series Editor

Foreword

Human assessments of the dignity of human life range from views reflecting moral darkness to perspectives that sparkle with compassion. The Nazis devised the deadly dictum of "life unworthy of life," leading to their heinous death camps. More recently, Peter Singer, having rejected the Judeo-Christian "myth" of man's origin and fall in Genesis, has argued that animal life can have greater dignity than human life, for example in the case of the severely impaired. Even the great Reformer, Martin Luther, once shockingly described a profoundly handicapped person as "a mass of flesh without a soul," and suggested that the disabled yet ravenous being should be strangled rather than fed. The eugenics movement, sometimes even supported by the church, continues to challenge the classic Judeo-Christian view of the image of God and the value of all human life.

The classic Judeo-Christian evaluation of man, however, is found in the creation account in Genesis 1:26–27 that teaches that man is made in the image of God. Although humankind is fallen and broken (Genesis 3), the Scriptures portray man as still possessing in some measure the image and likeness of God (Genesis 9:6; James 3:9). Experientially, we have learned from others such as Joni Eareckson Tada, the modern Disability Rights movement and l'Arche that there is beauty and dignity in those who are severely disabled. Moreover, did not Jesus teach that when his disciples cared for "the least" of Christ's brethren, by clothing, feeding visiting and serving them, that they were doing the same for Him?

While we are grateful for the beauty that emanates from handicapped individuals such as Joni Eareckson Tada, does not an emphasis on a hierarchy of ability in the midst of disability eventually exclude the significance of those who are so severely disabled that they will never speak, never consciously communicate or create and never relate interpersonally? How do we explain the theological significance of those who have severe cognitive disabilities? Do the severely disabled and especially those with severe cognitive disabilities reflect the lofty biblical anthropology that man is made in the image of God? For example, Augustine's fascinating Trinitarian understanding of the *imago Dei* in terms of intellect, memory and will can clearly apply to many handicapped people; but not to those with severe cognitive disabilities.

The Rev. Dr. George Hammond, a Presbyterian pastor and an alumnus of Westminster Seminary, Philadelphia, has sought to engage these questions. His study begins with a deeply moving account of his fatherly love for his daughter. Rebecca, his fourth child, was born with severe cognitive disabilities. Her very existence created a stunning theological crisis, compelling him to wrestle with the traditional understandings of what it means to be made in the image of God. From his heart-rending questioning, his research was born. His scholarly investigation pulses with a passionate quest to address the possibility that his beloved yet helpless child was perhaps only an image bearer of God by "exception".

"It Has Not Yet Appeared What We Shall Be": A Reconsideration of the Imago Dei in Light of Those with Severe Cognitive Disabilities is the result of his scholarly labors. This well written and sanctifying D. Min. project was completed at Gordon-Conwell Seminary. Herein, Hammond offers a valuable survey of the historical views concerning the image of God including the Patristic Period, the Medieval Period, the Reformation Period and the Nineteenth and Twentieth Centuries. He also supplies a survey of recent literature touching on this question. He summarizes the categories held by theologians concerning the image of God by the following positions:

- The identification of the *imago Dei* is identified as some *constituent* or component part of man.
- If this is understood *substantively*, it is likely interpreted as the soul or the intellect of man.
- If it is taken *formally*, it is generally seen as the human body and the human's upright posture.
- If the *imago Dei* is taken *functionally*, it is usually identified as mankind's rule or dominion over the creation.
- More recently, the view of Barth is that the *imago* is to be understood in an I-Thou *relationship* between God and man. In this, Barth has rejected the traditional substantive and functional views. An analogy of relationship is seen in the relationships between man and man as well as between male and female. Thus for Barth's understanding of the *imago Dei*, the analogy of being between God and man in the *imago* is replaced by the analogy of relationship.
- Is there an eschatological element to the *imago Dei*? If so, perhaps the image points into the future to what mankind will become when all of God's purposes are finally fulfilled in redemptive history. The eschatological significance of the image means that there is a forward look to the once coming person and work of Christ and now to the hope established by His resurrection and the consummation of that hope in the final resurrection.

The historian and the systematic theologian will benefit by the succinct summary of the views of the *imago Dei* provided in this study. The exegete will also find suggestive and helpful analyses of such passages as Genesis 1:26–27; 3:1–5; 1 Corinthians 15:45–49; Colossians 3:9–10; 2 Peter 1:4. Hammond's research also provides sources for understanding contemporary compassion ministries and relevant literature and resources. His extensive survey of current American pastoral views regarding the *imago Dei* demonstrates how the various understandings of the *imago* have impacted contemporary

Christian ecclesiastical traditions. His study is also eminently practical in regard to the church's role in caring for the severely disabled, providing substantial insights for both pastors and professors.

While the Scriptures teach that man is made "in the image of God", Hammond argues that they do not insist that the image of God is "in" man. Rather, Hammond argues that the Hebrew can well be translated that man was created "*as* the image of God". His conclusion is that the image of God is not substantive (something humans possess such as intellect or posture), or functional (dominion), or relational (conscious interpersonal interaction), or even ultimately telic or eschatological (the final glorification of the believer in Christ). While such things may well and do distinguish humans from animals or angels, and can be seen as part of the multi-perspectival understanding of the *imago Dei*, they are not its precise expression. Rather, he asserts that the *imago Dei* is "what God created human beings to be. Because man-the-image-of-God is predicated upon the creative purpose and action of God, human beings, regardless of how broken in body or soul, cannot be anything other than *imago Dei*." He explains, "Connecting all the data points in Scripture, we conclude that from the moment of conception human beings are constituted as 'living souls' and are thus *imago Dei*. Whatever distortions of body or soul take place in their development *in utero* or *ex utero*, they are still the image of God. Because of sin in the world, all people bear distortions, some more notable and visible than others; but all are no less the image of God despite the distortions. *Imago Dei* is simply what man *qua* man is constituted."

I gratefully and highly recommend Dr. Hammond's work. It is a rare gem of pastoral and theological scholarship. Its facets unite the pathos of a father, the ethos of a long-term care giver and the logos of a pastoral theologian. His persuasive study sparkles with insight as it deepens our understanding of a precious doctrine and how it can and should be more fully understood and more deeply applied.

As a result, Rebecca has proved to be an exception after all. Not in regard to the *imago Dei*, but in regard to how her precious yet

Foreword

fragile life has blessed the church through her father's penetrating investigation and her mother's and family's loving care. Hammond's *Reconsideration* provides a fuller understanding of who all of us humans are now *as* the image of God as well as "what we shall be" when Christ, the true and ultimate image of God, appears.

Dr. Peter A. Lillback
President, Westminster Theological Seminary
Philadelphia

Preface

This book encompasses much of the work of my doctoral thesis for Gordon-Conwell Theological Seminary with minor changes. The third chapter of the original thesis containing a study I conducted to better understand the thinking of modern Protestant clergy in the U.S. regarding the doctrine of the image of God has been relocated to the appendix for those to whom the data collected and collated may be of interest.

The other major change has been the addition of an appendix dedicated to a treatment of Herman Bavinck's discussion of the image of God in his *Reformed Dogmatics*. Bavinck's work is important and deserves to be treated. However, in this book I deal specifically with modern systematic theologians starting with Barth, and as Bavinck predates Barth by a few years, he was omitted. I was persuaded by Dr. Chad Van Dixhoorn that Bavinck's work with respect to the question under consideration needed to be analyzed, and I have done so in Appendix 4.

To write about the doctrine of image of God necessarily requires referring to human beings, but in the post-modern world questions of how to do so can be vexing. According to Merriam Webster's Collegiate Dictionary Tenth Edition, the primary meaning of the word "man" is "an individual human." For centuries the English word "man" has been understood to have at least two meanings. While it could be used to refer to the male member of the human species, it has often been used to indicate an individual human being of either gender. In recent years, sensitivity has developed toward language that is suspected of being gender exclusive.

Preface

The word "man" has thus come to be viewed with misgivings, despite its lexical meaning.

This work endeavors to employ the inclusive nouns "humanity," "humankind," and "people" when possible. However, to say "humanity is made in the image of God" may convey that only the human race collectively, and not individuals, is made in the image of God. The inclusivity of nouns such as "humanity" and "humankind" is found in their collective nature, but it is precisely their collective nature which connotes that what is in view are human beings jointly, rather than human beings severally. The word "man" is often employed in this book as being the most accurate expression of the thought being conveyed, or for stylistic reasons. The reader should understand that unless the clause is gender conditioned, "man" as it is used here is employed in its lexical sense of "an individual human" without respect to gender.

Acknowledgments

This book and the reconsideration is presents would not have possible without my daughter Rebecca. Her presence in my life has brought me great, though not easily come by, joy. Because of her I have come to learn more deeply and lean more greatly upon the grace of God. She has opened my eyes to an aspect of the world I was ignorant of, and forced me to re-examine what it means for human beings to be made in the image of God.

It would be impossible to express too much gratitude to my wife Donna. Because of the difficulties that attend Rebecca's care, I had given up the hope of pursuing any further formal education or writing. Her insistence that I do both was undergirded by her taking up more than her share in caring for Rebecca and our other children to make time for me for this work. She epitomizes the word *ezer*, and the woman described in Proverbs 31:10–31.

Introduction

The doctrine of the image of God in its dominant contours throughout history has been criticized for being technically exclusive of persons with severe cognitive disabilities. Modern disability theologians have dealt with this by normalizing disability, seeing disability as a "good" of creation and discounting the disastrous effects of the fall on all faculties of body and soul.

This book reconsiders the doctrine of the image of God in light of those with severe cognitive disabilities. The study critically examines the literature ancient to modern dealing with the *imago* doctrine. It evaluates the attitudes of society and of the church with respect to those with cognitive disabilities in light of the *imago* doctrine. It interacts with modern disability theologians and examines their assumptions in the light of the Scripture. An exegetical analysis of pertinent texts serves as the basis to recast previous theological insights and to establish a more accurate and inclusive *imago* theology.

Abbreviations

ALGNT	Friberg, *Analytical Lexicon of the Greek New Testament*
BDAG	Bauer, Danker, Arndt, and Gingrich, *Greek English Lexicon of the New Testament and Other Early Christian Literature*
BDB	Brown, Driver, Briggs, *Hebrew and English Lexicon*
CHALOT	Holladay, *Concise Hebrew-Aramaic Lexicon of the Old Testament*
ESV	English Standard Version Bible
HALOT	Koehler and Baumgartner, *Hebrew Aramaic Lexicon of the Old Testament*
KJV	King James Version of the Bible
LSJ	Liddell and Scott, *Greek English Lexicon*
LXX	Septuagint (from BibleWorks 9)
NASB	New American Standard Bible
NIV	New International Version Bible, 1984 (unless otherwise noted)
RSV	Revised Standard Version Bible
TDOT	*Theological Dictionary of the Old Testament*
TGELNT	Thayer, *Greek-English Lexicon of the New Testament*
TWOT	*Theological Wordbook of the Old Testament*
VUL	Latin Vulgate
WCF	Westminster Confession of Faith
WLC	Westminster Larger Catechism
WSC	Westminster Shorter Catechism

Prologue

"Come here, Rebecca."

She was oblivious to my voice. She was busily engaged in rocking back and forth, making a monotonous droning sound. In her right hand was a Little People's truck which she held by one of the wheels and which she was incessantly spinning. She looked intently at the rows of books on the shelves. Not the titles, just the fact that they stood in orderly rows.

"Come here, Rebecca."

She continued to ignore me, lost in her own world. I got up and walked over to her. "What are you doing, Honey?" Her actions indicated that she was completely unaware of my presence. I reached my hand down and stroked her hair. She did not notice. She was bent on spinning the truck, rocking, making the monotonous sound, and looking at rows of books for no reason I could tell. She looked busy but not happy.

I hugged her from behind. "Honey, come over here with Daddy." She stopped for a moment and turned her face approximately toward me, but I wasn't really sure that she saw me. She seemed to look past me. She must have been aware of me, though, because she reached out her unoccupied hand and placed it on my face. I felt a rush of joy at this expression of love and intimacy. But my feelings were premature. She had reached for my face only to push it away.

It was not an unusual day.

My daughter Rebecca was born with severe cognitive disabilities. That something was wrong was manifest by the onset of seizures when she was eight months old. At four years old she was still diagnosed as having cognitive delays, but by time she was eight we realized that these were no mere delays. Rebecca would contend her whole life with her disabilities.

Sometimes Rebecca will look at me. Sometimes she will hug me. Sometimes she will even seek me out to sit by me. But not very often. And when it happens it is for a very short duration. For much of her life, Rebecca lives in her own world oblivious to my existence. The activities she busies herself with are not productive. Her undertakings are not a help; they simply cause more work.

Rebecca has no idea where her food and clothing comes from. She is helpless to do anything to care for herself; to get food or drink, to get dressed, to get washed, to use the toilet. She accepts all of these things without gratitude and without any discernible cognizance that they are provided by the love of others (most often her mother).

Meaningless, repetitive behavior. Existence in her own world without too much acknowledgment or regard for others. An expectation that she and all her needs will be taken care of without gratitude, and in fact with frequent complaining on her part.

The world calls people like Rebecca "special." I much prefer that label to "useless eater," the alternative proposed by the National Socialist Party of Germany in the 1930s and endorsed in concept today by Peter Singer who teaches ethics at Princeton University.

Rebecca is special to me, but it is not her condition that makes her special. She is broken. Utterly and profoundly broken. What makes her special to me is that she is my daughter and, dimmed and diminished by her disabilities as it may be, she is made in the image of God.

I see Rebecca's brokenness because she stands out as being unable to do for herself and others what other people can typically do. I don't see my own brokenness so easily because it's not very different from yours. We tell ourselves, perhaps even congratulate ourselves, that we are "normal."

But it occurs to me as I watch Rebecca . . .

Prologue

I wonder if God sees me very much like I see Rebecca. Meaninglessly spinning things for no apparent reason, back and forth here and there, droning on incessantly, intently observing things that don't matter. Too busy for my Father. Too occupied in my own world to acknowledge his goodness, except sporadically, assuming that all the good things that come to me in life just appear. Too intently occupied with my affairs to listen to his voice except for a moment here or there. Too absorbed in my world to listen to his call to fellowship and intimacy, and seeking his face only to push it away.

Too self-focused to understand that he longs for my healing and wholeness. And yet ...

He is patient with me in my brokenness, not rewarding me according to my ingratitude or obliviousness to him. He loves me because he's made me his son, and broken as I am, he sees in me his own image which he will restore.

That work was started and will be completed by what he did two thousand years ago. He sent his only-begotten Son to live with the consequences of my brokenness in a broken world. He was very busy while he walked among us, and yet he was never too busy for his Father, never too occupied with the world to acknowledge his Father's goodness; not employed with his own affairs, but doing the will of his Father. Finally, having been himself battered and broken on the cross, he rose from the dead for my healing, for my health, for my restoration. All while I was oblivious, ungrateful, powerless. Worse than that, while I was an enemy.

And that's where the similarity ends. I am powerless to do anything about Rebecca's condition. He is all-powerful to do something about my condition and Rebecca's as well.

1

The Problem and Its Setting

Introduction

This study was born out of a crisis of my own faith. When I was a divinity student at Westminster Theological Seminary in Philadelphia in the early 1990s I was required to take a biblical anthropology course titled *The Doctrine of Man* taught by D. Clair Davis. It was in this class that I was introduced to some of the complexities associated with the consideration of the doctrine of the Image of God. *That* mankind was created in the image of God lays on the surface of the text. *What* exactly it means for mankind to be made in the image of God has been the occasion for on-going reflection from the patristic period to the present day.

The course introduced me to the various historical approaches to and perspectives on in what exactly the *imago Dei* consists. Generally, these approaches can be summarized under three headings: 1) The *imago Dei* may be seen as something *substantive* in man, a God-like component or aspect of man (*analogia entis*) often presented as being manifested in those qualities which separate man from the animals (e.g., faculties of rationality, spirituality, self-conscious volition, morality, etc.). 2) The *imago Dei* may be seen in terms of man's *function* in the world. In this view Genesis 1:26b often is seen to be the epexegetical commentary on Genesis 1:26a. "And let them rule over the fish of the sea and the birds of the air, over the livestock, over all the earth, and over all the creatures that move along the ground" is the explanation of what it means for mankind to be made "in our image, and after our likeness." 3) The *imago Dei* may be seen in terms of *relationship*. Following Barth, many modern theologians have seen the *imago Dei* as consisting in the ability of human beings to create and maintain complex interpersonal relationships (*analogia relationis*).

Having been favorably influenced by Poythress' multi-perspectival approach to theology,[1] I saw value in all of these approaches to the doctrine and no reason to choose among them. These perspectives were complementary, not mutually exclusive.

I was ordained to the ministry in 1993. In 2001 my fourth child, Rebecca, was born. It would not be until she was about a year old that we would be told that she had severe developmental delays. When she was about five years old these were reclassified as disabilities. Over the next few years it became apparent that short of miraculous intervention on the part of God, Rebecca would never speak, never calculate a math problem, never attend college, never live on her own or exercise authority over any sphere of her life, would never marry, and would never be a friend to anyone (if being a friend is defined as consciously and sacrificially giving of one's self for the good of another).

One day while I was watching Rebecca play by herself (the only way she plays) a thought occurred to me that filled me with horror: *My daughter does not bear the image of God.* The thought was abhorrent to me; every fiber of my being told me that my conclusion must be false. But there was no denying my theological grid. If the *imago Dei* is to be found substantively in those things which separate us from the animals such as language and intellect; if it is to be found functionally in the ability to exert dominion over the environment and other creatures; or if it is to

---

[1] See Vern S. Poythress, *Symphonic Theology* (Phillipsburg, NJ: P&R Publishing, 2001).

be found relationally in creating and maintaining intricate human relationships, then it was evident that Rebecca's life did not fit these criteria.

As I began to pay closer attention to what I heard and read about the image of God, I discovered that my theological grid of exclusion was not unique. In his book *Receiving the Gift of Friendship* Hans Reinders reaches much the same conclusion: by traditional definitions those with severe cognitive disabilities are disqualified from the image of God.[2] Yet Reinders also notes that Christians who care for or come in contact with those with such disabilities are not willing to bar them from humanity, and will in fact include them either inexplicably (i.e., "Such people may not fit my definition of the image of God, nor my definition of what it means to be human, but they still are in the image of God and human") or by exception.[3]

While it is encouraging that Christians intuitively will not exclude these people from humanity, it is problematic that they include them either by making an exception for them in their theology or with no theological basis at all. One would think that the doctrine of the image of God should surely provide the basis for the inclusion of some of humanity's neediest members. In fact, however, in dealing with this doctrine theologians throughout history have frequently (though perhaps inadvertently) presented the doctrine in such a way as to exclude those with severe intellectual disabilities from participation in the *imago Dei*. Reinders notes,

> When I first began thinking about this problem [i.e., the humanity of those with cognitive disabilities], my intuitive response—as a Christian theologian—was that the Christian tradition could handle it easily because of the doctrine

---

[2] Hans S. Reinders, *Receiving the Gift of Friendship* (Grand Rapids, MI: Eerdmans, 2008), 1–4.
[3] Ibid., 19–48.

of the *imago Dei*. . . . When I started to explore this question, however, it soon became clear to me that the Christian tradition might have been one of the major sources of the commonsense view [that humanity is to be found in certain intellectual, stewardship, and relational abilities].[4]

The sacrosanct nature of human life as it is presented in the Scriptures rests upon mankind being made in the image of God. The first instance of a *lex talionis* in the Scripture prescribes the death penalty for the one who (unjustly) takes a human life. The reason given for the severity of the penalty is that mankind is made *ad imago Dei*: "Whoever sheds the blood of man, by man shall his blood be shed; for in the image of God has he made man" (Gen. 9:6).

The secularized modern world began to speak of the universality of human dignity and rights after World War II, but it did so (and continues to do so) using the unacknowledged borrowed capital of the *imago Dei* doctrine. John Behr notes that before the wide-spread acceptance of the *imago* doctrine, Greco-Roman culture had no notion of the universal rights, dignity, or worth of all human beings.[5] He questions whether a modern philosophical anthropology uncoupled from the biblical *imago* doctrine can long bear the weight of the affirmation of universal human personhood, dignity, worth, and rights. His concerns are well-founded.

Dismissing the creation account as a "Hebrew myth,"[6] Peter Singer feels free to question whether severely cognitively disabled human beings really qualify as "persons."[7] With the myth of the *imago Dei* disposed of, Singer maintains that the right to life does

---

[4] Ibid., 2.

[5] John Behr, "The Promise of the Image," in *Imago Dei Human Dignity in Ecumenical Perspective*, ed. Thomas Albert Howard (Washington, DC: The Catholic University Press, 2013), 15–37.

[6] Peter Singer, *Rethinking Life and Death* (New York: St. Martin's Press, 1994), 171.

[7] Ibid., 183, 201, 219–22.

not extend to all innocent human beings.[8] Indeed, it could be argued that if mankind is not made in the image of God, the *right* to life does not extend to *any* human being. Similarly, Steven Pinker has argued that the notion of universal human dignity is "stupid," the invocation of "obstructionist bioethics," and "hardly up to the heavyweight moral demands assigned to it."[9]

Few Christians would question whether all human beings are "persons" and universally are possessed of dignity, rights, and worth. But are all human beings created in the image of God? The reflexive answer to this question by Christians is "of course." Yet the way in which the doctrine of the *imago Dei* has been conceived and set forth throughout history may leave doubt that this is the case.

The *Imago Dei*: A Brief Historical Overview

Theology may be defined as the human echo of the divine voice. The Scriptures themselves were not given in abstraction, but rather were given in and to particular and specific historical contexts. Good hermeneutics requires the consideration of the context of a given book or passage of Scripture for sound exegesis.[10]

Theology likewise has a context. Theologians engage in the task of understanding and applying the Scriptures to their particular situation and setting. In this regard there is no "pure theology" if that phrase means theological formulation uninfluenced by the theologian's own setting. There is always a "hermeneutical spiral" between the text and the reader's context which affects, limits, and gives insights into what one concludes from a given text of Scripture.[11]

---

[8] Peter Singer, *Practical Ethics* (Cambridge: Cambridge University Press, 1980), 71–93, 123–90.

[9] Steven Pinker, "The Stupidity of Dignity," *The New Republic* (May 28, 2008): 28–31.

[10] See Louis Berkhof, *Principles of Biblical Interpretation* (Grand Rapids, MI: Baker, 1988), 60–65, 113–32.

[11] See Harvie M. Conn, *Inerrancy and Hermeneutic* (Grand Rapids, MI:

As the *imago Dei* is considered in the light of those with severe cognitive disabilities, it is important to note that until the twentieth century such people were not as visible, and perhaps not as prevalent, as they are today.[12] This is so not only because factors in the modern world may actually increase the risk of cognitive disability,[13] but also because before the advent of modern medicine many of the underlying or concomitant physical conditions of severe cognitive disability made it less likely for such people to survive childhood.

Even apart from underlying physical conditions, severe cognitive disability carries its own risk of mortality. In the wake of the Second World War, First World nations have seen a marked increase in both the number of labor saving devices and the amount of living space. Practically speaking, this means that parents of ambulatory severely cognitively disabled children are able to keep them in safer and more spacious confines, and are freed from many of the labor-intensive tasks that consumed their ancestors' time and attention. This has allowed them to be more attentive to the safety of their children than was possible in the past. The risk that cognitively disabled people can pose to themselves is seen anecdotally in the first encounter Jesus had when he came down from the mount of transfiguration: "'Lord, have mercy on my son,' he said. 'He has seizures[14]

Baker, 1988), 194*ff*; and J. Richard Middleton, *The Liberating Image* (Grand Rapids, MI: Brazos Press, 2005), 34–40.

[12] For a North American history of those with disabilities from pre-Columbian until present times, see Kim E. Neilson, *A Disability History of the United States* (Boston: Beacon Press, 2012).

[13] According to a report by the Centers for Disease Control, rates of Autism Spectrum Disorder rose from 1 in 150 in 2000 (birth year of subjects was 1992) to 1 in 88 in 2008 (birth year of subjects was 2000). It is unclear whether the increased rate is due to better diagnosis and reporting, but many believe that environmental factors have increased the actual rates. See Centers for Disease Control, "Autism Spectrum Disorders, Data and Statistics," http://www.cdc.gov/ncbddd/autism/data.html (accessed February 15, 2013).

[14] Σεληνιάζομαι; many who suffer from severe cognitive disabilities also have seizure disorders.

and is suffering greatly. He often falls into the fire or into the water'" (Matt. 17:15 NIV).

The Christian doctrine of the *imago Dei* traces its history back to the earliest Christian centuries. For much of the history of the church, theologians did not regularly encounter and thus did not much consider those with severe cognitive disabilities in their formulations of the doctrine. Not until the 1960s and the advent of the l'Arche communities did such people come to the attention of theologians in any notable way. It has only been in the last two or three decades that any thought has been given to a theology of severe cognitive disability.

What follows is a brief historical sketch of the contours of the development of the *imago Dei* doctrine. The purpose of the sketch is to set a background for this study. It is indicative, not exhaustive, delineating the ideas of the *imago Dei* that have widely shaped the doctrinal contours of the Christian community in the west.

For the purposes of this study it is important to understand, not the subtleties of well-known theologians with regard to this doctrine, but how these theologians have been understood by their interpreters, and the broad contours of the development of the *imago* doctrine. In the history of the church there have been lesser known theologians in the Renaissance period whose synthesis of an Augustinian substantivism and an Eastern telic theosis may have taken the discussion in a different direction, but the names of Ficino, Morandi, and Mirandola are not widely known, much less their theological reflections on the *imago Dei*.[15]

The Patristic Period

Although their understanding of the image of God is not monolithic, almost without exception the early church fathers expressed a substantive understanding of the doctrine of the *imago Dei*. "Sometimes the Fathers attribute the character of the 'image of

---

[15] See Middleton, 29.

God' to the Kingly office of mankind.... Sometimes the Fathers see the 'image' in the spiritual aspect of human nature, in the soul, or in the governing aspect of our nature. They have seen it in the mind, the higher powers, such as the intellect or human self-determination . . . ."[16] The patristic writers largely localized the *imago* in some component or aspect of man, focusing on those attributes which man shared in common with God and which distinguished man from the rest of the terrestrial creation. Most made a sharp distinction between "image" (*imago*) and "likeness" (*similitudo*),[17] though what attributes and characteristics they assigned to either word differed significantly.[18]

Irenaeus of Lyons (d. 200) believed that man was created in the image and likeness of God, that he retained the image of God after the fall, but that the likeness of God was lost and was being restored in the redemption of Christ. Irenaeus identified the image of God specifically with rational thought, freedom, and responsibility. He identified the likeness with sanctity which was lost in the fall.[19]

David Cotter notes that for Origen (d. 254), the "image" was given to man in his creation, but the "likeness" awaited the consummation for fulfillment, thus showing an eschatological orientation.[20] In sharp distinction from Irenaeus, Origen believed that the image was not to be found in any way in the physical frame of man: "We do not understand, however, this man whom Scripture said was made 'According to the image of God' to be corporeal. For the form of the body does not contain the image of God.... But it is the inner man,

---

[16] Christoforos Stavropoulos, *Partakers of the Divine Nature*, trans. Stanley Harakas (Minneapolis, MN: Light and Life Publishing, 1976), 25.

[17] Εἰκών and ὁμοίωσις respectively among the Eastern fathers.

[18] See David W. Cotter, *Berit Olam Studies in Hebrew Narrative & Poetry in Genesis* (Collegeville, MN: The Liturgical Press, 2003). "[Early] Christian commentators were very much taken with Genesis 1:26–27, the creation of humanity in the image and likeness of God. Customarily they distinguished between the two," 21.

[19] See Anthony A. Hoekema, *Created in God's Image* (Grand Rapids, MI: Eerdmans, 1986), 33–35.

[20] Cotter, 21.

incorporeal, incorruptible, and immortal, that is made 'According to the image of God.'"²¹

The great Cappadocian father Basil (d. 379) saw elements of the image of God functionally in man's ruling over the beasts of the field, and somatically in his upward gaze,²² but even in these aspects of the *imago* the human intellect is the primary and prominent substance. Contemplating mankind's task to exercise dominion over the animals, Basil asks, "By the body or by the mind? . . . The flesh is weaker than that of many animals. . . . But in what is the ruling principle? In the superiority of reason. What is lacking in strength of body is encompassed by the employment of reason."²³ Basil distinguishes between image and likeness in the following way: "By our creation we have the [image] and by our free choice we build the [likeness]. . . . For I have that which is according to the image in being a rational being, but I become according to the likeness in becoming a Christian."²⁴

Diadochus of Photice (d. 486) believed that "All men are made in God's image; but to be in his likeness is granted only to those who through great love have brought their own freedom into subjection to God."²⁵ Thus while the image of God is present in man by virtue of his creation, the likeness has an eschatological orientation even in the pre-fallen Adam.

---

[21] Origen, *Ancient Christian Commentary on the Scripture Genesis 1–11*, vol. 1, *Old Testament* ed. Andrew Louth (Downers Grove, IL: InterVarsity Press, 2008), 31.

[22] "God created you upright. He gave this special structure to you as distinct from the rest of the animals. . . . grazing animals are structured according to the things toward which they aim by nature. . . .[The sheep] has his head inclined downward looking at the stomach . . . since the fulfillment of the happiness of these animals is filling the stomach. But the human being['s] . . . head is lifted high toward things above, that he may look up to what is akin to him." St. Basil the Great, *On the Human Condition*, trans. Nonna Verna Harrison (Crestwood, NY: St. Vladimir's Seminary Press, 2005), 61.

[23] St. Basil the Great, 35.

[24] Ibid., 43–44.

[25] Diadochus in Louth, 30.

The Problem and Its Setting

For Gregory of Nyssa (d. 395), the "image" is what man presently is; the "likeness" is what man aspires to.[26] Here again man's full affinity to God has an eschatological orientation.

Severian of Gabala (d. *circa* 408) also saw a distinction between image and likeness. Diverging slightly from others before him, Severian saw in the image not a possession but a potential. The image of God consists in virtues that people are called to exhibit, and in exhibiting them they will show forth the image of God. Severian sees the likeness as associated specifically with man's dominion. He is thus one of the earliest theologians to propose a functional view, though of the *similitudo Dei* rather than of the *imago Dei*.[27]

Augustine of Hippo (d. 430) maintained that since God was the archetype of being, all of creation—everything that *is*—in some way reflects the nature of God. By simply being, creation participates in the nature of "*the* Being" (ὁ ὤν, Ex. 3:14 LXX). This participation is hierarchical, and so those creatures which are living bear greater resemblance to God than does the inanimate creation. Similarly, those living creatures which can perceive other living creatures are more like God than those which cannot. Pelikan notes that for Augustine too the apex of the image of God is found in reason:

> But among the creatures that perceived other creatures, those that were able to *reason* [italics added] about this perception were in a unique position in relation to the divine Origin and bore his image in a special way. Therefore "that which is rational [bears the likeness of the supreme nature] more than that which is incapable of reasoning." God has put his image into man so that he might be aware of him, ponder him, and love him. Man could not do this because of his sin, unless God "renewed and reformed" the image. And yet the rational

---

[26] Cotter, 21.

[27] Severian, *The Ancient Christian Texts Commentaries on Genesis 1–3: Severian of Gabala and Bede the Venerable*, ed. Michael Glerup (Downers Grove, IL: InterVarsity Press, 2008), 64–65.

mind continued to be created "according to the likeness" of the supreme wisdom of God. Therefore it was incumbent on any "rational creature . . . to express by its voluntary activity this image that has been impressed on it by natural power." This it did when it applied all its power to "remembering, understanding and loving the Summum Bonum."[28]

Augustine is the first theologian to suggest that the *imago Dei* should be understood in terms of *imago trinitatis*. He sees a reflection of the Trinity in the constitution of man-made-in-God's-image, and thus posits that man is made in the image of God because there is within him a trinity-like intellect, memory, and will.[29]

Brian Brock, a theologian who works with people who are cognitively disabled, has pointed out that Augustine sees a strong association between rationality and what it means in essence to be human. He notes that "Augustine *wants* to say that all human life is valuable, but his basic account of God and humanity problematizes his achieving this aim. . . . [The most] worrying implication of such an intellect-focused account of the human . . . is that it appears to allow that those without intellect are sub-human."[30]

While there are numerous differences between the patristic writers with regard to the *imago Dei*, there are three similarities: 1) The patristic writers nearly uniformly make a distinction between the "image" and the "likeness," 2) although some patristic writers highlight a functional aspect of the *imago Dei*, all the patristic writers in one way or another identify the image of God substantively,

---

[28] Jaroslav Pelikan, *The Christian Tradition: A History of the Development of Doctrine*, vol. 3, *The Growth of Medieval Theology* (Chicago: University of Chicago Press, 1978), 260.

[29] See Augustine, *The Trinity*, Books X and XIV, trans. Edmund Hill (Hyde Park, NY: New City Press, 1991), 286–303, 370–94.

[30] Brian Brock, "Augustine's Hierarchy of Human Wholeness and Their Healing," in *Disability in the Christian Tradition A Reader*, ed. Brian Brock and John Swinton (Grand Rapids, MI: Eerdmans, 2012), 71.

identifying it with something *in* man (and nearly always associated with rationality and intellect), and 3) nearly all of the patristic writers see an eschatological, unrealized, and potential telos that characterized man in his creation. This unfulfilled telos is a part of the make-up of the pre-fallen Adam; the eschatological orientation is particularly seen among the Greek fathers, a precursor to the theosis doctrine. Among them the image (εἰκών) was understood to be what man possessed statically and the likeness (ὁμοίωσις) was what he dynamically aspired to:

> This static description of the image of God in man is coupled with a dynamic description of the likeness of God in man. Man was created perfect, not in finality, but in the sense of perfect potentiality. He did not possess his end, union with God, but was rather called to it. Thus "[t]he perfection of our first nature lay above all in this capacity to ... be united more and more with the fullness of the Godhead." As a result of this unrealized capacity, we can say that "man at his first creation was innocent and capable of spiritual development." Hence, according to the Eastern church, humanity's perfection was something it was called to realize fully. The image is "a gift within man but at the same time a goal set before him, a possession but also a destiny...."[31]

The Medieval Period

Theologians throughout the medieval period largely retained the distinction between *imago* and *similitudo*. The western writers particularly put even more emphasis on man's intellect as the locus of the *imago Dei*.

Bede (d. 735) indicated that the *imago Dei* entails dominion (functional) which is possible because man excels in reason over

---

[31] Jonathan D. Jacobs, "An Eastern Orthodox Conception of Theosis and Human Nature," *Faith and Philosophy* 26 (5), (2009): 617–18.

the beasts. He states, "Put in this place of honor, if he does not understand that he should live well, he will be put on the same level as senseless creatures over which he has been placed, just as the Psalmist testified."[32]

Greatly influenced by Augustine, Bonaventure (d. 1274) emphasized man's intellect with regard to his fellowship and interaction with God, and what it means for man to be made in the image of God. He believed that by introspection it was possible for God to lead us "to the point of entering into ourselves, that is, into our minds in which the divine image shines."[33] Through one of the faculties of reason, specifically memory, it becomes evident that ". . . the soul itself is the image of God and His likeness . . . ."[34] For Bonaventure the image of God is conceived of substantively, and identified with something that is *in* man.

Anselm of Canterbury (d. 1109) also stressed the importance of the mind. Although not dealing directly with the *imago Dei* he nonetheless speaks of apprehending the divine image by the intellect. Visser and Williams note that for Anselm "The most excellent created essence, the one that is most like God, is the rational mind. For the mind is the only creature that can remember, understand, and love itself—or better still, remember, understand, and love God—and is thus 'a true image of that essence who through his memory and understanding, and love of himself constitutes an ineffable Trinity.'"[35]

From his *Summa Theologica* Thomas has been interpreted to have maintained that the image of God is virtually identified with

---

[32] Bede, *The Ancient Christian Texts Commentaries on Genesis 1–3 Severian of Gabala and Bede the Venerable*, ed. Michael Glerup (Downers Grove, IL: InterVarsity Press, 2008)129. Bede refers to Psalm 38:12 (Vulgate).

[33] Bonaventura, *The Mind's Road to God*, trans. George Boas (Indianapolis: Bobs-Merrill, 1953), 22.

[34] Ibid., 23.

[35] Sandra Visser & Thomas Williams, *Anselm* (New York: Oxford University Press, 2009), 195.

the intellect. While all people bear the image of God there is a hierarchy: "The first stage [of the image of God] is to be found in all men, the second only in the just [believers], and the third only in the blessed [saints]."[36] These stages have been widely understood to reflect a hierarchical sanctification of the intellect in which the image bearer is more or less cognizant of God, is more or less possessed of sound reason, and thus more or less reflects the divine image. With complete logical consistency (if questionable exegesis), Thomas maintains that since the *imago Dei* is located in the intellect, the image of God must be found more perfectly in angels than in men because by nature "angels are more perfectly intelligent than men."[37]

More recent writers like John Berkman[38] and Miguel Romero[39] have argued that Thomas did not exclude the *amentes* (severely cognitively disabled) from participation in the *imago Dei*. Their theses, and the arguments and evidence they put forth are intriguing and (in the case of Romero) convincing. However, the tide of Thomastic scholarship has generally seen Thomas as exalting the intellect above other considerations, and it is this understanding that has influenced the church's disposition toward the doctrine of the *imago Dei*.

The medieval theologians span a millennium and thus it would be difficult to say in any monolithic sense what they believed about the image of God. In general, however, it may be concluded that

---

[36] *Summa Theologica I.93.12* quoted in Hoekema, 36.

[37] Ibid.

[38] John Berkman, "Are Persons with Profound Intellectual Disabilities Sacramental Icons of Heavenly Life? Aquinas on Impairment," *Studies in Christian Ethics* 26 (1) (2013): 83–96. Berkman's discussion is helpful in providing a balance to Hans Reinder's conclusion that since severely cognitively disabled people cannot reach a telos of intellect in this life, Thomas excludes them from consideration. Berkman points out that for Thomas, the telos is in the resurrection. Reinders' understanding of Thomas is, however, the common one.

[39] Miguel J. Romero, "St. Thomas Aquinas on Disability and Profound Cognitive Impairment" (Th.D. diss., Duke University, 2012).

they maintained a substantive view of the *imago Dei*, identifying it with some component found within man. During this period there is an even greater emphasis on the intellect of man as the specific locus of the *imago Dei*.

The Reformation Period

The Protestant Reformation of the fifteenth and sixteenth centuries was originally rooted in practical and ethical matters. As the movement progressed, however, an unbridgeable chasm opened between Rome and the Reformers around the doctrine of justification and how people are made acceptable to God. This inevitably led to a reconsideration of the doctrine of the *imago Dei*.

Luther himself rejected the notion that the *imago* was to be identified solely with the intellect. Taking issue with the patristic version of the substantive view of the image of God, he nonetheless replaced it with an ethical substantive view, i.e., the image of God existed in original righteousness.[40] He pointed out that if the *imago Dei* was to be located in the intellect then Satan was more the image of God than any man.[41] Although Luther says that the image of God was lost in the fall, it is clear that he did not thereby mean that the image was completely obliterated.[42] Although not prominent in his theology, Luther maintained that the *imago Dei* has a telic and eschatological orientation. Even in the unfallen Adam, the *imago Dei* was a potential that was not yet fully realized.[43]

Luther's rejection of the intellect as the *imago Dei* seems to have been a polemic against the schoolmen, the intelligentsia of the day. It clearly was not a rejection of the patristic and medieval idea

---

[40] Martin Luther, *A Critical and Devotional Commentary on Genesis*, trans. John Nicholas Lenker (Minneapolis, MN: Lutherans in All Lands, 1904), 115–24.

[41] Ibid., 115. Luther seems to thus have profoundly disagreed with Thomas Aquinas that the angels were created *ad imago Dei*.

[42] Ibid.

[43] Ibid., 120.

that the intellect was necessary to the *imago*. In discussing severe birth defects with his table fellows, his disciple Dietrich recorded, "When someone asked him whether monstrosities of this kind ought to be baptized, he replied, 'No, because I hold that they are only animal life.'"[44]

Eight years later in a discussion in the same setting, the topic came up of a boy whose described symptoms may indicate a severe form of Prader-Willi syndrome: "In Dessau there was a twelve-year-old boy like this: he devoured as much as four farmers did, and did nothing else than eat and excrete. Luther suggested that he be suffocated. Somebody asked, "for what reason?" He [Luther] replied, 'Because I think he is simply a mass of flesh without a soul.'"[45]

Although Calvin maintained that the image of God was displayed in some ways in the body of man, it was to be primarily identified with the soul,[46] and the human soul was identified specifically with rational faculties. Thus the image of God was expressed by "... full possession of right understanding, when he had his affections kept within the bounds of reason ...."[47] This image was deformed in the fall, but Calvin believed that the *imago* had not been lost.[48] *Contra* the patristic and medieval writers, Calvin saw the *imago* and the *similitudo* as synonymous.[49] For Calvin, the *imago Dei*, damaged by the fall, was being restored in Christ progressively. Although its full restoration awaited an eschatological *telos*,[50] Calvin's clear focus

---

[44] "Table Talk," LW 54:44–45 (1532) reprinted in Stefan Heuser, "Luther and Disability," in Brock and Swinton, 211.

[45] "Table Talk," LW 54:396–97 (1540) reprinted in Heuser, in Ibid., 214.

[46] John Calvin, *Institutes of the Christian Religion*, trans. Ford Lewis Battles, ed. John T. McNeill (Philadelphia: Westminster Press, 1960), 1:15.3.

[47] Ibid., 1:15.3.

[48] Ibid., 1:15.4.

[49] Ibid., 3:7.6.; John Calvin, *Commentary on Genesis 1–31*, vol. 1 (Grand Rapids, MI: Christian Classics Ethereal Library, 2005), http://www.ccel.org/ccel/calvin/calcom01.vii.i.html (accessed February 16, 2013).

[50] See Hoekema, 46–48.

was on the *imago* as a present possession. For Calvin also, the image was conceived of substantively. He, like Luther, saw the image of God as something *in* man.

Unlike Luther, Calvin did not address disability in any direct way. Deborah Creamer points out, "Calvin tends to discuss issues of impairment . . . in ways that relate to all people (e.g., that none of us can clearly see or understand God's grace). . . . He rarely talks about disability in and of itself, making it seem that he had little interest in disability either as a concept or as an experience."[51] In this regard, Calvin is not different from theologians prior to or contemporary with him. As theology is an intellectual endeavor, done with a view to engaging other intellects, there is usually little impetus for theologians to consider lack of intellect.

Ulrich Zwingli took a novel approach to the doctrine of the *imago Dei*. He saw the image of God in man in terms of a desire for justice. This image, distorted by the fall, is restored in Christ and seen in those who strive to live innocent and good lives.

> Some refer to [the image as] dominion over the creatures, that humans should preside over all, just as God does; others connect it to the mind. But I think this image and likeness is what we call the law (*ius*) of nature: "What you would have done to you, do to others!" This image is inscribed and impressed on our hearts. . . . Those who attend to justice, who seek God, who imitate God and Christ in innocence of life toward all as well as doing good to them in turn—these are the ones in the final analysis, who bear that ancient image of God, which has been cleansed and restored by Christ.[52]

---

[51] Deborah Beth Creamer, "John Calvin and Disability," in Brock and Swinton, 219.

[52] Ulrich Zwingli, *Reformation Commentary on the Scriptures of the Old Testament*, vol. 1, *Genesis 1–11*, ed. John L. Thompson (Downers Grove, IL: InterVarsity Press, 2012), 44.

Zwingli's approach to the doctrine is notable for giving no consideration (and perhaps no credence) to the image of God in terms of a telos. For him, the *imago Dei* is something that was bestowed in man's creation, damaged in the fall, and restored presently in Christ.

Departing from Luther, the Lutheran theologian David Chytraeus' (d. 1600) expression of the doctrine more closely approached the Reformed doctrine:

> So while human beings ought to be a polished mirror and the express image of God, through the fall of our first parents we've become the devil's fright mask. And yet just as a mirror spattered with mud still renders some image, however obscure, so too in us do some marks of the traces of God remain even after the fall, and these are gradually given luster in this life by the Son of God, until the entire image of God is restored.[53]

As in the patristic and medieval periods, in the Reformation there was a divergence of opinion as to what the *imago Dei* consisted in. However, there was a certain commonality of trajectory: 1) there was wide agreement that the image and the likeness were synonyms and did not have two separate referents. 2) Although the reformers were beginning to broaden their consideration of what exactly the *imago* is, there was a residual tendency to locate the *imago Dei* substantively in the intellect. The doctrine of the *imago Dei* in this period is best understood in terms of a substantive view, viz. the image is something that is *in* man. 3) Among many of the Reformers there was an emphasis on the telic and eschatological orientation of the *imago Dei*. This seems to have been overshadowed, though, by the focus on the *imago Dei* as a present possession of even fallen man (Luther being the exception).

---

[53] David Chytraeus, *Reformation Commentary on the Scriptures of the Old Testament*, vol. 1, *Genesis 1–11*, ed. John L. Thompson)Downers Grove, IL: InterVarsity Press, 2012), 51.

The Nineteenth and Twentieth Centuries

Old Princeton Seminary was the bastion of rigorous Protestant orthodox scholarship through the nineteen and early twentieth centuries. Her theologians thus represent a good pulse for the Protestant understanding of the *imago Dei* of that time.

From 1851 until his death in 1878, Charles Hodge was principal of Princeton Seminary. Though Hodge taught many disciplines at Princeton, he is best remembered as a systematic theologian. In his three-volume *Systematic Theology* Hodge discusses the image of God, summing up the discussion in this way: "[Man] is the image of God, and bears and reflects the divine likeness among the inhabitants of the earth, because he is a spirit, an intelligent, voluntary agent . . . ."[54] Hodge expresses a modified substantive view of the *imago Dei*, clearly identifying it in some way with intellect.

James Orr served as professor of theology and apologetics at Free Church College (now Trinity College) in Glasgow from 1900 until his death in 1913. In 1905 he published the book *God's Image in Man*, a compilation of addresses given for the Stone lecture series at Princeton Seminary in September and October 1903. In taking up the question of what exactly constitutes the image of God in man, Orr says, "The image of God . . . is a mental and moral image. It is to be sought for in the fact that man is a person—a spiritual, self-conscious being; and in the attributes of that personality—his rationality and capacity for moral life . . . ."[55] Orr proceeds to identify the image with rationality, specifically the rationality that separates man from the "lower animals." "It is the ground of man's capacity for rising to general truths, and of framing such higher ideas as infinity, eternity, God, duty, religion. This power, almost every psychologist will acknowledge, the animals do not possess. It

---

[54] Charles Hodge, *Systematic Theology*, vol. 2 (Grand Rapids, MI: Eerdmans, reprinted 1982), 99.

[55] James Orr, *God's Image in Man* (New York: A. C. Armstrong & Son, 1905), 57.

belongs to that true, self-conscious rationality in which man is the image of God."⁵⁶

J. Gresham Machen taught at Princeton Seminary from 1906 until its reorganization in 1929. At that time Machen withdrew to found Westminster Seminary with the expressed goal of carrying on the old Princeton tradition. Shortly before his death in 1936 Machen did a series of popular radio broadcasts entitled "The Christian View of Man." These were collected into a book that was published posthumously. Machen writes, "The 'image of God' cannot well refer to man's body, because God is spirit; it must therefore refer to man's soul. It is man's soul which is made in the image or likeness of God."⁵⁷

Machen spoke of the image of God as consisting in man's personhood, freedom, and goodness. Perhaps most telling is the title of the chapter "God's Image in Man," which seems to indicate that Machen, like Orr, thought of the *imago Dei* as something located somewhere *in* man, and not man himself *as* the image.

As late as the early twentieth century, there is thus in evidence an increasing tendency to identify the *imago Dei* with intellect or rationality. During this time, however, there were also some lines of emerging theological thought which would eventually take the consideration of what it meant to be made in the image of God in a different direction.

Notable in this period is the seminal work of Geerhardus Vos. In a departure from traditional theological methods, Vos brought the discipline of biblical theology to the North American dogmatic landscape. This precipitated a slow but significant shift away from a systematic theological *ordo salutis* to a biblical-theological *historia salutis*.⁵⁸ The approach was marked by less emphasis on abstract

---

⁵⁶ Ibid., 64.

⁵⁷ J. Gresham Machen, *The Christian View of Man* (Carlisle, PA: Banner of Truth, reprinted 1984), 145.

⁵⁸ See Geerhardus Vos, *Biblical Theology Old and New Testaments* (Carlisle, PA: Banner of Truth, reprinted 1975).

thought and philosophical methodology, and more emphasis on biblical grammatical-historical exegesis set in the context of a metanarrative. This and other influences led to an increased emphasis on an intertextual approach to Genesis 1:26–27, the consideration of historical contexts, and the use of cognate languages. These considerations have supplied grist for the theological mill as modern theologians attempt to grind out the ingredients for a doctrine of the *imago Dei*.

Karl Barth has been perhaps the most universally influential theologian since Friedrich Schleiermacher. His work on creation in *Church Dogmatics* represents a turning point in the consideration of the doctrine of the image of God.

Barth specifically rejected the idea that the *imago Dei* was to be found in man's intellect, or indeed in any "part" of man. In contrast to theologians before him who maintained a substantive or substantive/functional view of the image of God, Barth was the wellspring of the *relational* understanding of the image of God. He believed that the image of God was to be found specifically in the "I-Thou" relationship of confrontation. This "I-Thou" relationship exists within the Godhead ("I" because there is one God; "Thou" because this one God exists eternally in three distinct persons). The "I-Thou" relationship also exists in man ("I," in both men and women as human; "Thou" in both men and women as distinguished by gender; and in the distinction between God and mankind). Thus the image of God is not to be found in an analogy of being (substantive), but rather in an analogy of relationship.[59] For Barth, the *imago Dei* was not something that is *in* human beings. The image of God *is* mankind-in-relationship. The influence of Barth is evident in the thought of Stanley Hauerwas, John Swinton, Hans Reinders, Nancy Eiesland, and others doing theological work with regard to severe cognitive disability.

---

[59] See Karl Barth, *Church Dogmatics*, 3:1 "The Doctrine of Creation" (Peabody, MA: Hendrickson, 2010), 176–88.

In more recent years biblical scholars such as D. J. A. Clines, Meredith Kline, J. Richard Middleton, and Catherine Beckerleg have sought to incorporate the discoveries of scholars in the field of Old Testament and ancient Near Eastern studies in the on-going discussion of the *imago Dei*. The watershed contribution of Karl Barth coupled with these newer approaches have had a notable effect on modern systematic theologians such as G. C. Berkouwer, Wolfhart Pannenberg, Jürgen Moltmann, Herman Hoekema, Douglas Hall, Charles Sherlock, and Philip Edgcombe Hughes.

While there is a divergence of emphases in these later writers spanning the substantive, functional, and relational aspects of man in the image of God, two concepts commonly appear in all of them: 1) there is wide agreement that the use of the word צֶלֶם (cf. *imago*) does not allow for the exclusion of the human body from consideration of the doctrine of the *imago Dei*, and 2) modern theologians increasingly do not look for the image of God in some atomized component or aspect of man, but have a greater appreciation for considering the whole man with respect to the image of God.

Societal and Ecclesiastical Acceptance of Those with Disabilities: A Historical Overview

In seeing the *imago Dei* in substantive terms as something *in* man, in associating the image with those abilities that make mankind different from the animals, and generally identifying the image with the intellect, the contours of theology through much of the church's history has laid an unintended groundwork that could be construed as virtually excluding those with cognitive disabilities from being deemed full participants in humanity.

Moltmann has indicated what is at the root of the problem. Taking up the question "What constitutes the human being's likeness to God?" he delineates how theologians have tended to identify the *imago Dei* as some constituent part or component in man, either substantively (in the soul or intellect of man), formally (in the body and upright posture of man), or functionally (in the dominion of man). He is also critical of Barth's relational identification of the image of God. He states,

> We find the starting point for all these answers in 'the phenomenon human being.' They all begin with characteristics which distinguish the human being from animals, and interpret whatever is specifically human about men and women in religious terms as their likeness to God. Likeness to God then means the human being's general relationship to God, which distinguishes him from the animals. But this point of departure is based on a false inference. The human being's likeness to God is a theological term before it becomes an anthropological one. It first of all says something about the God who creates his image for himself, and who enters into a particular relationship with that image, before it says anything about the human being who is created in this form.[60]

Hans Reinders points out that despite the recent acceptance by society at large of those who are disabled there is a definite "hierarchy of disabilities." Those who are capable of self-sufficiency, self-direction, and achievement (generally those with physical or mild cognitive disabilities) are regarded to be superior in the hierarchy to those who are not capable of those things (generally those with severe cognitive disabilities).

> ... the hierarchy of disability reflects the hierarchy of moral values in our culture. People move upward on the ladder of cultural attraction because of what they are capable of achieving. ... this hierarchy of moral values reflects a basic assumption about our human nature, namely that selfhood

---

[60] Jürgen Moltmann, *God in Creation* (San Francisco: Harper & Row, 1985), 220.

[i.e., a self-consciousness] and purposive agency are crucial to what makes our lives human in the first place.[61]

The recognition of an implicit hierarchy is not limited to the typical or non-disabled population, but is evident even among that portion of the population that has disabling conditions in common. Anita Cameron who herself has multiple disabilities has noted, "There is an unspoken hierarchy in our community [i.e., people with disabilities], with well-heeled, well educated, good looking, clear speaking athletic types at the top and folks who are less able, poor, not so good looking ..., less educated or intellectually challenged at or near the bottom.... Of all of the discrimination I've experienced, disability on disability discrimination is hardest to understand and deal with."[62]

The presence of such a hierarchy means that the worth of a person, in fact his or her right to be regarded as a participant in humanity, is contingent (although not often explicitly stated) upon what place in the hierarchy the individual is capable of achieving. Increasingly in the modern world a "moral taxonomy" (Reinders) is developing which includes in or excludes from participation in human dignity those with severe cognitive disabilities.

Eugenics in the United States and Germany

The Eugenics movement had its origin in the work of Sir Francis Galton. Eugenics was conceived to be the science of improving the human race through good breeding. Galton was the cousin of Charles Darwin, and he drew upon Darwin's work to develop his ideas. Despite Darwin's tip of the hat to God at the end

---

[61] Reinders, *Receiving the Gift of Friendship*, 27.
[62] Anita Cameron, "A Call to Action for the Disability Community to Come Together," *The Mobility Resource*, entry posted October 25, 2013, http://www.themobilityresource.com/the-disability-community-need-to-come-together/ (accessed October 31, 2013).

The Problem and Its Setting

of *The Origin of Species*,[63] Darwin's natural selection was presented as a substitute for a Designer, and quickly became regarded as the cause for the emergence of all life, including human life, among intellectuals. God's existence was not denied, but he was relegated to the status of "irrelevant" for biology. Given the Scientific Revolution and its practical outworking in the emerging Industrial Revolution, and an increasing sense of progress and optimism, the development of the Eugenics movement was inevitable. Being at the cutting edge of progress, the United States embraced the "science" of Eugenics with vigor.

In 1919 William E. Kellicott, professor of biology at Goucher College, published a book entitled *The Social Direction of Human Evolution: An Outline of the Science of Eugenics*. Kellicott's work indicates that although Eugenics was largely focused on racial issues, there was also a goal of increasing the intelligence of the population.[64] It is important to note that for Kellicott and other eugenicists working in the U.S. the focus was on reducing the number of "idiots, imbeciles, and the feeble-minded"[65] in the future, and not on eliminating such people in the present. However, it is a short step from eliminating such people in the future to eliminating them in the present. The Eugenics movement in Germany in the 1940s eventually led to the cognitively

---

[63] Charles Darwin, *The Origin of Species* (New York: Signet Classics, reprinted 2010), 459. *"There is a grandeur in this view of life, with its several powers, having been originally breathed by the Creator into a few forms or into one; and that, whilst this planet has gone cycling on according to the fixed law of gravity, from so simple a beginning endless life forms most beautiful and most wonderful have been, and are being evolved."*

[64] See William E. Kellicott, *The Social Direction of Human Evolution An Outline of the Science of Eugenics* (New York: D. Appleton & Company, 1919), e-reader, under "The Sources and Aims of the Science of Eugenics."

[65] Ibid. Shocking as these terms sound to modern ears, they were technical terms in the day used for those with cognitive disabilities, and not intended to be insulting. They do, however, indicate a sense of superiority on the part of those who so designate other people.

disabled being labeled as "useless eaters" who took resources from society and returned nothing, and were thus targeted for systematic elimination.[66]

In 1921 Horatio Pollock published an article entitled "Eugenics as a Factor in the Prevention of Mental Disease" in the journal *Mental Hygiene*. Pollock begins the article by pointing out the enormous costs society bears—$200,000,000 annually, a huge sum in 1921—as a significant reason why society must strive to prevent cognitive disability in the future.[67] In keeping within the generally accepted ethical guidelines, Pollock does not suggest that those with cognitive disabilities should be eliminated. It is clear, however, that given the then (and now) current abilities of medical science, the only way to prevent cognitive disabilities in the future is to prevent those with such disabilities from being born, a likely factor in why Stanley Hauerwas has answered the question "Should we prevent retardation?" with a resounding "no."[68]

The Church's Support of the Eugenics Movement

Galton coined the term "eugenics" (good birth) in *An Inquiry into Human Faculty and Development* published in 1833.[69] The discipline remained largely theoretical until it was embraced in the United States by Charles Davenport, a man who came from a long

---

[66] See Richard Weikart, "The Specter of Inferiority: Devaluing the Disabled and 'Unproductive,'" and "Killing the 'Unfit'" in *From Darwin to Hitler: Evolutionary Ethics, Eugenics, and Racism in Germany* (New York: Palgrave Macmillan, 2004), 89–102 and 145–62. See also Henry Friedlander, *Origins of Nazi Genocide From Euthanasia to the Final Solution*, (n.l.: Henry Friedlander, 1995). The title is somewhat misleading as the book in its entirety outlines the systematic exclusion, isolation, and murder of the handicapped.

[67] Horatio Pollock, "Eugenics as a Factor in the Prevention of Mental Disease," *Mental Hygiene* 4, 4 (October 1921): 807–12, e-reader.

[68] Stanley Hauerwas, "Suffering the Retarded: Should We Prevent Retardation?" *Journal of Religion, Disability, and Health* 8, 3/4 (2004), 87–106.

[69] See Edwin Black, *War Against the Weak: Eugenics and America's Campaign to Create a Master Race*, (Washington, DC: Dialog Press, 2012), 12–16.

line of New England Puritan ministers. Davenport sought to escape the austerity of his religious upbringing by retreating into academia. Davenport pursued doctoral studies at Harvard, eventually teaching zoology at his alma mater and later at the University of Chicago.[70] It was Davenport who brought Eugenics out of the realm of the theoretical at the turn of the twentieth century.

With funding from the Carnegie Institute, Davenport was able to establish the Eugenics Record Office. A tireless advocate for "elevating humanity," Davenport persuaded the federal and state governments to institute programs of sterilization for "unfit" people.[71] The effectiveness of his efforts is evidenced in the case of *Buck v. Bell* adjudicated by the United States Supreme Court in 1927. Carrie Buck, a "feeble minded" woman, was institutionalized against her will, became pregnant in the institution and was being compelled against her will to be sterilized. Justice Oliver Wendell Holmes wrote the opinion for the eight judge majority:

> Carrie Buck is a feeble minded white woman who was committed to the State Colony.... She is the daughter of a feeble minded mother in the same institution, and the mother of an illegitimate feeble minded child.... The Commonwealth [of Virginia] is supporting in various institutions many defective persons who if now discharged would become a menace but if incapable of procreating might be discharged with safety and become self-supporting with benefit to themselves and society.... It is better for all the world, if instead of waiting to execute degenerate offspring for crime, or let them starve for their imbecility, society can prevent those who are manifestly unfit from continuing their kind.... Three generations of imbeciles is enough.[72]

---

[70] Ibid., 32–33.
[71] Ibid., 43–62, 87–124.
[72] Buck v. Bell 274 U.S. 200 (1927) quoted in Ibid., 120–121.

Partnering with Davenport, John Merriam, president of the Carnegie Institute, enlisted the aid of Harry H. Laughlin to spread the eugenics message abroad to Europe in the hope of stemming the flow of "unfit" immigrants at the source.[73] Less than a decade later, in 1933, Adolph Hitler became chancellor of Germany. Over the next ten years he would consolidate power, tap into a cultural and ideological meme taking the title of *Führer* ("leader"), and require an oath of personal fealty. The church in Germany was not immune to Hitler's jingoistic spell. A large segment of the church in Germany aligned itself with Hitler against the "godless Bolsheviks." Prostituting herself in service to the state, this segment of the church ". . . boldly called themselves the *Deutsche Christens* and referred to their brand of Christianity as 'positive Christianity.'"[74] Hitler used the church to his advantage, creating a *Reichskirche*, with Ludwig Müller being elected *Reichsbischof* over the church through political maneuvering. This new consolidated church was to be grounded in "love," Müller maintained, but the "love" of the *Deutsche Christens* had

> . . . a hard, warrior-like face. It hates everything soft and weak because it knows that all life can only then remain healthy and fit for life when everything antagonistic to life, the rotten and indecent, is cleared out of the way and destroyed.[75]

This philosophy dovetailed with Hitler's own. As early as 1929, Hitler had proposed that 700,000 of the "weakest" Germans be "removed" from society each year. In 1939 the T-4 euthanasia program was instituted to eliminate "life unworthy of life." The removal began in earnest, though mercifully not in the numbers that Hitler had hoped for:

---

[73] Ibid., 185–205.
[74] Eric Metaxas, *Bonhoeffer: Pastor, Martyr, Prophet, Spy* (Nashville, TN: Thomas Nelson, 2010), 151.
[75] Ibid., 173.

In August 1939 every doctor and midwife in the country was notified that they must register all children born with genetic defects—retroactive to 1936. In September when the war began, the killing of these "defectives" began. In the next few years five thousand small children were killed.[76]

All totaled, some 200,000 disabled people of all ages were the objects of "mercy killing" by the Nazis before Hitler rescinded the policy in August of 1941. Even after that time, however, the killing of such people continued passively by withholding medical treatment, medication, or food.[77]

Not all of the church in Germany was party to these atrocities. The Theological Declaration of Barmen in 1934 distinguished the Confessing Church from the *Deutsche Christens* and repudiated the movement, including its denigration of those with disabilities. The Roman Catholic Bishop of Münster, Clemens August von Galen, called upon all Christians to actively oppose the killing of the handicapped.[78] But it should not escape notice that at least some segment of the church in Germany found little objectionable in "removing" those with cognitive disabilities for the good of society.

Martin Luther had rejected the notion that the intellect was the seat of the *imago Dei*, but he had made unguarded statements that would later be used by the Nazis to justify killing those with intellectual handicaps. Later Lutheran theologians continued to promote the idea that the image of God was substantive, something *in* man that could be observed and distinguished. That observable distinction was often set forth as those abilities that separate human

---

[76] Ibid., 354.

[77] Doris Zames Fleisher and Frieda Zames, *The Disabilities Rights Movement* (Philadelphia: Temple University Press, 2011), 139.

[78] See Encyclopaedia Britannica Online, s.v. "T4 Program," http://www.britannica.com/EBchecked/topic/714411/T4-Program and s.v. "Blessed Clemens August, Graf von Galen," http://www.britannica.com/EBchecked/topic/223894/Blessed-Clemens-August-Graf-von-Galen (accessed February 25, 2013).

beings from animals. As the German *volk* longed for a return to the days of Germany's glory, they saw as an impediment to that goal a class of people in whom there were no observable abilities that distinguished them from animals.

It would be saying too much to claim that the contours of the doctrine of the *imago Dei* from the Fathers through the Reformation were at the root of the eugenics movement and some of the atrocities that it spawned. What can be said is that the doctrinal formulations, conceiving as they did the *imago Dei* as some component within man, left the church with scant defense for those who were evidently unable to contribute to society or even to their own care due to intellectual disability. Genesis 9:6 gives as the rationale for the prohibition against taking human life: "Whoever sheds man's blood, by man his blood shall be shed, for in the image of God he made man." If the *imago Dei* is conceived of as something to be found *in* mankind, and that something is not present, or is at least not discernible, there is little direct theological reason for not "removing" them if they become a burden to society. Luther himself had said that certain people were "masses of flesh without souls," a hitherto little known quote from the great reformer that the Nazis made (in)famous.

The atrocities of Nazi Germany brought the United States' flirtation with eugenics to a swift halt, but America had been the world leader in the eugenics movement from the late nineteenth through the early twentieth centuries. With aims little different than those of the *Deutsche Christens*, advocates of the Social Gospel embraced the eugenics movement in the interests of the betterment of American society.

Christine Rosen has demonstrated that it was a certain kind of minister in the U.S. who gravitated toward the eugenics movement in the early twentieth century, "... ministers anxious about the changing culture but also eager to find solutions to its diagnosable ills."[79] In 1917 Walter Rauschenbusch published his *Theology for the*

---

[79] Christine Rosen, *Preaching Eugenics: Religious Leaders and the American*

The Problem and Its Setting

Social Gospel. Fifteen years before that he had warned an audience at Rochester Theological Seminary that immigrants from southern and eastern Europe were "introducing 'alien strains of blood' into American society."[80]

> ... in 1926, hundreds of ... clerics representing nearly every major Protestant denomination ... preached eugenics across the country. ... They grafted elements of the eugenics message onto their own efforts to pursue religious based charity in their churches and adopted eugenic solutions to the social problems that beset their communities. They explored the eugenic implications of the biblical Ten Commandments and investigated the heredity lessons embedded in the parables of Jesus.[81]

It bears repeating that eugenics as conceived by Galton and embraced by Progressives in the U.S. sought to control the population by making sure that certain kinds of people, among them the cognitively disabled, did not reproduce. Advocacy for the logical conclusion of eugenics as practiced by the Nazis (eliminating living persons who were severely cognitively disabled) was entirely lacking.

Foreshadowing the pushback of the Confessing Christians against the *Deutsche Christens*, the theological conservatives in the U.S. opposed the eugenic enthusiasm of their progressive and Modernist fellow clergyman, but seldom for any reason other than a suspicion and distrust of the extravagant claims of modern(ist) science. A consideration of the *imago Dei* with regard to those who were "severely retarded" was not in evidence.

Eugenics Movement (New York: Oxford University Press, 2004), e-reader under "Fervent Charity."
 [80] Ibid.
 [81] Ibid., under "Introduction."

The Disability Rights Movement: The Divide between Physical and Cognitive

Temple University has published a timeline of significant events in the Disabilities Rights Movement.[82] Although there were precursors to the movement dating back to the early nineteenth century, the Civil Rights Movement of the early 1960s provided a pattern and impetus for organizing the movement. The movement continued to gain strength and culminated in the Americans with Disabilities Act (ADA) which was signed into law in 1990. Since that time elements of the law have been strengthened.

The Disabilities Rights Movement advocated mainly for the physically handicapped, although those with cognitive disabilities were not entirely overlooked. The focus of the movement has been on access and enablement. Although those with severe cognitive disabilities are (gratuitously) mentioned, the drive of the movement is summed up in the ADA text: "[T]he Nation's proper goals regarding individuals with disabilities are to assure equality of opportunity, full participation, independent living, and economic self-sufficiency for such individuals".[83]

For all the good the Disabilities Rights Movement in general and the ADA in particular has done for those with *physical* disabilities, it has done little good for those with severe *cognitive* disabilities. The focus of the movement has been to enable those with disabilities the opportunity to become full participants in and contributors to society. But what about those who have such profound cognitive

---

[82] Temple University, "Disability History Timeline," http://isc.temple.edu/neighbor/ds/disabilityrightstimeline.htm (accessed February 25, 2013). Although the website notes that the author of this timeline is unknown, and indicates that the dates and events have been verified by Dr. Paul Longmore, in fact what appears is an abridged version of the timeline compiled by Fleischer and Zames, xv—xxxii.

[83] Americans with Disabilities Act of 1990, amended 2008, Title 42, Chapter 126, Section 12101 (a) (7).

disabilities that they cannot participate in, or contribute (in any economic or artistic way) to society? Norman Cantor has pointed out that the value of human beings as persons is often assigned on the basis of criteria that assesses that human being's ability for certain psychological or social characteristics and interactions.[84]

A perusal of the book *The Disabilities Rights Movement* (Fleischer and Zames) makes clear that the focus of the movement has been on providing those with disabilities the opportunities and access to be self-sufficient, contributing members of society. It is also clear, however, that society's tolerance of people with disabilities has its limits:

> Bioethicist Dr. Alan Fleischman observed the tension in the dominant [i.e., non-disabled] culture—increasing accommodations of the disabilities in adults while simultaneously decreasing tolerance of abnormality in children: "We'll blame families if they knew there would be an abnormal child but chose not to abort," Fleishman fears.[85]

This may be particularly true if the child's disabilities are profound and cognitive, or physical of a kind that would require life-long care, and prevent the ability to be a self-sufficient, contributing member of society.

Consideration of the *imago Dei* with regard to those with severe cognitive disabilities is not contemplated by the dominant secularizing culture. Why should it be? With the Disabilities Rights Movement and its capstone legislation, the Americans with Disabilities Act, haven't we progressed beyond the need to invoke arcane metaphysical constructs in order to recognize the value of all people, both the disabled and the abled?

---

[84] Norman L. Cantor, *Making Medical Decisions for the Profoundly Mentally Disabled* (Cambridge, MA: MIT Press, 2005), 17–18.

[85] Fleischer and Zames, 161–62.

Norman Cantor believes this is so.[86] He argues that all human beings should be fully regarded as persons, because this is in fact what American society, legislatures, and the courts have done. This, however, is a very precarious argument upon which to base the value of people with severe cognitive disabilities. As Reinders has pointed out in his critique of Cantor, "One cannot defend personhood for the profoundly disabled by referring to what people believe about them, because if adherence to certain beliefs justifies the ascription of personhood, then a change in these beliefs may do the opposite."[87]

The Church's More Recent Response to Those with Disabilities

Throughout her history the church has exhibited concern and care for those with disabilities.[88] Almost reflexively, the church shows compassion to those in need, and cares for "the least of these." Local churches typically have ministries aimed at relieving the suffering and hardship of the hungry, the homeless, the poorly-clothed. Some congregations are proactive in these ministries. Others are welcoming to those who providentially come to them in difficult situations, sharing with them the love of Jesus and the good news of the gospel, rendering material aid, and embracing, discipling, and enfolding those who trust in Christ.

The Disabilities Rights Movement of the 1970s and 80s has led to a greater visible presence and participation in society and the church by those with disabilities. The Americans with Disabilities Act has increased access to participation in society for those with disabilities. While not discounting the good accomplished by the Disabilities Rights Movement and ADA, the church should

---

[86] Cantor, 20–23.
[87] Reinders, *Receiving the Gift of Friendship*, 35.
[88] See Brock and Swinton.

The Problem and Its Setting

be cognizant of their inadequacies. Reinders has noted that while the Disabilities Rights Movement has certainly increased *access* for people with disabilities, it has not necessarily increased *acceptance* in any meaningful way. Kenneth Campbell has observed, "Architectural barriers have been falling due to the passage of the ADA and the incorporation of accessibility design into building codes. But no law of man can mandate a change of heart."[89]

The Nazi atrocities took away the zeal for attempts to realize an impeccably athletic and intelligent race. The movement toward the deinstitutionalization of the physically disabled in the late 1950s and early 1960s brought society at large into contact with those who had been systematically hidden away "for their own good."[90]

Undoubtedly the person to bring those with disabilities to light for the church in the modern age was Joni Eareckson. Her autobiography *Joni*, first published in 1976, chronicled the confusion, heartache, despair, spiritual growth, and tremendous success of a young lady who, having been avidly athletic, was at seventeen years of age rendered a quadriplegic by a diving accident. Eareckson (now Tada) became an advocate for those with disabilities, eventually being appointed by President George W. Bush to the National Council on Disability and being present when the ADA legislation was signed.[91]

The unmistakable message of the book *Joni*, however, is the same as that of the Disabilities Rights Movement: with the proper tools and technology, those with disabilities can be valuable, contributing members of society. A conversation is recorded that took place between Eareckson and her friend Chris regarding Eareckson's artistic ability:

---

[89] Kenneth J. Campbell, "That My House May be Full: Implementing a Church Ministry With People Impacted by Disabilities" (D.Min. Thesis, Gordon-Conwell Theological Seminary, 2010), 25.
[90] See Fleischer and Zames, 33–48.
[91] Joni Eareckson Tada, *Joni*, (Grand Rapids, MI: Zondervan, 2001 ed.), 195.

Chris seemed amazed at my first attempt. "Joni, that's great! You've got real talent." She grinned and said, "You should have done this before. You need to get back to your art."

"But that was when I had hands," I protested.

She shook her head. "Doesn't matter. Hands are tools. That's all. The skill, the talent, is in the brain. Once you've practiced, you can do as well with your mouth as with your hands!"

... It was an enormously satisfying day for me. For the first time in almost a year and a half, I was able to express myself in a productive creative way.[92]

Eareckson hoped that people would admire her art because it was good, not because it was ". . . drawn by someone in a wheelchair holding a pen in her mouth."[93] That desire was realized as her art began to capture first local, then national attention. Being interviewed at her first widely attended art show in Baltimore, Eareckson told a reporter for the *Baltimore News America*, "My art is a reflection of how God can use a person like me to rise above circumstances."[94]

Eareckson has become an important and tireless advocate for people with disabilities, and a successful evangelist and Bible teacher. This, however, is precisely the point. While it is certainly the case that everyone should develop his or her gifts to the best of the person's abilities, Eareckson's success would be the envy of people without disabilities. She is an attractive, articulate, intelligent, and talented, artist, singer, speaker and writer with international recognition.

While Eareckson has used this talent for the glory of God and the good of her fellow human beings, her story inadvertently sends the same message as does the Disabilities Rights Movement: given the proper therapy and technology, people with disabilities can be

---

[92] Ibid., 94.
[93] Ibid., 170.
[94] Ibid., 179.

productive members of society who contribute more than they take. While this may indeed be true for the majority of those with physical disabilities, and even for those with mild to moderate cognitive disabilities, it is simply not true for that very small percentage of the population that has profound cognitive disabilities.[95] Those with the most severe cognitive disabilities will never be successful, productive, contributing members of society.

Perhaps the largest and most well-known modern ministry of inclusion for people with intellectual disabilities is l'Arche. Founded by Jean Vanier in 1964 in Trosly-Breuil, France, l'Arche is a collection of communities where those with and without cognitive disabilities live together: "We are people, with and without developmental disabilities, sharing life in communities belonging to an International Federation. Mutual relationships and trust in God are at the heart of our journey together. We celebrate the unique value of every person and recognize our need of one another."[96] Since its inception, l'Arche has grown to include some 5,000 disabled people in 140 communities in thirty-six countries.[97]

The work of l'Arche is laudable, but it is significant to note that it is not inclusive of the most profoundly cognitively disabled people. Its charter states, "L'Arche knows that it cannot welcome everyone who has a mental handicap. It seeks to offer not a solution but a sign, a sign that a society, to be truly human, must be founded on welcome and respect for the weak and downtrodden."[98] Those who are invited

---

[95] As the Joni and Friends ministry has expanded, it has included families with children with severe cognitive disabilities, specifically in the ministry of their family camps. Typing the words "intellectual disabilities" returns forty-seven results; the words "cognitive disabilities" returns fifty-three results at www.joniandfriends.org (accessed on March 1, 2013).

[96] L'Arche USA, "Identity and Mission," http://www.larcheusa.org/who-we-are/identity-and-mission/ (accessed February 2, 2013).

[97] Ibid., "Who We Are," http://www.larcheusa.org/who-we-are/larche-international-2/ (accessed February 2, 2013).

[98] L'Arche Internationale, "Charter of the Communities of L'Arche," Quebec: General Assembly of the Federation, May 1993, 2, http://www.larcheusa

to participate in l'Arche are those who are able to "... develop their abilities and talents to the full."[99] The charter continues, "The fundamental rights of each person include the right to life, to care, to a home, to education and to work. Also, since the deepest need of a human being is to love and to be loved, each person has a right to friendship, to communion and to a spiritual life."[100] This assumes an ability to work, to be educable, to experience friendship, and to have the capacity for an inner or spiritual life.

L'Arche communities accommodate those who are able to contribute in some way, but are largely exclusive of those who are not able to in any way be productive or contribute to the community, i.e., those who are the most severely cognitively disabled. This is not pointed out to denigrate the important ministry that l'Arche communities have, but simply to highlight that the most severely cognitively disabled are often not considered in discussions of "the disabled." Work, contribution, participation, success, relative independence—all of these things are important and necessary for typical human beings and for those with disabilities that do not profoundly affect the intellect. But for the most profoundly intellectually disabled, these concepts have no meaning.

For people like Oliver de Vinck, who was his whole life blind, deaf, mute, and paralyzed, and who was unable to do anything but breath, eat, and excrete;[101] like Kelly, a twelve-year old red-head with microcephaly who "stares without seeing," for whom "... words like 'I', 'me,' or 'myself,' will never mean anything to her, nor will any

---

.org//wp-content/uploads/2011/03/Charter-of-LArche.pdf, 1 (accessed February 2, 2013).

[99] Ibid., "Charter of the Communities of L'Arche," Quebec: General Assembly of the Federation, May 1993, 2, http://www.larcheusa.org/wp-content/uploads/2011/03/Charter-of-LArche.pdf, 2 (accessed February 2, 2013).

[100] Ibid., "Charter of the Communities of L'Arche," Quebec: General Assembly of the Federation, May 1993, 2, http://www.larcheusa.org//wp-content/uploads/2011/03/Charter-of-LArche.pdf, 3 (accessed February 2, 2013).

[101] Christopher de Vinck, *The Power of the Powerless: A Brother's Legacy of Love* (New York: Doubleday, 1988).

word for that matter," and for whom by any criteria of hierarchy of being would cast doubt on her actually being human;[102] and like my daughter Rebecca, for whom work, contribution, participation, success, and relative independence will not be a part of life in this age, the Disabilities Rights Movement may occasion more danger than protection. The movement by its very nature with its emphasis on self-determination, independence, and meaningful contribution inadvertently devalues people such as Oliver, Kelly, and Rebecca. If such people are included in the scope of humanity it is by exception, for they fall outside of the hierarchy of human value that the movement has created. Although in modern times the church has reflexively valued and been protective of such people, the reasons for doing so have been vague.

Resource Allocation, "Persons," and Hierarchy of Value

Since the conclusion of the Second World War resources in the U.S. have become increasingly abundant. This abundance has facilitated the rise of the Disabilities Rights Movement. When resources are plentiful, a society can afford to be sympathetic to those with disabilities, and is willing to allocate resources to aid those with physical or mild intellectual handicaps to actualize their potential. Plenteous resources will incline a society to be kindly disposed and sympathetic toward those relatively few human beings who consume resources but cannot contribute to the material wellbeing of the society.

All other things being equal, people with disabilities will consume a greater number of resources than those without disabilities. These include physical accommodations of access and their attendant costs, cost in terms of time (those with disabilities as an aggregate require more time to carry out tasks than do those without disabilities, and in many cases they require the time of others without

---

[102] Reinders, *Receiving the Gift of Friendship*, 19–24.

disabilities to help them) and medical resources (those with disabilities often require more, and more costly medical care than those without disabilities).

When resources become scarce, however, a hierarchy of value emerges. This was the impetus behind Hitler's desire to eliminate "useless eaters." As he tried to return Germany to a place of greatness in the wake of the First World War and the resulting economic collapse and on-going distress, he faced a resource shortage. Those with disabilities consumed a greater amount of those scarce resources than others, and contributed less (or nothing) to the material well-being of the society.

Resource allocation is a current topic of discussion in the medical community throughout the world. As medical technology advances, life expectancies increase among populations at large and among those with disabilities. These technologies exist because of considerable monetary investment, and at the time of this writing many developed nations find themselves on the verge of serious economic distress.

At the lowest level of medical resource allocation, "bedside rationing" occurs. Strech, Synofzik, and Marckmann at Eberhard-Karls Univerity in Tübingen have observed that "Priority setting and rationing occur at all levels in almost all health-care systems around the world."[103] "Our review confirms that physicians see rationing as a matter of fact that is widely prevalent in everyday medical practices. This supports the view that the crucial question in the current debate is not *whether* we should ration or not, but *how* we can ration in a fair and efficient manner."[104] In most cases in democratic nations this rationing is left to the discretion of physicians, but the criteria they use is not favorable to those with severe cognitive disabilities: ". . . the individual characteristics and capabilities of a patient can strongly influence BSR [bed-side rationing]. For example, a patient's ability to articulate his/

---

[103] Daniel Strech, Matthis Synofzik, and Georg Marckmann, "How Physicians Allocate Scarce Resources at the Bedside: A Systematic Review of Qualitative Studies" *Journal of Medicine and Philosophy* 33 (2008): 80.

[104] Ibid., 95.

her wishes . . . might be a decisive factor in whether he/she gets a certain measure or not."[105] Doctors may ". . . draw on the—likewise controversial—criterion of an individual's 'contribution to society.'"[106]

Furnham, Thomas, and Petrides at University College London conducted a study in 2002 to determine what criteria would be used by a sample of the general population to determine who should receive life-preserving medical treatment if resources were limited (in the hypothetical case presented, access to a dialysis machine). They found in part that an individual's level of intelligence affected the consideration. "[T]he highly intelligent [were preferred] over the moderately intelligent."[107] "Participants favored those described as highly intelligent possibly because it was believed that they could make more substantial contributions to society. . . . [T]he distinction here was between people of high versus people of average, not high versus low, intelligence, which presumably would have shown even greater difference."[108]

In an attempt to make allocations equitably, since the 1970s the medical community has often employed John Rawls' concept of "The Veil of Ignorance" set forth in his book *A Theory of Justice*."[109] In this ethical model any personal knowledge of the individuals among whom resources must be distributed is "veiled" and the determinations are made on the basis of an agreed upon set of criteria. Only after the decisions are made is the "veil lifted" to see to whom the resources have been allocated.

Recently Carlos Soto has argued against this concept for medical resource allocation.[110] He believes that a certain knowledge

[105] Ibid., 91.
[106] Ibid., 92.
[107] A. Furnham, C. Thomas, and K. V. Petrides, "Patient Characteristics and the Allocation of Scarce Medical Resources," *Psychology, Health, & Medicine* 7, 1 (2002): 103.
[108] Ibid., 105.
[109] John Rawls, *A Theory of Justice* (Cambridge, MA: President & Fellows of Harvard College, 1971).
[110] Carlos Soto, "The Veil of Ignorance and Health Resource Allocation"

of the people to be treated is necessary in order to make truly ethical decisions. "... [W]e must decide which features are morally relevant to any given distributive problem. The veil cannot help us with this question because it presupposes an answer to it. There is no reason we *must* use the veil and there is ample reason why we should not."[111]

Soto's approach is not unlike the approach of Peter Singer to the question of scarce resource allocation. But Soto is not sympathetic to Singer. He attacks the premise of Singer's arguments for its discrimination against the handicapped. However, unlike Soto's, Singer's approach to ethical questions regarding those with severe cognitive disabilities is internally consistent. He is willing to draw the conclusions that his presuppositions demand whether or not they are popular or pleasant.

Singer himself points out that the western notion of the sanctity of human life rests upon a belief that man was created in the image of God.[112] "Human beings are here [i.e., in Genesis 1 and 2] seen as special because they alone of all living things were made in the image of God."[113] He says that this idea has lost credibility. "No intelligent and unbiased student of the evidence could any longer believe in the literal truth of Genesis. With the disproof of the Hebrew myth of creation, the belief that human beings were specially created by God, in his own image was also undermined."[114]

Free from the constraints imposed by the notion that human beings are made in God's image, Singer distinguishes between human beings (*homo sapiens*) and persons (*persona*).[115] He maintains that a profoundly intellectually disabled child and a newborn infant

---

Journal of Medicine and Philosophy 37 (2012), 387–404.

[111] Ibid., 401.

[112] Peter Singer, "In God's Image and at the Centre of the Universe" in *Rethinking Life and Death*, 165–69.

[113] Ibid., 166.

[114] Ibid., 170.

[115] Peter Singer, *Practical Ethics*, 3rd ed. (New York: Cambridge University Press, 2011), 74ff.

"... are indisputably members of the species *homo sapiens*, but [they] are not] self-aware, [do not] have a sense of future, [nor] the capacity to relate to others."[116] Whether or not one is a human being, one is only to be considered a *person* if one attains to a certain intellectual capacity that enables him or her to have a sense of continuity, self-consciousness, and a desire to continue living (a summary of Singer's thesis in *Rethinking Life and Death*).

For Singer, the hierarchy of value is explicit: "Hardly anyone really believes that all human life is of equal worth. The rhetoric that flows so easily from the pens and mouths of popes, theologians, ethicists, and some doctors is belied every time these same people accept that we need not go all out to save a severely malformed baby."[117] Thus we should rather "... treat human beings in accordance with their ethically relevant characteristics" which include "consciousness, the capacity for physical, social, and mental interaction with other beings, having conscious preferences for continued life, and having enjoyable experiences."[118]

It is not necessarily the aim of this study to advocate for medical resources for those with severe cognitive disabilities in times of scarcity. Questions of resource allocation are difficult in the best of times, and resist simple formulas. But *contra* Singer, such decisions need not be made by resorting to a hierarchy of the value of human beings.

Whether or not society at large will be influenced by the thinking of Peter Singer and others like him, the church must not be persuaded to a hierarchy of value for human beings, particularly with respect to those with severe cognitive disabilities. However, the trajectory of the "commonsense understanding" of the *imago Dei* which identifies the image with the human intellect is not inconsistent with Singer's conclusions.[119]

---

[116] Ibid., 74.
[117] Singer, *Rethinking Life and Death*, 190.
[118] Ibid., 191.
[119] Nor is a Barthian *analogia relationis*; this will be taken up later.

The Problem and Its Setting

The Contours of This Study

The biblical doctrine that mankind has been created in the image of God is foundational to the value of every person. The biblical paradigm of a good creation (Gen. 1:31), the fall of man and the consequent deleterious spiritual, physical, and noetic/intellectual effects upon creation (Gen. 3, Rom. 8:20–21), and the redemption that has come in Christ and awaits consummation (Luke 2:8–11, Rev. 21:1–5) provides the basis for: 1) the conviction that God is good, and that the world originally reflected this goodness and still bears remnants of it; 2) a reason why evil in general, and specifically the surd evil of profound disability, exists in our world; and 3) faith to pray, hope, long for, and expect the healing of those with severe cognitive disabilities, repudiating the notion set forth by segments of the Disabilities Rights Movement and by some of the "disability theologians" that their condition is "normal."

This study will be set forth in four subsequent chapters. The literature review of the second chapter will examine the more recent theological reflection on the doctrine of the *imago Dei* from the time of Karl Barth. Barth's seminal work broke the log-jam of consideration of the *imago* in substantive and functional terms, and opened the way for a more plenary consideration of the doctrine. Although in the last several decades there has been profound insight with regard to the *imago* doctrine, few modern theologians have included those with intellectual disabilities in their exegetical contexts and theological models, a reality that calls for critical interaction with them.

The second chapter will also critically interact with the still small but growing body of literature that seeks to contribute to a theology of severe cognitive disability. Many of these writers approach the topic from a theologically liberal and higher critical perspective, and while their desire to affirm the value of persons with disabilities is laudable, their failure to take into account the reality of sin's effects on the creation, and a physical resurrection of the body and a renewed earth, leaves some of them arguing for the "good" of disabilities and against any need for remedy or healing.

Lastly, Chapter Two will examine some of the representative literature regarding the modern Historical Adam debate. Those who represent the traditional position have undergirded the idea that the definition of humanity is to be found in what separates mankind from the animals, specifically the powers of intellect, an approach that moves us in the wrong direction for affirming the value of those with cognitive disabilities.

The third chapter will comprise an exegetical analysis of key passages for reconsidering the *imago Dei* doctrine in light of those with severe cognitive disabilities. While many of the passages to be exegeted will be those commonly discussed when dealing with the *imago* doctrine, some passages will not be those typical for an exegetical undergirding of the doctrine.

Chapter Three will consider that not only theology but also exegesis is done contextually, the theologian or exegete doing his work in the context of a constructed model which represents the world he or she lives in. Most of these models do not include severely cognitively disabled people. The exegesis done here will be set in the context of a model that includes such people consciously, if not always manifestly.

The fourth chapter attempts to synthesize the historical research, theological research, field research, and exegetical work into a reconsideration of the *imago Dei* in the light of those with severe cognitive disabilities. The goal in doing so is to provide at least the seeds of an *imago* theology that is rooted in a more accurate model of the world, a model which includes not only abstract exegetical and theological considerations, but a model in which disability is a reality. The hope is to contribute to an *imago* theology that includes all people, and in a way more deliberately than by exception.

The fifth and final section draws conclusions from the study and makes suggestions to seminary professors and pastors for teaching the doctrine of the *imago Dei* in a way that is not inadvertently exclusive of people with the most severe cognitive disabilities. It also makes suggestions to churches in order to form communities that are inclusive of people with severe cognitive disabilities, based not upon their ability to be independent and contribute to the life of the church in any way that would lessen the work of each member, but based upon their value as human beings made in the image of God.

The appendices contain raw data and an analysis gathered from a sample of Protestant clergy from across the United States. This study seeks to understand current trends in the thoughts about the *imago Dei* by said clergy, stratified by theological tradition, level of theological education, and other demographic data, and to understand and analyze these findings with respect to those with cognitive disabilities.

Justification for a Reconsideration of the Doctrine of the *Imago Dei*

The doctrine of the *imago Dei* has largely been understood throughout history in terms of some actual or reified element or capacity *within* people. Often it is those characteristics that distinguish human beings from the animals which are set forth as the seat of the image of God, chief among them being the intellect. Although it is possible to find allowances for those with severe intellectually disabilities in the historical theological literature, those with intellectual disabilities are often considered as exceptions, anomalies in the *imago* theories. There has not been a generally recognized approach to the doctrine of the *imago Dei* that is inclusive of those with such disabilities.

Statistically speaking, the need for a study like this is small. The Center for International Rehabilitation Research Information & Exchange (CIRRIE), maintained by the State University of New York at Buffalo indicates that instances of cognitive disability, and in particular severe and profound cognitive disability, are quite low. Data compiled there indicate the cumulative incidents of all intellectual disabilities in the United States are .91% of the population. Of these,

> The distribution of the affected population depends on the severity of the disorder. Among those with a diagnosis of I[ntellectual] D[isability], mild mental retardation affects about 85% of the population, moderate mental retardation about 10%, severe mental retardation about 4%, and profound mental retardation about 2%.[120]

Given these statistics, no case can be made that there is a broad need for a reconsideration of the doctrine in a way that includes those with severe cognitive disabilities. The population of those classified as severely and profoundly intellectually disabled is so small that it is possible that a typical person might go his or her entire life without meeting such a person. However, for those who care for and love those with severe cognitive disabilities, there is a *deep* need.

Those with severe cognitive disabilities cannot be "productive" or "contributing" members of society. They are often given gratuitous mention in the disability (and sometimes the theological) literature and then forgotten. Because they are in the social position of being the weakest of the weak, it is reasonable to conclude from Scripture that those with severe cognitive disabilities occupy a place of high concern for the God who "executes justice for the orphan and the widow, and shows his love for the alien by giving him food and clothing" (Deut. 10:18). This God who in his incarnation had compassion on those who were sick and healed them, told his disciples that whenever they cared for "the least" by clothing them, feeding them, giving them drink, taking them in, and visiting them, they were rendering that service to him (Matt. 25:34–40).

---

[120] Pallab K. Maulik and Catherine K. Harbour, "Epidemiology of Intellectual Disability," *International Encyclopedia of Rehabilitation*, under "Severity of Disorder," http://cirrie.buffalo.edu/encyclopedia/en/article/144/ (accessed March 8, 2013).

Those with severe cognitive disabilities are the most vulnerable human beings living outside of the womb. Historical precedent indicates that in times of want or distress, their position is low on the hierarchy of value. The secularized world likely will not care much about considerations relating to the image of God, but the church should.

Disability considerations among theologians often do not take into account those with severe intellectual impairment in any but the most cursory way. Those who do take them into account focus on practical issues or virtue ethics, or speak of the worth of such people as though this were a universally accepted given. An inclusive doctrine of the *imago Dei* would provide a sound basis for the church's advocacy for the value of those with severe cognitive disabilities.

Peter Singer has advocated the moral acceptability of taking the lives of the intellectually disabled who are not "persons," inside or outside of the womb. "If these conclusions seem too shocking to take seriously, it may be worth remembering that our present absolute protection of the lives of infants is a distinctly Christian attitude . . . ."[121] Thus "If we can put aside these emotionally moving but strictly irrelevant aspects of the killing of a baby, we can see that the grounds for not killing persons do not apply to newborn infants."[122] It is ironic that it is Peter Singer who has pointed out that the doctrine of the *imago Dei* is foundational to the sanctity of all human life, and that emotionalism cannot forever be the grounds on which to base the value of human beings.

The need for a reconsideration of the *imago Dei* with regard to those with severe cognitive disabilities is simply this: the church needs a basis for valuing and protecting such people that transcends a compassion born of mere sentiment and emotion.

---

[121] Singer, *Practical Ethics*, 153.
[122] Ibid., 152.

2

Literature Review

The literature relevant to this study falls into three categories. The first section will survey modern approaches to the doctrine of the *imago Dei* from Karl Barth to the present. Barth's approach represents a radical departure from the cumulative trajectory of the doctrine, and his pioneering analysis was at the root of later theologians employing new *imago* paradigms.

The second section will review a sample of the body of literature dealing with the theology of disability, and specifically cognitive disability. Theological consideration of severe cognitive disability is recent, beginning with the work of Jean Vanier. He and a number of theologians coming after him with divergent approaches to disability will be considered. It is significant to note, however, that all of the "disability theologians" have in common a paucity in their consideration of the *imago Dei* doctrine.

Finally, brief consideration will be given to a sample of the literature dealing with the modern historical Adam debate within Evangelicalism. The importance of this literature for the current study lies in the fact that many of those on both sides of the debate are moving the understanding of *imago Dei* back in the direction of an association with language, intellect, and higher cognitive abilities, thus potentially (if unintentionally) excluding those with severe cognitive disabilities.

Literature Review

A Survey of Modern Approaches to the *Imago Dei*

Approaches to the *imago* doctrine since Karl Barth fall into three categories: consideration given by historical theologians who consider the doctrine abstractly in its historical/systematic theological context; ancient Near Eastern scholars who seek to understand the doctrine in and from its ancient Near Eastern context; and contextual theologians who explore the doctrine in light of a particular contextual or existential issue. What follows is a sampling of the significant literature in each category.[1]

Historical/Systematic Theologians

In 1932 Karl Barth published the first volume of his *Church Dogmatics*. He would continue to add to this work, completing fourteen total volumes shortly before his death in 1968. Barth's influence has been enormous. It is all but impossible to read any work of theology in any locus that does not interact with Barth, either with approbation or criticism.

Barth's doctrine of the *imago Dei* is spread throughout four parts of the second volume of *Church Dogmatics*, "The Doctrine of Creation." He notes that the very fact that man is created in the image of God shows man's utter dependence upon God: "That God will create man in His image implies that it is not man but God who is first a Living Person.... Thus the creature in its totality was allied to the living, divine Person, being wholly referred to it for its existence and essence, its survival and sustenance."[2] While it is true that this may be said of all creatures, Barth's point is that mankind being

---

[1] W. Randall Garr's work *In His Own Image and Likeness: Humanity, Divinity, and Monotheism* (Boston: Brill, 2003), considered by many to be the authoritative work on Gen 1:26–27 and the concept of the image of God, is not reviewed in this section because his work is solely exegetical. The work is drawn upon and interacted with in Chapter Four of this book.

[2] Barth, *Church Dogmatics*, 3.1 (Peabody, MA: Hendrickson Publishers, reprinted 2010), 110.

made in the image of God does not constitute an autonomous, independent, intrinsic condition, but one of dependency upon God. In opposition to thinkers such as Descartes and Kant there can be no consideration of man *qua* man. "'In our image' means to be created as a being which has its ground and possibility in the fact that in 'us,' *i.e.*, in God's own sphere and being, there exists a divine and therefore self-grounded prototype to which this being can correspond."[3] Barth believes that it is the *imago Dei* that is the very ground for the possibility of fallen man's justification.[4]

Barth is critical of the attempts of theologians who find the image of God in some analogy of being between God and man. Instead, he believes that the image is located in an analogy of relationship. Thus there is

> . . . not a correspondence and similarity of being, an *analogia entis*. The being of God cannot be compared to that of man. . . . It is a question of the relationship within the being of God [as triune] on the one side and between the being of God and that of man on the other. Between the two relationships as such—and it is in this sense that the second is the image of the first—there is a correspondence and similarity. There is an *analogia relationis*.[5]

Man lives in relation to God in a way that the animals cannot, but also in relationship to other human beings in the male-female relationship in a way that angels cannot:

> God created [mankind] in His own image in the fact that He did not create him alone but in connexion and fellowship. . . . It is inevitable that we should recall the triune being

---

[3] Ibid., 183.
[4] Ibid.
[5] Ibid., 3.2: 220.

of God at this point. God exists in relationship and fellowship. As the Father of the Son and the Son of the Father He is Himself I and Thou, confronting Himself and yet always one and the same in the Holy Ghost. God created man in His own image, in correspondence with His own being and essence.... Because He is not solitary in Himself and therefore does not wish to be so *ad extra*, it is not good for man to be alone and God created him in His own image as male and female.... there can be no question of an analogy of being, but of relationship. God is in relationship, and so too is the man created by Him. This is the divine likeness.[6]

For Barth, to be human is to be human-in-relationship, and to be human-in-relationship is the essence of the image of God.

Humanity, the characteristic and essential mode of man's being, is in its root fellow-humanity. Humanity which is not fellow-humanity is inhumanity. For it cannot reflect but only contradict the determination of man to be God's covenant-partner, nor can the God who is no *Deus solitarius* but *Deus triunus*, God in relationship, be mirrored in a *homo solitarius*. As God offers man humanity, and therefore freedom in fellowship, God summons him to prove and express himself as the image of God—for as such He has created him.[7]

For Barth, that the *imago Dei* is to be found in mankind as an "I" and also as an "I—Thou" of the male-female relationship is the self-evident exegesis of Genesis 1:26–27. "This is what is emphatically said in Gen. I[27] and all other explanations of the *imago Dei* suffer from the fact that they do not do justice to this

---

[6] Ibid., 324.
[7] Ibid., 3.4: 117.

decisive statement."[8] God's statement of intention to make man "in our image, and according to our likeness" in Genesis 1:26 is, Barth believes, fully explained by the statement of 1:27, "So God created man in his own image, in the image of God he created him; male and female he created them."

While Barth may have overestimated the self-evident nature of the exegesis of Genesis 1:26–27, the communal aspect of man as God's image bearer and the consequent necessity of life-in-community has had an evident and marked influence on contemporary theologians working in the area of severe cognitive disability, notably Jean Vanier and Hans Reinders. However, although Barth was acquainted with the Bethel community of 1,600 disabled persons in Beisenthal,[9] such people do not seem to be a part of his conscious theological frame of reference.

The relationships that Barth envisions as encompassing the *imago Dei* require a certain level of intellect. Although mild and moderate forms of intellectual disability such as Down syndrome may allow for complex relationships (in some cases, perhaps even marriage), the most severe forms of intellectual disability stemming from conditions such as anencephaly or lissencephaly preclude complex relationships. In many cases, care-givers may have relationships with such people, but such people may not be cognizant that others outside of themselves exist. Barth may be read in such a way as to understand such people as examples of "inhumanity."

Barth has not been universally praised. Reinhold Neibuhr took issue with the notion that the *imago Dei* should be conceived as humanity-in-relationship. Niebuhr states, "In their crudest forms the purely social and historical interpretations of [human] life bid the individual to fulfill his life in community. The breadth of the communal life and the majesty of its power supposedly complete

[8] Ibid., 3.2: 324.
[9] See Eric Metaxas, *Bonhoeffer: Pastor, Martyr, Prophet, Spy* (Nashville, TN: Thomas Nelson, 2010), 183–85.

the partial interests and inadequate power of the individual."[10] The crux of Niebuhr's opposition to Barth was his belief that it is not man-in-community, but each human being individually that is in the image of God. "... the meaning of [man's] life is derived from his relation to the historical process.... Each individual has a direct relation to eternity."[11]

Like Barth, Niebuhr is critical of what he calls the classical view of man which sees the image of God in terms of intellect, and the idea that "... man is to be understood primarily from the standpoint of his rational faculties. What is unique in man is his νοῦς. Νοῦς may be translated as 'spirit' but the primary emphasis lies upon the capacity for thought and reason."[12] The Christian view of man, he contends, ought to be different from the classical view but has been perennially plagued by it, particularly when it seeks to understand man as an abstraction:

> [Human rationality's] most natural inclination is to make itself that ultimate principle, and thus in effect to declare itself God.... [But man is to be] understood primarily from the standpoint of God, rather than the uniqueness of his rational faculties or his relation to nature. He is made "in the image of God." It has been the mistake of many Christian rationalists to assume that this term is no more than a religious-pictorial expression of what philosophy intends when it defines man as a rational animal.[13]

Niebuhr avers that "The Christian view of man [must be] sharply distinguished from all alternative views ... in its doctrine

---

[10] Reinhold Neibuhr, *The Nature and Destiny of Man*, vol. 2 (New York: Charles Scribner's Sons, 1948), 309.
[11] Ibid., 2:308.
[12] Ibid., 1:6.
[13] Ibid., 1:12–13.

of the 'image of God.'"[14] He notes the difficulty of clarifying the doctrine because it is given "no precise psychological elaboration in the Bible itself."[15] Attempts to explain the doctrine, ". . . particularly in the early period of strong Platonic influence and in the latter Middle Ages, when Aristotle shared with Augustine and the Bible the position of ultimate arbiter of theological truth, sometimes define the 'imago Dei' in terms which do not advance beyond the limits of the Aristotelian conception of man as a rational creature."[16]

Departing from an orthodox explanation for man's fallen condition, Niebuhr believes that since man as created was, and continues to be the image bearer of God, this logically requires a denial of the historical fall of man from a state of original righteousness into rebellion and sin:

> The disavowal of the historical-literalistic illusion, which places the original perfection of man in a period before an historical Fall, thus clarifies and corrects both Catholic and Protestant thought. Against Protestant thought it becomes possible to maintain that the image of God is preserved in spite of man's sin. In distinction from Catholic thought it is possible to eliminate the unwarranted distinction between a completely lost original justice and an uncorrupted natural justice.[17]

Furthermore,

> In placing the consciousness of "original righteousness" in a moment of the self which transcends history . . . it may be relevant to observe that this conforms perfectly to the myth of the Fall when interpreted symbolically. The myth

---

[14] Ibid., 150.
[15] Ibid., 151.
[16] Ibid., 152–53.
[17] Ibid., 276.

does not record any actions of Adam which were sinless.... His sinlessness, in other words, preceded his first significant action and his sinfulness came to light in that action. This is symbolic of the whole of human history. The original righteousness of man stands, as it were, outside of history.[18]

Although Neihbur believes that a denial of the historicity of the fall is necessary to preserve the doctrine of the *imago Dei*, his approach causes more problems than it ostensibly solves. The influence of Neibuhr (and others who share his higher critical views) can be seen in the writings of many of the contemporary "disability theologians," notably Nancy Eiesland. Niebuhr's denial of the fall as a historical event makes it difficult to attribute disability to something gone wrong, and modern theologians who follow him struggle, sometimes tortuously, to ascribe and make sense of the divine pronouncement of "very good" (Gen. 1:31) upon such conditions.

Barth had cautioned that trying to precisely define the *imago* may in fact be a violation of the second commandment. Similarly G. C. Berkouwer recognized the inherent difficulty of formulating a systematic doctrine of the *imago Dei*: "If we examine the Biblical witness regarding man, we soon discover that it never gives us any systematic theory about man in the image of God."[19] There is necessity to develop such a theory, however, because "... Scripture's references to the image of God, whenever there are such, have a special urgency and importance."[20]

In agreement with Barth, Berkouwer sees the designation of "man as the image of God" as contingent upon man's relationship to God,[21] but is unconvinced by Barth's argument that the image is to

---

[18] Ibid., 279.

[19] G. C. Berkouwer, *Man: The Image of God* (Grand Rapids, MI: Eerdmans, 1962), 67.

[20] Ibid., 67.

[21] Ibid., 35.

be found specifically in the creation of mankind as male and female: "We are of the opinion that what Barth calls his 'straight forward defining explanation of the text' actually involves constructive interpretation...he is wrong in...concluding this relation [of male-female, I-Thou] is the specific content of the image of God...."[22]

In dealing with the difficulty of what it means for man to be created in the image of God and yet corrupted by sin in all of the faculties of body and soul, Berkhouwer follows Calvin in positing a broader and narrower sense of the image of God. In the broader sense, "... man, despite his fall into sin and corruption, was not bestialized or demonized, but remained man."[23] In this broader sense, the image of God is found in those aspects of "... man's being that forever makes man different on the one hand from angels, and on the other from animals."[24] Berkouwer maintains that it is this broader sense that has received the lion's share of the attention. However, it may be said that the narrower sense of the image of God—man's knowledge of God and his original righteousness and holiness—has indeed been lost.[25] He believes that although the patristic theologians were mistaken in distinguishing between the image and the likeness as referring respectively to the static image of what man is and the dynamic likeness of what man may become, "The fact remains ... that this duel terminology was certainly not the only reason for the idea of the double usage of the term 'image of God.'"[26] In this narrower sense, it can legitimately be said that the image of God has been lost in fallen mankind, but is being renewed through the grace of God in Christ as a "new *comformitas cum Deo*" in humanity's being "renewed unto knowledge after the image of him that created him' (Col. 3:10)."[27]

---

[22] Ibid., 73.
[23] Ibid., 38.
[24] Ibid., 39.
[25] Ibid., 38, 42.
[26] Ibid., 43.
[27] Ibid., 45.

Berkouwer believes it is an error to identify the *imago Dei* with the intellect, or indeed any specific faculty, aspect, or constituent part of man. Rather, the *imago* is in the whole man, or more accurately the whole man is in the *imago Dei*. He alludes to von Rad with approbation that there is a "... real, concrete meaning of the image.... Von Rad would not rule out man's body as part of the image in man; quite the contrary, he thinks that the idea of the image sets out from corporeality as something *visible*. According to the story in Genesis, the whole man is made in the image of God, and Genesis certainly does not imply that certain 'higher' qualities, in contrast to 'lower' bodily qualities, exclusively make up the content of the image."[28] Indeed, "Scripture's emphasis on the whole man as the image of God has triumphed time and time again over opposing principles. Scripture never makes a distinction between man's spiritual and bodily attributes in order to limit the image of God to the spiritual, as furnishing the only possible analogy between God and man."[29]

For Berkouwer, man in his entirety as a human being is created in the image of God and retains that image in the broad sense even in the fall. However, the entirety of man, soul and body, "higher" functions (such as intellect) as well as "lower" functions has been corrupted by the fall, and Berkouwer is not shy about speaking of the loss of the image of God in the narrower sense. The image of God in this narrower sense is restored and being restored in Christ only for those who are redeemed. Thus the *imago Dei* ultimately has an eschatological and telic orientation.

Berkouwer's emphasis on the physicality of the *imago Dei* is shared with disability theologians such as Vaneir and Nouwen, who (though not specifically addressing *imago* issues) speak of a theology not of word (*logos*, cf. those things having to do with the intellect) but of body. Berkouwer is theoretical and abstract in his *imago* theology,

[28] Ibid., 74–75.
[29] Ibid., 77.

and thus how his views relate to people with disabilities is not in evidence as being a conscious part of his theological reference point.

Foundational to Anthony Hoekema's theological anthropology is the tensioned balance of man as a *created person*. Because personality has its origin in God, the fact that man is a created person is ". . . the central mystery of man: how can man be both a creature and a person at the same time? To be a creature means . . . absolute dependence on God; to be a person means relative independence."[30]

In his exegesis of Genesis 1:26–27, Hoekema takes issue with the patristic and medieval notion that the "image" and the "likeness" are two distinct things, noting that while both the Septuagint and the Vulgate render the passage syndetically with an "and" between the "image" and "likeness," the Hebrew text is asyndetic.[31]

While his approach to the *imago* has eclectic elements, there is a propensity toward a functional understanding of the image. Hoekema indicates that the meaning of the text is that man "images God" functionally by his dominion over the animals, in his personality (i.e., his being a person), and (with obvious allusion to Barth) in the male-female relationship.[32] Sin has had a serious effect on the image of God but has not destroyed it: "We may indeed think of the image of God as having been tarnished through man's fall into sin, but to affirm that by this time man had completely lost the image of God is to affirm something that the sacred text does not say."[33]

While the Scriptures do not tell us precisely what the image of God is, nor precisely what effect the fall had upon it, Hoekema echoes the patristic writers in pointing out that the Scriptures in referring to Christ as "the image of God" show us "the perfect

---

[30] Anthony Hoekema, *Created in God's Image* (Grand Rapids, MI: Eerdmans, 1986), 6.

[31] Ibid., 13.

[32] Ibid., 13–14, 75–82.

[33] Ibid., 15. He alludes to Gen. 9:6 and James 3:9 as proof that the image of God is not lost in fallen man.

man—the unsurpassed example of what God wants us to be like."[34] Hoekema believes that the incarnation was possible only because man is created in the image of God: "That God could become flesh is the greatest of all mysteries, which will always transcend our finite human understanding. But presumably, it was only because man had been created in the image of God that the Second Person of the Trinity could assume human nature.... the Incarnation confirms the doctrine of the image of God."[35]

For Hoekema, this mystery creates a kind of feedback loop: man is made in the image of God and therefore the incarnation is possible, but to know what the image of God really is we must look at the incarnate Christ. Thus, "... the best way to understand the image of God is not to contrast man with animals, as so often has been done, and then to find the divine image to consist in those qualities, abilities, and gifts that man has in distinction from the animals. Rather, we must learn to know what the image of God is by looking at Jesus Christ."[36]

There is an eschatological component to Hoekema's understanding of the *imago Dei*. The image of God is being restored in the redeemed, for in the fall "we no longer image God as we should."[37] In distinction from those theologians like Niebuhr who want to remove "... the 'fall' from the dimension of historical beginnings of the human race 'into a suprahistorical, supratemporal, supraemperical dimension, a dimension called *origin*,'"[38] Hoekema contemplates the image of God in terms of the "original image," the "perverted image," and the "renewed and perfected image."[39] The original image, though perfect, was not yet perfected: "Man, to be

---

[34] Ibid., 20.
[35] Ibid., 22.
[36] Ibid., 22.
[37] Ibid., 28.
[38] Wolfhart Pannenberg, *Anthropology in Theological Perspective* (Edinburgh: T&T Clark, 1985), 56.
[39] Hoekema, 82–96.

sure, was created in the image of God at the beginning, but he was not yet a 'finished product.'"[40]

In contemplating the "perverted image," that is, mankind in the consequences of the historical fall, Hoekema does not consider any deleterious effect on natural human ability, but takes into account only the moral dimensions. He speaks of man's propensity to worship idols rather than the true God, to be self-centered and alienated from other persons, and to misuse and sinfully exploit natural resources for personal gain at the expense of the environment and others.[41]

Hoekema regards the image renewed with respect to the new birth and its outworking in sanctification. He only considers typical human beings, and gives no attention to those whose handicaps may prevent them from showing manifestations or evidences of regeneration.[42] The perfection of the image of God will ultimately be connected with Christ's people participating in his glorification, and the restoration of the three-fold relationship (man with God, man with other people, and man with his environment).[43]

Jürgen Moltmann's understanding of the *imago Dei* has a prominent eschatological orientation. Like Hoekema, Moltmann sees anthropology as antecedent to Christology, but not something that can be divorced from it: "anthropology is 'deficient Christology' and Christology is 'realized anthropology.'"[44] The problem with the early approaches to the doctrine of the *imago Dei*, according to Moltmann, is that they were too anthropocentric. He believes that the difficulty of the doctrine (which, he concedes, has little explanation in the biblical texts[45]) stems from not sufficiently giving due weight to the fact that in the conciliar fiat speech of "Let us

---

[40] Ibid., 83.
[41] Ibid., 84–85.
[42] See ibid., 85–91.
[43] Ibid., 91–96.
[44] Jürgen Moltmann, *God in Creation* (San Francisco: Harper & Row, 1985), 7.
[45] Ibid., 215.

make man,""... God designates himself as the Creator of the image before he creates the image."⁴⁶ The perennial error of the church in approaching the doctrine has been a matter of emphasis. It has been approached as the ***imago*** Dei rather than as the *imago* **Dei**.

With questionable exegesis, Moltmann distinguishes between the image and likeness in that "... the first expresses more the outward [concrete, visible] representation, the second rather the reflexive inward relationship [to God].⁴⁷ In a polemic against the near universal ancient Near Eastern tradition in which only kings were thought to be the image and representation of the gods, the Genesis account democratizes the *imago Dei* to all human beings.⁴⁸

In seeking to analyze what exactly constitutes the divine likeness, Moltmann denies that it is to be found in any analogy of substance (i.e., the human soul), any analogy of form (i.e., his upright walk and upward gaze), any analogy of function (i.e., his dominion over the earth⁴⁹), or (*contra* Barth) in any analogy of relationship between a man and his wife as a reflection of the persons of the Godhead.⁵⁰ All of these, says Moltmann, are based on a false inference of beginning with "characteristics which distinguish human beings from animals."⁵¹ "The human being's likeness to God is a theological term before it becomes an anthropological one. It first of all says something about the God who creates his image for himself, and who enters into a particular relationship with that image, before it says anything about the human being who is created in that form."⁵² Therefore, "what makes the human being God's image is not his possession of any particular characteristic or

---

⁴⁶ Ibid., 217.

⁴⁷ Ibid., 218–19.

⁴⁸ Ibid., 219.

⁴⁹ Ibid. He curiously uses the phrase "analogy of proportionality" to describe this, 220.

⁵⁰ Ibid., 219–20.

⁵¹ Ibid., 220.

⁵² Ibid.

other—something which distinguishes him above other creatures; it is his *whole existence*."⁵³ Thus, "Only the human being is *imago Dei*. Neither animals nor angels . . . may be either feared or worshipped as God's image or his appearance or his revelation."⁵⁴

For Moltmann, the *imago Dei* is eschatologically oriented, with Christ as the pattern to which redeemed humanity will be conformed. Because it is to be found in God's relationship to man bestowed in and by virtue of creation, it cannot be destroyed by sin: "Human sin may certainly pervert human beings' relationship to God, but not God's relationship to human beings. That relationship was resolved upon by God, and was created by him, and can therefore never be abrogated or withdrawn except by God himself."⁵⁵

Moltmann is one of the few theologians who, though not writing specifically about the implications of the *imago Dei* for those with severe handicaps, nevertheless addresses the issue: "Even the human being who is totally *in*human remains a human being and cannot escape his responsibility. By virtue of the relationship in which God puts himself to men and women, the handicapped person is also God's image in the fullest sense of the word; the image is in no way a diminished one. The dignity of human beings is unforfeitable, irrelinquishable and indestructible, thanks to the abiding presence of God."⁵⁶

Moltmann believes that the *imago Dei* is now in process and is telic. The completion and fulfillment of it is to be found at the end of history and is brought about only in Christ. "The restoration or the new creation of the likeness of God comes about in the fellowship of believers with Christ. Since he is the messianic *imago Dei*, believers become *imago Christi*, and through this enter upon the path which will make them *gloria Dei* on earth."⁵⁷

⁵³ Ibid., 221.
⁵⁴ Ibid.
⁵⁵ Ibid., 233.
⁵⁶ Ibid.
⁵⁷ Ibid., 226.

With regard to the study under consideration, Moltmann's approach allows us to recognize without minimization the devastating effects of the fall upon humanity, and especially upon those with severe cognitive disabilities, without despair. "In the messianic light of the gospel, the human being's likeness to God appears as a historical process with an eschatological termination. *Being* human means *becoming* human in the process. Here too the image of God is the whole person, the embodied person, the person in community with other people, because in the messianic fellowship of Jesus, people become whole, embodied, and social human beings . . ."[58]

Unlike Berkouwer, who deprecates the ancient theosis doctrine,[59] Moltmann has a deep appreciation for it. In the appearing of Christ the redeemed will be transformed from *imago per conformitatem gratiae* to *imago similitudinem gloriae*. "The eschatological becoming-one-with-God of human beings (*theosis*) is inherent in the concept of 'seeing,' for the seeing face to face and the seeing him as he is transforms the seer into the One seen and allows him to participate in the divine life and beauty."[60] For those who feel the weight of the effects of the fall in themselves and in their loved ones it is a comforting thought that the image of God ". . . is never fixed, once and for all, but is transformed . . . . What human beings are is not thoroughly determined. It will only be known out of this divine history."[61]

In the book *The True Image*, Philip Hughes insists that the *imago Dei* is not to be found in mankind collectively, but in people individually. Man as an individual, abstracted from any relationship save that of his relationship with God (because he is a creature and therefore necessarily dependent on that antecedent condition), is made in the image of God. Interfacing with Barth's theology, Hughes writes, "[W]e conclude that male and female duality does

---

[58] Ibid., 227.
[59] Berkouwer, *Man: The Image of God*, 48–52.
[60] Moltmann, 229.
[61] Ibid., 229.

not provide the key to the understanding of the divine image in which man was formed."[62]

For Hughes, the *imago Dei* is to be found precisely in mankind's discontinuity with the rest of the terrestrial creation: "Because he is made in the image of God, man differs in radical manner from the rest of animate creation."[63] Hughes tries to identify and expound those aspects of mankind's "surpassing excellence" over the rest of the creation, and arrives at the attributes of personality, spirituality, rationality, morality, authority, and creativity. For the purposes of this study the most germane of these is Hughes' understanding of rationality as a (not *the*) seat of the *imago Dei*. It is significant to note that Hughes reflexively criticizes those who would place human beings on a hierarchy of value based upon their abilities. He speaks scathingly of evolutionary theory that would assign individuals to varying levels along a hierarchy of value based upon intelligence or other criteria, and would "open the door . . . [to] the ungodly conclusion . . . that for the improvement of society . . . euthanasia may be administered to . . . the handicapped and the unproductive members of the race."[64] Yet such a statement is difficult to reconcile with his emphasis on rationality and intellect as a seat of the divine image:

> The excellence by which man is superior to the animals is seen . . . in the fact that he is constituted as a rational creature, and this too is an aspect of the image of God in which he has been created. The animals are called dumb or brute beasts because of the irrationality of their nature. Man, in striking contrast, is not dumb and uncomprehending, but is

---

[62] Philip Edgcumbe Hughes, *The True Image: The Origin and Destiny of Man in Christ* (Grand Rapids, MI: Eerdmans, 1989), 20. Hughes does not appear to understand Barth at this juncture. Barth does not base the *imago* on sexuality, as Hughes intimates, but in sameness (*adam*) and differentiation (the *zakar* of *ish* and the *n'qebah* of *ishah*), "I" and "Thou."

[63] Ibid., 51.

[64] Ibid., 6–7.

endowed with mental faculty that enables him to use language for the rational expression and communication of his thoughts and wishes, to pursue intellectual studies, to investigate the connection between things, and to appreciate the rationality of God's creation, of which he himself is a part. And man is not dumb because God is not dumb. God is a God who speaks, and his speaking is the declaration of his mind and his will.... Being exclusively formed in the divine image, man alone of earth's creatures is endowed with the faculty of rationality which enables him, as a reflector of the Creator's rationality, to think and to plan and to speak. His rationality is another strand in the bond that binds him to his Maker. The personal intercommunion between God and man is rational as well as spiritual.[65]

For Hughes too, the *imago Dei* ultimately is eschatological. "The question regarding the significance of man's creation in the divine image is raised on the opening pages of the Bible, but it is not clearly resolved until we come to the revelation in the New Testament that Christ himself, the Son, is the Image of God."[66] Thus Hughes sees significance in the Hebrew preposition that he believes distances man from the *imago Dei* itself: "It is not without significance that man is described as having been created *in* the image of God, and not as being himself that image."[67] *Imago Dei* is, he believes, closely associated with being a son.[68] Thus whatever remnants and expressions of the *imago Dei* continue to exist in fallen man, the reality of what it means to be made in the image of God will not be realized apart from Christ and his appearing at the end of history.

Hughes does not understand human beings to be the image of God but to be made *in* the image of God. He understands Christ to

[65] Ibid., 57.
[66] Ibid., 3.
[67] Ibid., 15.
[68] Ibid., 29–35.

have eternally been the image of God, and thus the image of God is understood to be a prior (indeed, an eternal) reality, antecedent to the creation of mankind. As Chapter Four will demonstrate, Hughes' exegetical treatment of the Hebrew prepositions is unfounded, and his work exhibits an inconsistency with regard to whether or not the intellect is the seat of the *imago Dei*.

Like early theologians such as Augustine and Bonaventure, Thomas Smail attempts to elucidate the *imago Dei* in specifically Trinitarian terms. Smail contends that "For Christians *imago Dei* means *imago Trinitatis*."[69] Unlike the earlier writers, however, Smail does not seek to find the Trinitarian image in constituent or substantive non-corporeal components within man. He is critical of theories of the *imago* in which humans are said to be ". . . like God because we stand upright, because we have immortal souls, and, dominating Western anthropology, the distinctive and God-like thing about us is our rationality."[70]

Smail is critical of the exegesis of the Eastern fathers who sought to draw a distinction between the *image* as being a basic relatedness to God that is indelible, and the *likeness* which has been lost and is only recovered in Christ's redemption. Although he maintains sound exegesis will not support this division between "two obviously synonymous terms," Smail contends that the theological instincts of the Eastern fathers were good, in that there is something eschatological about this doctrine that finds its fulfillment only in Christ.[71] He states,

> If the first Adam shows us what we are, the last Adam promises what we shall be . . . . [I]mage of God language . . . [is] of course affirmed once in Genesis 1 and then largely ignored in the rest of the Old Testament, where image language is used largely in a negative and pejorative way. . . . It

---

[69] Thomas Smail, "In the Image of the Triune God" *International Journal of Systematic Theology* 5, 1 (March 2003): 22.
[70] Ibid., 24.
[71] See Ibid., 25.

is significant that this thought is taken up only in the New Testament with its conviction that God's life and character have been perfectly reflected in the human life of Jesus. In him the mirror of our humanity loses its distortions and gains its proper focus on God, so that in Christ the image is restored and through him can be restored in us as well.[72]

Thus, ". . . the Genesis passage stands at the protological and the Pauline passages at the eschatological horizon of the way the biblical witnesses think of the *imago Dei* . . . ."[73]

Smail makes the intriguing observation that Jesus Christ ". . . is not only the man who images God, he himself is the incarnation of the God he images . . . ,"[74] and the God that he images is triune. He attempts to use the economic activities of the divine hypostases as a basis for the ontological reflection of the *imago Dei* to establish a functional view in which man consciously and deliberately images God. Thus as the Father sent the Son into the world because of a proactive love,

> So to be in the image and likeness of the Father . . . there are to be areas of life . . . where we are to be proactive and not merely reactive . . . , to intervene in situations and accept responsibility for turning them in directions that they would not otherwise take. . . . The image of the Father is the image of the leader. [Conversely], the image of the initiating Father is inhibited and distorted when people are oppressed or when they become oppressors.[75]

With regard to the Second Person, "*willing responsiveness* is the *proprium* of the Son," whose responsiveness "is not constrained by

---

[72] Ibid., 23.
[73] Ibid.
[74] Ibid., 24.
[75] Ibid., 28.

rigid law, superior force or threatened sanctions; it is his loving, self-giving response to the loving self-giving of the Father." This means that for us to be in the image of the Son is to be "bound to others in relationships in which we are not first but second, where we are not leading but following...." Conversely, "The image of the Son in us is repressed and denied when ... accountability is refused in a rebellion against ... authority.... Alternately the image is fatally distorted by any subservience to authority that is hostile to and destructive of a life lived in the freedom of love."[76]

Lastly, with regard to reflecting the image of God the Holy Spirit, Smail writes,

> ... to live in the *imago Dei* is also to be caught up in the *creative fulfillment* that characterizes the person and action of the Holy Spirit.... the *proprium* of the Spirit is to take what has been achieved by the Son's obedience and the Father's initiative and to achieve the purpose for which it was undertaken.... The faithful ... creativity of the Spirit is to be distinguished from the initiating creativity of the Father. The Father starts it all, but the Spirit completes it all.[77]

"So we image the Spirit ... in the way we interact" with situations and people in our lives when we seek to move them "step by step nearer the goals that God has for them in Christ."[78] Smail believes that we inhibit the image of the Spirit when we give in to the sin of sloth or apathy, and distance ourselves from what is challenging and requires courage or creativity to complete.

With the acknowledged influence of Barth, Smail maintains the essential nature of relationship in bearing the *imago Dei*. "Even at our worst we seek and want the friendship and support of other

---

[76] Ibid., 29–30.
[77] Ibid., 30–31.
[78] Ibid., 31.

people and will, in however limited a way, be ready to offer friendship and support to others, so that, *in as far as we remain human at all, we reflect the fundamental relationality that is at the heart of our creation* [italics added].[79]

This approach to the *imago Dei* raises questions when considered with regard to those with severe cognitive disabilities. Although Smail disagrees with those who see substantive rationality as the seat of the *imago Dei*, his approach to the *imago* emphasizes the functional and volitional aspects of the *imago*, i.e., how we deliberately image God, or how we deliberately diminish, counterfeit or bastardize that image. But volition presupposes a certain level of cognition. Depending on the severity of the disability, those of cognitively diminished capacity may be unable ever to lead, to serve another, or to be creative.

Hans Reinders has argued that what those with severe cognitive disabilities need most of all is for other human beings to choose them as friends, but some very severely disabled people may not have the capacity to reciprocate friendship. It is therefore troubling when considering the *imago Dei vis-à-vis* those with severe cognitive disabilities that Smail believes that a "fundamental relationality" must be reflected by people if they are to "remain human at all."

John Frame's treatment of mankind in the image of God likewise does not consciously consider any other than typical human beings, and many of the statements he makes are thus technically exclusive of those with severe cognitive disabilities.

After speaking of the uniqueness of humankind as being made in the image of God, Frame notes that "theologians have long puzzled over what exactly the image of God consists of."[80] He briefly mentions several examples, concluding "There is truth in all of these representations. But there are so many of them that it is

---

[79] Ibid., 26.

[80] John M. Frame, John M. Frame, *Systematic Theology; An Introduction to Christian Belief* (Phillipsburg, NJ: P&R Publishing, 2013), 784.

important for us to try to understand the conceptual patterns that bring them together."[81]

Frame then goes on to search for those qualities in human beings that separate them from the rest of creation, qualities that "lift man above other creatures," and which "constitute finite replicas of God's infinite qualities."[82] He concludes that the image of God itself "consists of those qualities that equip man to be lord of the world under God."[83]

Frame invokes a (familiar) triperspectival paradigm to present what is essentially a functional approach to the image of God, specifically Control (kingly function); Authority (prophetic function); and Presence (priestly function).

Under the heading of Control, Frame speaks of the cultural mandate. He maintains that the body of man must be included in the image of God for the reason that physical strength and activity is necessary to the task of subduing and ruling the earth.[84] Under the head of Authority, he notes, "Language is also fundamental to human nature in the image of God."[85] For Frame, language is crucial, so much so that he says that it is necessary to the image. "It makes man like God in an important way, and it lifts man above the other creatures so that he may have dominion over them."[86] Under Presence, Frame notes "Since [man] is not omnipresent as God is, he can fill [the earth] only by marrying and having children."[87]

Frame is critical but not dismissive of Barth's relational view. He sees God's image as "mirrored" or "pictured" in such things as human sexuality and love.[88] While Frame asserts that the primary

---

[81] Ibid. 785.
[82] Ibid.
[83] Ibid. 786.
[84] Ibid. 786–87.
[85] Ibid. 788.
[86] Ibid. 790.
[87] Ibid.
[88] Ibid. 794.

meaning of "image" is resemblance rather than representation, it is a distinction without a demonstrated difference (Frame states that distinction is between structure and function).[89]

Although elsewhere in the book Frame is cautious about exalting reason above other human faculties,[90] his approach is unsettling when looked at from the perspective of those with the most sever intellectual disabilities. For Frame, the *imago Dei* consists in certain criteria. But if the image of God "consists in" those qualities which "lift man above other creatures," and equip him to be "lord of the world under God," where does that leave human beings who do not possess qualities that lift them above other creatures or equip them to be lord of anything?[91] If the human body is included in the *imago* only because it's strength allows the person to carry out certain functions, what does this mean for those who do not have use of or control over their bodies?

Frame expresses his belief that language is "fundamental" (*viz.* essential, vital) to human nature in the image of God. Again we may ask, what of those human beings who do not possess expressive language, or do not possessive receptive language, or do not possess either? If language is fundamental to the *imago*, are they thereby excluded from it?

Frame deals with the *imago Dei* only in terms of the creation. His work contains no eschatological orientation of the image of God. His statements taken at face value would be exclusive of individuals with various forms and levels of disability. I suspect that Frame did not intend this, and would concede an exception for such people, but including those with severe cognitive disabilities in a theological paradigm of the *imago Dei* by way exception is no less a part of the problem.

---

[89] Ibid. 795.

[90] Ibid. 751–53.

[91] The author once heard the father of a child with very severe intellectual disabilities say in tears, "Our dog is able to obey more commands, and exert more physical control over his environment than is my son."

Literature Review

Ancient Near Eastern Scholars

D. J. A. Clines' work in the image of God was seminal in bringing the ancient Near Eastern context to bear on the question of the Genesis texts on a broadly popular level. "The meaning of the image of God in Genesis 1 cannot be understood without reference to the significance of the image in the ancient Near East."[92] Drawing on the scholarship of von Rad, Bernhardt, and others, Clines is adamant that the image cannot be limited to the incorporeal aspects of mankind. "We mention first the fact that צֶלֶם and its cognates in other Semitic languages are used predominantly in a literal sense, of three dimensional objects which represent gods, men, or other living things."[93]

Clines maintains that the way in which images were used in the ancient Near East suggests that man as God's image indicates that humanity represents God to creation. "The image does not primarily mean similarity, but the representation of the one who is imaged in the place where he is not. . . . The king puts his statue in a conquered land to signify his real, though not his physical, presence there. . . . According to Genesis 1:26f. man is set on earth in order to be the representative there of the absent God who is nevertheless present by His image."[94]

In regard to the difference between the "image" and the "likeness" Clines writes, "In suggesting here that a difference in meaning can be established between צֶלֶם and דְּמוּת we are by no means asserting that they . . . refer to different elements in the image. Rather we are suggesting that דְּמוּת refers entirely to צֶלֶם; it has no referential meaning in itself, but only specifies the kind of image, namely a representational image."[95]

Based on his research of the ancient Near East, Clines maintains that it is not possible for the image of God to be lost, despite man's

---

[92] D. J. A. Clines, "The Image of God in Man" *Tyndale Bulletin*, 19, (1968): 85
[93] Ibid., 73.
[94] Ibid., 88.
[95] Ibid., 92.

fall. "Once a divine image in the Ancient Near East has become the dwelling-place of the divine fluid, it remains the image of the god, regardless of the vicissitudes to which it is subjected.... In Genesis also man remains, from the moment of his creation, the image of God."[96]

Dealing with the difficulty of translating and exegeting the Hebrew particle preposition בּ, Clines concludes that the traditional translation of "in the image of God" is mistaken, and should be abandoned in favor of "as the image of God."[97] Thus, "Man is created not in God's image, since God has no image of His own, but as God's image" for the purpose of representing "the transcendent God who remains outside the world order.... The whole man is the image of God, without distinction of spirit or body. All mankind, without distinction, are the image of God."[98]

Clines concludes his monograph by applying the conclusions of his ancient Near Eastern studies to the consideration of the *imago Dei* in the New Testament. He points out that all image language there (εἰκών, ὁμοίωσις, μορφή, χαρακτήρ) refers predominately to the incarnate Christ. As Adam shared his image with his descendants (cf. Gen. 5:3), so Christ shares his image with his descendants, "... namely, those who are 'in Christ.'" The redeemed are thus conformed to the image of Christ, who is himself the image of God, and although believers take part in that renewed image now, "Bearing the image of Christ is an eschatological concept; it contains elements both now and not yet."[99]

> The protological doctrine of the image, which retains its existential implications, has become transformed in the New Testament into an eschatological doctrine itself with existential implications.... In Christ man sees what manhood was meant to be. In the New, where Christ is the one true

[96] Ibid., 99.
[97] Ibid., 70–85.
[98] Ibid., 101.
[99] Ibid., 102.

image, men are the image of God in so far as they are like Christ. The image is fully realized only through obedience to Christ; this is how man, the image of God, who is already man, already the image of God, can become fully man, fully the image of God.[100]

Clines insists that physicality is not the totality of, but certainly an important aspect of, the image of God even more adamantly than does Berkouwer. Particularly in his argument for the translation that man has been created *as* the image of God, Clines moves the discussion away from a substantivism which would see the image of God as something *within* man.

While Clines' work is useful for considering the image of God *vis-à-vis* those with severe cognitive disabilities, clearly such people are not within his exegetical or theological consideration. His approach to conformity to Christ as a realization of the *imago Dei* is focused in this age, and not in the eschaton. While nothing Clines writes would exclude those with disabilities from participation in the *imago*, his theology would clearly preclude those with intellectual disabilities from making observable progress in the *imago* which is evidently open to people of more typical intellect.

Meredith Kline likewise incorporates considerations from ancient Near Eastern and Second Temple studies into a unique approach to the doctrine. Kline indicates that his book *Images of the Spirit* was the result of "exegetical studies . . . sprout[ing] in unexpected directions," which, though not meant to be a systematic theology, he hopes "will contribute to the doctrine of the *imago Dei* in systematic theology."[101]

Kline's thesis is that the theophanic glory-Spirit is the archetype for man who is made in the image of God.[102] The widely held

---

[100] Ibid., 103.
[101] Meredith G. Kline, *Images of the Spirit* (South Hamilton, MA: Meredith G. Kline, 1986), 10–11.
[102] Ibid., 17, 20–25.

idea that the Scriptures speak of God in anthropomorphisms is incorrect; rather, the Scriptures present man as a theomorphism, although the archetypical *imago* (the pre-incarnate Son) is realized only in relationship to creation.[103]

Like many ancient Near Eastern scholars, Kline maintains that the "Let us" of Genesis 1:26 is a reference to the heavenly court, that is, God and the angels (or "gods"). He argues that the image of God is to be found precisely in a reflection of the judicial function of the heavenly court, and in the decision-making process in mankind's kingly function in ruling over the rest of creation.[104] But his view of the *imago* is not merely functional. He notes that "Under the concept of man as the glory-image of God the Bible includes functional (or official), formal (or physical), and ethical components, corresponding to the composition of the archetypical Glory."[105]

Kline's perspective is helpful specifically in that it is not myopic. Rather than seeking to identify the *imago* with one component, aspect, or perspective, there is a totality in viewing the whole man in all of his dimensions as the *imago Dei*.

Kline sees the pre-incarnate Son as the image of God,[106] an idea that Clines and others have noted is not supported by the words used in Genesis 1:26–27. His assertion that angels are also made in the image of God[107] is exegetically dubious at best. Because he sees the *imago* archetypically as the pre-incarnate Christ, Kline makes a distinction between humanity and the image of God. "When defining the *imago Dei*, dogmatic theology has traditionally tended to engage in an analysis of what constitutes humanness. But to answer

---

[103] "The description of the likeness of the Son to the Father does not refer to eternal ontological reality of God apart from creation but to the revelation of the Father by the son in creation," but the manifestation of the image is ". . . not . . . a reference to the incarnation." Ibid., 16.

[104] Ibid., 27–31.

[105] Ibid., 31.

[106] Ibid., 16.

[107] Ibid., 22.

Literature Review

the question, "What is man?" is not the same thing as answering the precise question, "What is the image of God?"[108] Although Kline means this metaphysically, the statement raises the possibility that there could be human beings who do not participate in the image of God (cf. the discussion of Martin Luther in Chapter One).

In her doctoral dissertation Catherine Beckerleg considers the concept of the image of God in Genesis 1:26–27 and other texts where it occurs explicitly (and, she believes, implicitly) in light of *mīs pî pīt pî* ("washing the mouth, opening the mouth") and *wpt-r* rituals in Mesopotamia and ancient Egypt. The main idea of her thesis is that Genesis 2:5–3:24 contains the concept of the image of God, even though the phrase is not used in this section, in light of ancient Near Eastern practices in which kings in their installation are washed and consecrated (*mīs pî*), and idols are ritualistically endowed with life (*pīt pî*, i.e., their mouths are opened). Beckerleg argues that "Genesis 2:5–3:24 draws on features common to vivification rituals," though unlike in those rituals, "Mankind was not a 'living statue of the deity' in the same way that a divine statue became the god once its mouth was washed and opened. Rather, man was, in some way, created in the image of God yet distinct from God himself."[109]

Beckerleg sees parallels between these rituals and the Eden account of Genesis 2–3 in light of mankind's having been made in the image of God (Gen. 1:26–27).

> In ancient Mesopotamia the creation, animation, and installation of a divine statue in its temple was a complex task requiring a skilled set of craftsmen and priests. The materials used to manufacture the image and the ritual space in which the creative activity took place had to be prepared and purified

---

[108] Ibid., 13.

[109] Catherine Leigh Beckerleg, "The 'Image of God' in Eden: The Creation of Mankind in Genesis 2:5–3:24 in Light of the *mīs pî pīt pî* and *wpt-r* Rituals in Mesopotamia and Ancient Egypt" (Ph.D. diss., Harvard University, 2009), 23.

according to strict confidential guidelines. After the image was created it had to be "brought to life" through the appropriate incantations and rituals, dressed, adorned with proper insignia, installed in its temple, and fed its first meal before it could be effective.... The *mīs pî* was performed not only on divine statues, but also on the king and his royal insignia, royal statues, priests, individual humans, and various animals and sacred objects. By contrast, the mouth-opening rite (*pīt pî*) was apparently reserved for inanimate objects, including figurines and larger divine images .... It was thought to consecrate, activate, and/or enliven the object in preparation for cultic use.[110]

Likewise for the similar Egyptian ritual: "... the *wpt-r* was a ritual chiefly concerned with the creation and animation of a divine image."[111]

If she is correct, the Genesis account would constitute a polemic against these ancient Near Eastern rituals, for the "vivification" of the Eden account comes about by the fall of man: "It is clear that in eating the forbidden fruit and *becoming like elohim* the man and woman had transgressed a very significant boundary between human and divine spheres. In the Mesopotamian *pīt pî* and the Egyptian *wpt-r*, however, the opening of the eyes, which signified the image's (re-)birth and the transformation of the image into a living manifestation of an *'el* (*ilu*) was precisely the goal."[112] Beckerleg believes that these rituals shed light on the continuity of Genesis 1 and 2 (often considered to be separate, distinct, and by some contradictory creation stories). The temptation of man by the serpent and his subsequent fall in Genesis 3 unpack the *tselem* and *demuth* of Genesis 1:26–27.

---

[110] Ibid., 61–62.
[111] Ibid., 146.
[112] Ibid., 58.

Treating the words in question, Beckerleg says of *tselem*, "In the Hebrew Bible the term *selem* appears seventeen times and generally refers to a statue, figure or replica."[113] In almost every case of Aramaic cognates, "the term describes anthropomorphic statues. We conclude therefore that [the term and its cognates] typically refer to a concrete object made of metal, painted stone, or human flesh, which is a representation, likeness, or copy of the original."[114]

She notes that the noun *demut* derives from the verb *dmt*, "to resemble, be like. [It] occurs twenty-five times in the Hebrew Bible. It expresses similarity. . . ." She points out that the word is most frequently employed in Ezekiel where it is used "to relate the unfamiliar to the familiar . . . He did not see a man but something *like* a man. He did not see a throne but something *resembling* a throne. . . . Thus, *demut* refers to correspondence and likeness, but it does not seem to indicate a copy nor a facsimile, as can *selem*."[115] Yet while "*demut* and *selem* are not always semantic equivalents . . . Gen. 5:3 may be an example of where the terms are, more or less, interchangeable."[116]

Beckerleg concludes that humankind as God's image does not mean that he is an avatar, a manifestation of God. Like Clines, she is inclined toward a representative understanding of the image of God. Mankind represents God's ruling presence on earth. Whatever distinctly human attributes mankind may have, however, they are not the essence of the image of God, but are consequent of it. ". . . . mankind's intellectual abilities, his unique relationship with God, and even his status as divinely appointed administrator over creation seems to be a result of the being created in God's image rather than a definition of what it means to be made [in the image of God]."[117]

---

[113] Ibid., 163.
[114] Ibid., 163–64.
[115] Ibid., 169–70.
[116] Ibid., 170–71.
[117] Ibid., 178–79.

Reshuffling the familiar triad of Adam as prophet, priest, and king under God and over the rest of creation, Beckerleg asserts the expression of the image in terms of kingship (king), cult (priest), and *kinship*. It is in the last of these that Beckerleg's work has the most applicability to the present study.

Drawing on the work of Meredith Kline, Beckerleg affirms that "Image of God and son of God are mutually explanatory concepts." "That man is . . . depicted as a 'royal son' of God seems much closer to the sense of *selem* and *demut* in Gen. 1:26–27."[118] Although careful to make a distinction between man as creature and God as creator, she asserts that in Genesis 1 man is presented as "God's kind":

> In Gen. 1:11–12 God creates vegetation, plants and fruit trees, all of which are reproduced "each according to its kind . . . ." God also created the sea creatures and birds "according to their kind." . . . God then made all the living creatures inhabit the earth, each "according to its kind." . . . Clearly the author is emphasizing the creation and reproduction of each species *according to its own distinctive type or class*. [But] the creation of man is described not "according to his kind" as [we] might have expected, but "in the image of" and "according to the likeness of" Elohim. This juxtaposition of the oft-repeated "according to its/their kind" with "image and likeness of God" suggests that the author was drawing a sharp distinction between man and the other created beings. However, it also implies that just as the plants and animals were created according to their own type, man was made, at some level, according to *Elohim's kind*. . . . being created in the image and likeness of God is both comparable to being created "according to God's kind," yet distinct from it. In other words, man is not divine. . . . Yet at some level, man

---

[118] Ibid., 179.

belongs to the divine class or species, that is, humanity's kind or type is God.[119]

For this reason, while the other earthly creatures reproduce "after their kind," Adam begets Seth "in his own likeness (*demut*) according to his image (*selem*)" (Gen. 5:3) just as God had created Adam "in his ("our") own image (*selem*) and according to his ("our") likeness (*demut*)" (Gen. 1:26).

Although the scope of Beckerleg's dissertation is not conducive to her exploration of the ramifications of her thesis in light of the redemption of Christ, the connection is not hard to make. Man was originally made in the image of God, but believed the lie that by disobeying God he would become "like God" (Gen. 3:5). When the Son of God came into the world, he by contrast "though being in very nature God, did not regard equality with God a thing to be grasped" (Phil. 2:6). Whatever remnants of the *imago Dei* remain for fallen man, sonship has been lost (cf. Eph. 2:3–7, John 1:12–13). Although carefully qualified, the goal and result of Christ's redemption is that those who participate in it "become partakers of the divine nature" (2 Peter 1:4) by becoming sons and daughters, thus being restored to the perceptible and evident status of being "after God's kind."

Contextual Theologians

Beginning with the Augustinian idea that all of creation in some way reflects the being of God, Douglas Hall takes a functional approach to the *imago Dei* but seeks to cast the approach in a new light. Concerned that the doctrine has historically been misappropriated as justification for exploitation of both other human beings and the environment ("dominion"), Hall borrows concepts from Barth[120] to establish a relational approach to humankind's functionality in

---

[119] Ibid., 181–82.
[120] Douglas Hall, *Imaging God Dominion as Stewardship* (Grand Rapids, MI:

the world with respect to the biosphere, other creatures, and other human beings. Although not specifically his topic, in developing his thesis Hall touches on some aspects of the *imago Dei* that are insightful and significant for the consideration of the doctrine with regard to those with severe cognitive disabilities.

A protégé of Reinhold Niebuhr, Hall does not understand the fall to be a historical event, but recognizes existentially that something is amiss. The first subsection of the first chapter of his book Imaging God: Dominion as Stewardship is entitled "Something is Wrong." He is critical of Christians for turning a blind eye to problems beyond their own experience, even while theoretically embracing the notion of sin. "[W]hen so many of us citizens of First World countries—where it is still possible, with a little luck, to sustain the illusion of well-being—make it our aim to assure ourselves that nothing is seriously amiss, we simply compound the deepening crises of our own planet. Not only do we deceive ourselves, but we perpetuate systems of injustice, oppression, and want by which other human beings are daily humiliated."[121] Hall believes that this is both unbecoming and unnecessary for Christians. "Optimism is the product of a frantic need to think exclusively 'positive' . . . thoughts about reality. . . . Christian hope, which is first of all hope in God and not in human institutions, systems, ideologies, and 'dreams,' does not have to lie to itself about what is really there in the world."[122]

Hall's discussion of sin signals a cautionary note when dealing with the doctrine of the image of God. Significant for his contextual approach, Hall maintains that the *imago Dei* is no mere exegesis of צֶלֶם אֱלֹהִים, but the phrase has become a symbol, and symbols require caution, for they can become shorthand for extra-conciliary dogma:

Eerdmans, 1986), 72 ff.
[121] Ibid., 2.
[122] Ibid., 3.

It could be said about every aspect of Christian theology that it is burdened by its own past. Everyone who works seriously in the discipline of systematic or dogmatic theology knows that the theological tradition is both a great gift and a great encumbrance. Without the tradition, theology would be at the mercy of immediate religious experience, and this would soon destroy whatever unity of truth practitioners of this discipline are allowed to glimpse. For that unity depends in large measure on common tradition of reflection and experience. At the same time, the tradition is theology's burden because human nature being what it is, the past continuously imposes itself on the present, discouraging the frail faith of the *koinonia* from venturing out into the unknown, and tempting it instead to remain within the familiar confines of past expressions of belief.[123]

Yet it is precisely in the *imago Dei* being symbol that it has broad applicability and a certain plasticity in dealing with various and newly considered aspects of human existence. "The advantage of symbol, as opposed to dogma or doctrine, is that it lends itself more readily to the contextualization that is a necessary dimension of theological thought."[124]

It is in his encouragement to extend beyond the familiar confines of historical expressions of theology, and in his rejection of the substantive concept of the *imago Dei* found in the patristic and medieval theologians that Hall's observations are most applicable to this study. Hall sums up the substantive view of the *imago* in this way: "Human kind in God's image, according to this view, means that . . . the human species possesses certain characteristics or qualities that render it similar to the divine being" often conceived of in what "distinguishes man from nature and from other

---

[123] Ibid., 64–65.
[124] Ibid., 64.

animals."¹²⁵ The problem with this approach, according to Hall, is that it baptizes those "qualities lauded by the dominant culture of one's society"¹²⁶ as being the essence of the *imago Dei*. Given the prevalence of a substantive understanding of the *imago* which so often associates the image of God with intellect, Hall notes,

> The notion that it is human reason that constitutes *Homo sapiens*, God's earthly *imago*, is so firmly entrenched in the conventions of Christendom that it is hardly possible for anyone who is part of the intellectual stream of our culture to read Genesis 1:26–27 without immediately and subconsciously assuming that the ancient Hebraic author's phrase "image of God" specifically referred to the rational capacities of the human creature. . . . our civilization has been so persuaded that human rationality is humanity's absolute highest good that we automatically assume that this to be what the Hebrew writer must have had in mind. . . . Hence, we suppose, *imago Dei* obviously refers to our capacity to think.¹²⁷

Furthermore, there are implications for approaching the doctrine in this way.

> If we look for the essence of the human in rationality . . . we automatically assume a hierarchical structure of the world. . . . this valuation process is prejudicial . . . to all humans who on account of their condition or their innate abilities are not capable of "measuring up" to the highest conceptions of what it means to reason. One could speculate endlessly how much damage has been done . . . to the mentally handicapped . . . on

---

¹²⁵ Ibid., 89.
¹²⁶ Ibid., 92.
¹²⁷ Ibid.

this avowedly "Christian" practice of identifying the highest and best—and truly human!—with rationality.[128]

In his critique of the traditional understanding of the *imago Dei* Hall does not denigrate reason; he does not advocate a "Dionysian frenzy of antirationality;"[129] but he believes that the *imago Dei* is to be found primarily in the "relatedness" of human beings to God, human beings to fellow human beings, and human beings to the rest of creation.[130] *Contra* Berkouwer, Hall believes that we cannot find the essence of humanity by examining individuals (humanity-in-the-abstract); we must rather study human beings "in the context of their many-dimensioned relationships."[131]

Hall considers this "withness" (Heidegger's *Mitsein*; Hall reflects on the significance of the German language's removal from Latin and the numerous compound *mit* nouns and verbs found in it[132]) to be the core of the *imago Dei*. "It is, in fact, not very far away from the world-picture of ancient Israel. *Shalom*, a word used by the Hebrews to express what they believed to be 'God's intention for creation' is perhaps the most poignant of all human words aiming to articulate the mutuality of all being."[133]

In view of the reality (but inexplicability?) of human sin, Hall believes that the continued importance of the image of God is bound up with the incarnation and the redemption Christ came to bring.

> The explicitly Christian references to the *imago* as symbol can be summarized succinctly in two interrelated ideas. First, they affirm that Jesus as Christ is himself the image of God. Second, they affirm that those who through hearing,

---

[128] Ibid., 108–109.
[129] Ibid., 111.
[130] Ibid., 113 ff.
[131] Ibid., 115.
[132] Ibid., 116–23.
[133] Ibid., 118.

baptism, and the work of the divine Spirit are being incorporated into the life of Christ ... are being conformed to the image as revealed and embodied in Christ, and thus renewed according to the original intention of the Creator.[134]

Hall profoundly notes that (in light of passages such as Isa. 53 and Phil. 2) if Christ is the image of God, this turns the notion of what it means to be in the image of God on its head. For if Christ is the image of God, the image of God is to be found in humility, in weakness, and even in suffering. "If Jesus is the image of God ... then it will no longer suffice to put forward the most notable and exalted of human capacities and call them *imago Dei*. For the one who is exalted here is the one who is brought low . . . ."[135]

For Hall, the image of God beckons us to look, not back toward a speculative past, but forward to the future through an existential present. It is telic and eschatological in its orientation, or better, in orienting us. "God is at work in this unfinished history of ours. We are part of a great process of restoration and redemption."[136] Regarding the image of God in man now, however, Hall turns the doctrine in an unexpected direction: "In short, we are once more unable to pursue this equation of Jesus with *imago Dei* without undergoing a transmutation of our ordinary human and 'religious' presuppositions: expecting glory, we are shown humiliation . . . ."[137]

Hall's main thesis is not concerned with the *imago Dei* in regard to those with cognitive disabilities. He believes that the essence of the image of God is to be found in the relatedness of humankind to God, to one another, and to the rest of creation, and as it is expressed in Christ, humility to the point of humiliation. Man has evilly turned these relationships into struggle for control, domination, and exploitation, a condition that Jesus, *the* Image of God, has come to

---

[134] Ibid., 76.
[135] Ibid., 78.
[136] Ibid., 81.
[137] Ibid., 80.

remedy. Although not in the purview of his thesis, it could be said that given his concerns, Hall speaks implicitly to the place of those with severe cognitive disabilities in human society. His approach encourages the explicit consideration of the *imago Dei* in the light of all human relationships, and human suffering.

Charles Sherlock examines the biblical teaching of the *imago Dei* as foundational to the two foci he addresses in his book *The Doctrine of Humanity*. The first focus is mankind made in the image of God; the second focus considers the existential condition of humankind collectively (which he maintains is a more eastern focus), and in terms of individual persons (which he maintains is a more western focus, particularly after the Renaissance, Reformation, and Enlightenment).

Sherlock begins his consideration by stating, ". . . it is vital to be clear how we image God, before we begin to explore what being made in the image of God as human beings may mean."[138] Although the phrase "how we image God" could be taken to indicate a functional understanding of the *imago Dei*, Sherlock does not mean it in quite this way. He points out that the fall and consequent distortion of the *imago Dei* came about precisely because the first pair believed the lie that they must *do* something to be like God. "The serpent's craftiness is particularly seen in the comment that the man and woman would be 'like God' . . . if they ate the forbidden fruit (Gen. 3:5). This suggests that human beings need to achieve something to be 'like God,' whereas their status is *already* that of being made in the image and likeness of God."[139] Although the phrase "image of God" is found explicitly only in three passages in the Old Testament (Gen. 1:26–28; 5:1–2; 9:6–7), each of these come at significant and "critical turning-points in the Genesis account."[140] In fact, "The significance of our being made in the

---

[138] Charles Sherlock, *The Doctrine of Humanity* (Downers Grove, IL: InterVarsity, 1996), 19.

[139] Ibid., 42.

[140] Ibid., 31.

image of God is emphasized by its placement in the first chapter of the Scriptures."[141]

Germane to this study, Sherlock believes that it is a mistake to try to "localize" the image of God in some aspect or ability of man. "[M]any approaches to what the image of God entails are ruled out. The Scriptures do not locate the image of God in some aspect or other of human life, or in any combination of aspects . . . ."[142] While it is ". . . clearly legitimate to *describe* human beings in image terms, attempts to *define* the image of God precisely are fraught with danger."[143]

The image of God was badly distorted by man's sin. "Human beings no longer *live* as those made in the image of God; sin distorts and mars it at every point."[144] The problem is not that the image of God has been abolished in us. "It is far worse, namely that while [the *imago's*] structures of relationship [to God, creation, and one another] remain, they are distorted at every point . . . ."[145] According to Sherlock, we thus live in the hellish condition of having the structures and longing to live out the *imago Dei*, but having lost the ability to do so.

The situation is not hopeless, however, because the New Testament provides a forward-looking, telic, and new-creation alignment of the *imago Dei*. Sherlock notes that "The early church proclaimed the greatness of the human species, but with a future orientation rather than a past one, from the perspective of what we are to become rather than of what we were or are."[146] He maintains that the Old Testament doctrine of humanity as a whole being created in the image of God ". . . is not strongly affirmed in the New Testament, but it is certainly not contested. It pales into relative

---

[141] Ibid., 29.
[142] Ibid., 33.
[143] Ibid., 32.
[144] Ibid., 42.
[145] Ibid., 43.
[146] Ibid., 49.

insignificance in the light of what God has in store for humankind: the focus is now on Christ, then on those who are 'in Christ,' and their destiny. It is striking, for example, that the term 'image' (*eikôn*) is not used for humankind in the New Testament apart from reference to Christ."[147]

Sherlock sees as significant the fact that in the New Testament only Christ is the "image of God," and those who are his become the "image of Christ." Thus,

> The creaturely dignity of human beings, made in the image of God, was to be seen in creative relationship with God, with one another, and with the world. It was human rejection of relationship with God which brought about the corruption of the image, and so each of the relationships which flow from it. The New Testament proclaims that Christ brought, and through the Spirit continues to bring, a new reality: the reconciliation of our humanity to God.... Christ as *the* image of God restores all the relationships corrupted in and by sin.... Restoration of humankind to the divine image entailed Christ's full identification with sinners, his complete dealing with sin, and his being raised from death, as Lord of all.... Jesus lived out obedience which humanity did not, as the 'second Adam,' the 'new humanity.' In his death and resurrection has come about the prospect of the reconciliation of human beings—with God and each other, and of and in all things. We do not see that restoration fully yet, nor do we know what it may entail. We experience it to some degree in the church, the body of Christ, the new community of God's Spirit, who brings into the present both what Christ has accomplished and what he will accomplish, anticipating the future re-creation of humankind.[148]

---

[147] Ibid., 50.
[148] Ibid., 69–70.

Although not the emphasis of his study, this has tremendous implication for those who are members of the body of Christ[149] and who have severe cognitive disabilities. "Christ's life, death and resurrection mean that the picture of humanity in Genesis 1–3 now speaks of hope made possible rather than of grand beginnings spoiled. Instead of orienting human self-understanding toward the past, to what we once were, we are oriented toward the future, to what in Christ we are to become."[150] Although humankind was created in the image of God, and remains as such even in its fallen condition, "Human beings are not solely defined in terms of their past or present, but in the light of what we are destined to become in Christ. This goal is our being 'glorified' (cf. 1 Cor. 11:7). . . . It is *Christ* who is the image of God; those whom God calls in Christ are to come into conformity with the image of God's Son."[151]

The thesis of J. Richard Middleton's *The Liberating Image* is that God's Sabbath rest in creation was the start of the significant labor of mankind, who was made in the image of God to continue God's work. Beginning with a survey of the difficulty of explaining the *imago Dei* due to the paucity of texts making explicit reference to it (Gen. 1:26–27; 5:1; 9:6; and in the New Testament 1 Cor. 11:7 and James 3:9 in dealing with the *imago Dei* by virtue of creation),[152] Middleton concludes that it is the lack of textual data that has led "Most patristic, medieval, and modern interpreters typically [to] ask, not an exegetical, but a speculative question: In what ways are humans *like* God and *unlike* animals?"[153] Most often, he notes, the image of God was conceived as man's powers of reason, the exception being among some of the Greek fathers who "understood [the image] dynamically, as the progressive conformity of the soul (ψυχή,

---

[149] How different traditions understand this will be taken up in Chapter Five.
[150] Sherlock, 57.
[151] Ibid., 65–66.
[152] J. Richard Middleton, *The Liberating Image* (Grand Rapids, MI: Brazos Press, 2005), 16–17.
[153] Ibid., 19.

"life" cf. Matt. 20:28) to God or a salvific partaking of the divine nature, a process typically called 'divinization.'"[154]

Middleton believes that the failure of systematic theologians to deal properly with the doctrine stems from an over-reliance on philosophy and an under-appreciation of Old Testament scholarship, notably a lack of appreciation that kings were seen as the image bearers of the gods in the ancient Near East, and an exclusion of the physical body from the *imago Dei* (in evident disregard of the meaning of צֶלֶם).[155]

Although Middleton does not believe that study of the linguistic or syntactic uses of the Hebrew words will yield definitive answers to the question of what constitutes the *imago Dei*, he nonetheless maintains that such a study is a necessary precondition to considering the broader literary and intertextual studies, which he has confidence will yield fruitful results.[156] Acknowledging that the word "king" does not appear in the Genesis text as a reference to God, he nonetheless concludes that because the *imago Dei* is connected with the function of rule over the creatures (Gen. 1:26), "A royal-function reading of the *imago Dei* is essentially confirmed."[157] He is very concerned that this kingship not be understood in a Kuyperian manner[158] (which he believes to be exploitive of creation), but rather in such a way that the royal metaphor includes "wisdom and artful construction,"[159] as well as a priestly dimension in which man made in the image of God engages in "actively mediating divine blessing to the non-human world and—in a post-fall situation—interceding on behalf of a groaning creation until the day when heaven and earth are redemptively transformed to fulfill God's purpose of justice and shalom."[160]

---

[154] Ibid., 19–20.
[155] Ibid., 24–34.
[156] Ibid., 43–45.
[157] Ibid., 88.
[158] Ibid., 34–35.
[159] Ibid., 89.
[160] Ibid., 90.

Middleton considers the doctrine against the backdrop of its likely ancient Near Eastern context. He examines and rejects the Gilgamesh Epic as a reliable guide to understanding the biblical *imago Dei*,[161] but finds a more plausible context in two extant documents from the First Intermediate Period after the fall of the Old Kingdom of Egypt, dating from about 2200 B.C.: *The Instruction for Merikare* and *The Instruction of Ani*. Although these texts are damaged and their translation contested, Middleton maintains that they can be cited as "promoting a democratization of the royal Egyptian image of god."[162] Although speculative, Middleton concedes that an early dating of these texts may not "rule out historical influence on Genesis,"[163] but ". . . if either of these isolated texts . . . did, in fact, influence the notion of the *imago Dei* in Genesis, it is still quite unclear what light they shed on the interpretation of the biblical text."[164]

Surveying Akkadian, Mesopotamian, and Babylonian texts in aggregate with the Egyptian texts, Middleton concludes,

> It is my judgment that the description of ancient near eastern kings as the image of God, when understood as an integral component of Egyptian and/or Mesopotamian royal ideology, provides the most plausible set of parallels for interpreting the *imago Dei* in Genesis 1. If such texts—or the ideology behind them—influenced the biblical *imago Dei*, this suggests that humanity is dignified with a status and role vis-à-vis the nonhuman creation that is analogous to the status and role of kings in the ancient Near East vis-à-vis their subjects.[165]

---

[161] Ibid., 95–99.
[162] Ibid., 101.
[163] Ibid., 103.
[164] Ibid., 104.
[165] Ibid., 120.

The goal of the *imago Dei*, both in creation and redemption, is to set human beings free to reflect God's rule over creation and mediate creation's worship of God.

> Genesis 1 artfully shatters both ancient and contemporary rhetorical expectations and, instead, depicts God as a generous creator, sharing power with a variety of creatures (especially humanity), inviting them ... to participate in the creative (and historical) process.... In the end, the liberating character of the *imago Dei* is grounded in the nature of God, who calls the world into being as an act of generosity. This means that we cannot artificially separate our vision of God's redemptive love from an understanding of God's creative power. A careful reading of Genesis 1:1–2:3 thus converges on John 3:16. In both creation and redemption, "God so loved the world that he gave ..." [last ellipsis in the original].[166]

Middleton's work is wide-ranging, drawing on Old Testament and ancient Near Eastern scholarship, as well as the work of systematic and historical theologians as the basis of a practical exhortation to the church to fulfill what he believes is (redeemed) mankind's divinely appointed task of bringing peace, enablement and liberty to all of God's creation.

A Survey of the Theology of Disabilities Literature

Within the last two decades serious theological consideration has been given to the topic of disability, and more specifically, intellectual disability. While some of this theological reflection has been abstract and academic, the bulk of it has been reflection born out of the practical experiences of those who live or work with those

---

[166] Ibid., 296–97.

who have disabilities. Although these "disability theologians" bring a unique and helpful perspective, they largely consider only those with disabilities. A more comprehensive anthropology that encompasses all people, including those with handicaps, is not in their purview. Nevertheless, their contributions have been a seminal reminder to the church that people with disabilities exist and need to be considered.

Any survey of the literature regarding a theology of disabilities (and particularly cognitive disabilities) must start with Jean Vanier. A Canadian Roman Catholic, Vanier earned a Ph.D. in philosophy from the *Institut Catholique* in Paris, his doctoral work being in Aristotelian ethics. He taught philosophy at the University of Toronto before founding l'Arche in Trosly, France, in 1964.[167]

Because of his background, Vanier's philosophy and theology of intellectual disability is not systematic. His approach is very much consistent with his virtue ethic, which seeks primarily to discern what kind of person one's own actions make him or her.[168] Although Vanier's insights are philosophical and psychological, and although he does not deal explicitly with the doctrine of the *imago Dei*, from his writings one can tease out a theological anthropology. For Vanier, to "become human" means to recognize our condition as creatures which are not self-sufficient. This "becoming," however, does not imply that there are people who are not human, but rather that all can and should grow in the recognition of their own humanity: "all humans are sacred, whatever their culture, race or religion, whatever their capacities or incapacities, and whatever their weaknesses and strengths may be. Each of us has an instrument to bring to the vast

---

[167] Jean-Vanier.org, "Jean Vanier, Becoming Human: Brief Chronology," http://www.jean-vanier.org/en/the_man/brief_chronology (accessed April 22, 2013). See also Jean Vanier, *Becoming Human* (Toronto: Anansi Press, 2008), 1–4.

[168] See Aristotle, *Nichomachean Ethics*, trans. Terrance Irwin (Indianapolis: Hackett Publishing, 1985), or for a brief analysis see Dennis P. Hollinger, "Character or Virtue Ethics" in *Choosing the Good* (Grand Rapids, MI: Baker Academic, 2002), 45–60.

orchestra of humanity, and each of us needs help to become all that we might be."[169]

For Vanier, realizing our humanity is bound up with recognizing the humanity of those who are different, particularly those who are intellectually disabled. He laments bluntly that "Society regards people with disabilities as 'misfits,' 'sub-human;'"[170] and further that "Society often seeks to eliminate people who are weak, before their birth or through euthanasia, arguing that they are a nuisance and cost too much."[171] He is glad for the change in language over the years from speaking of "the mentally retarded" to "people with intellectual disabilities" because, although language is fickle, "Behind the change of language is a desire to affirm that a person with mental handicap is first and foremost a *person*."[172]

Although Vanier never speaks of the fall, and does not seem to consider the entrance of sin into the world as the ultimate source of disability, nor does he reflect on Jesus as the Image of God *vis-à-vis* humanity created in the image of God, he notes that God has a concern for "the poor." "The gospel message talks about the 'poor' which is frequently interpreted as the 'economically poor.' However . . . the poor person is one who is in need. . . . are we not all needy and weak in some way? We all have our vulnerabilities, our limits, and our disabilities."[173] Contemplating "the mystery of Jesus," he reflects on passages such as Philippians 2 and notes, "Jesus does not just serve the poor, he becomes one of them."[174]

Although his theological tradition has typically emphasized "the mind's road to God" (cf. Bonaventure), his work with l'Arche has led him to the conclusion that not all people do or can know God in this way: "People who have highly developed intellects often

---

[169] Vanier, *Becoming Human*, 14.
[170] Jean Vanier, *The Heart of L'Arche* (Toronto: Novalis Publishing, 2012), 9.
[171] Ibid., 10.
[172] Ibid., 14.
[173] Ibid.
[174] Ibid., 22.

try to reach God through their mind and thoughts. People who have limited intelligence are more open to simple presence, a heart-to-heart relationship of communion and love. They receive God in the peace of their hearts, although they are unable to put their experience into words."[175]

Because "The gospel . . . shows that God welcomes in a special way those whom society rejects,"[176] the church as the society of Jesus should do the same.

> We do not know [to] whom Paul was referring [in 1 Cor. 12:18–24] when he spoke of "those members that we think less honorable"—those whom one hides away or, as at the beginning of this same letter, "the foolish, the feeble, the outcast." But people with intellectual disabilities perfectly fulfill his criteria. So often through the ages they have been hidden away. Paul says that they are necessary to the body, and that they must be treated with special honor. They are important; they have a role to play . . . in the church.[177]

> When I talk about "inclusion" of people . . . with disabilities . . . I am not talking only about starting up special schools or residences or creating . . . new hospitals. These are, of course, necessary. I am not just saying that we should be kind to such people because they are human beings. Nor is it a question of "normalizing" them in order that they can be "like us," participate in church services, and go to the movies and the local swimming pool. When I speak of inclusion of those who are marginalized I am affirming that they have a gift to give us all.[178]

---

[175] Ibid., 39.
[176] Ibid., 44.
[177] Vanier, *The Heart of L'Arche*, 53.
[178] Vanier, *Becoming Human*, 83–84.

Through a lifetime at l'Arche, Vanier indicates that he has learned to slow down, to notice people, to not be so wrapped up in and enamored of achievement and accomplishment. He has learned the fundamental value of relationship. He tells the story of a young man with intellectual disabilities who wanted very badly to win the hundred-meter race at the Special Olympics. He writes, "he was running like crazy to get the gold medal. One of the others running with him slipped and fell; he turned around and picked him up and they ran across the finish line together last. Are we prepared to sacrifice the prize for solidarity? It's a big question. Do we want to win or do we want to be in solidarity with others?"[179]

Vanier's great contribution is not in the area of biblical exegesis, or a systematic theology of cognitive disability, or in a well thought out *imago Dei* doctrine. His contribution is rather in the area of a practical, hands-on compassion for those with intellectual disabilities and a reflection on the common neediness and humanity.

Henri Nouwen taught at Notre Dame, Yale, and Harvard before being invited by Jean Vanier to the Daybreak Community of l'Arche near Toronto where Nouwen lived for ten years before his death in 1996. Although he wrote some forty books on Christian spirituality, only his last book specifically reflected on spirituality and intellectual disability through the life of Adam Arnett, one of the core members at Daybreak. Like Vanier, Nouwen does not approach the question of intellectual disability in a systematic way, but reflects on it through the lens of a virtue ethic.

Nouwen speaks of his uncertainty and the discomfort he experienced when he first came to Daybreak and was assigned to Adam. However, Nouwen slowly came to realize the deep significance this relationship had on his and Adam's unfolding humanity. "Adam's humanity was not diminished by his disabilities, Adam's humanity was a full humanity, in which the fullness of love became visible for

---

[179] Jean Vanier, *Encountering the Other* (Mahwah, NJ: Paulist Press, 2005), 18.

me, and for others who grew to know him."[180] But Nouwen had to work through the unanswerable questions.

> Could Adam pray? Did he know who God is and what the name of Jesus means? Did he understand the mystery of God among us? For a long time I thought about these questions. For a long time I was curious about much of what I knew, Adam could know, and how much of what I understood Adam could understand. But now I see that these were for me questions from "below" [i.e., earthly], questions that reflected more my anxiety and uncertainty than God's love.[181]

For Nouwen, Adam's helplessness helped him to realize his own vulnerabilities and the implications of the gospel. He came to realize that he had believed that his acceptance with God rested on his success in academia, and then on his giving it all up to help "the poor." But at l'Arche he came face to face with his own vulnerabilities and sins: "I was challenged to believe that even when I had nothing to show for myself, I was still God's beloved son."[182]

It is notable that Nouwen, like Vanier, never speaks of the entrance of sin into the world, nor the fall's relationship to sickness and surd evil. He recalls an instance in which a woman who was visiting the community walked "... right up to Adam, saying, 'Poor man, poor man, why did this happen to you? Let me pray over you so that our dear Lord may heal you.' She motioned the assistants to make a circle around Adam to pray. But one of them gently tapped her on the shoulder and said, 'Adam doesn't need any healing; he is fine.'"[183]

---

[180] Henri Nouwen, *Adam God's Beloved* (Maryknoll, NY: Orbis Books, 1997), 50–51.
[181] Ibid., 55.
[182] Ibid., 79.
[183] Ibid., 68.

It is difficult to say whether the mild rebuke of the assistant gave Nouwen satisfaction because the rebuked woman did not recognize her own need and felt herself superior to Adam, or whether Nouwen discounted the fall, and thereby thought there was nothing wrong with Adam that needed to be remedied. Much of the rest of the book would give the latter impression, except that toward the end of the book Nouwen speaks of Adam's resurrection. He recounts the dream of Elizabeth, a longtime member of l'Arche: "In my dream I saw Adam running and dancing, jumping up and down, free as a bird. I saw him as a free spirit, laughing and talking and moving his head, arms, and legs like a beautiful athlete."[184] This vision was of a very different Adam than the one she knew at l'Arche, and constitutes a vision of healing.

Like Vanier, Nouwen's contribution to this discussion is not a systematic or doctrinal one. Rather it is a reflective consideration of what it means to be human, and the universal neediness of humankind.

With Vanier and Nouwen, Stanley Hauerwas stands in the virtue ethics tradition. His philosophical and theological reflections on cognitive disability are therefore practical and "earthy." He does not write on the doctrine of the image of God *per se*. In fact, although he has made a significant contribution to the literature concerning those with intellectual disabilities, he is palpably ill at ease with the whole endeavor. "Every time I write about the mentally handicapped, I make a promise to myself that it will be the last time I write about this subject."[185] He has great admiration for Vanier for never questioning the humanity of those with intellectual handicaps. For Hauerwas, l'Arche stands as a rebuke to the hypocritical "concern" that society has for those with handicaps. "No group exposes the pretensions of the humanism that shapes the practices

---

[184] Ibid., 118.

[185] Stanley Hauerwas, "Timeful Friends: Living With the Handicapped," *Critical Reflections on Stanley Hauerwas' Theology of Disability*, ed. John Swinton (New York: Routledge, 2004), 13.

of modernity more thoroughly than the mentally handicapped. Our humanism entails that we care for them once they are among us, once we are stuck with them; but the same humanism cannot help think that, all things considered, it would be better if they did not exist. . . . We live in cultures for which rationality and consciousness are taken to be the very essence of what makes us human."[186] Hauerwas believes that the great contribution of l'Arche is that it removes an attempt to establish criteria for who is to be accounted as a "person" and "truly human." In fact, the idea of establishing criteria for defining who is "human" (Fletcher) or "a person" (Singer) is an abhorrent notion to Hauerwas: "This assumption makes us forget how inappropriate it is for the preservation of our humanity to justify the exclusion of some men from human care and concern on the ground that they fail to meet such 'criteria.'" Consistent with his virtue ethics approach he continues, "The appropriate moral context for raising the question of the 'essentially' human should not be an attempt to determine if some men are or are not human, but rather what *we must be* if we are to preserve and advance what humanity we have"[187][italics added].

Like Vanier and Nouwen, Hauerwas does not seem to consider the fall as an ultimate source of disability, but he does recognize that utopian notions of the supposed innocence of those with severe cognitive disabilities can be maintained only by those who have never worked closely or lived with them: ". . . we can be captured by destructive accounts about the retarded—namely that they are more innocent or sweet than other children or people."[188]

Though not speaking of mankind as the *imago Dei*, nor of redemption as such, Hauerwas sees the importance of the church

---

[186] Ibid., 14.

[187] Stanley Hauerwas, "The Retarded and the Criteria for the Human," *Critical Reflections on Stanley Hauerwas' Theology of Disability*, ed. John Swinton (New York: Routledge, 2004), 128.

[188] Stanley Hauerwas, "Community and Diversity: The Tyranny of Normality," in Ibid., 39.

in manifesting the intrinsic value of those with severe cognitive disabilities. He takes issue with the fact that society (and at times the church) has "In their enthusiasm to assert the dignity of man . . . formulate[d] criteria of the human that appear in our cultural context as an *ideology* of the strong. . . . [the] assumption that man's rational and cognitive ability is what makes us human."[189] Because children with severe cognitive disabilities are born to Christian families and are baptized into the church,[190] they become a part of the body of Christ, challenging the church to rise to meet the world that really is, not the idyllic world that it may have created in its own mind.[191]

Because the body of Christ is a *body*, there is no question that the Christian faith must be formed *in community*, and so it is necessary to include in the life and worship of the church those of her number who have severe cognitive disabilities.

> . . . the first social task of the church is to help the world know that it is the world. For without the church, the world has no means to know that it is the world. The distinction between church and the world is not a distinction between nature and grace. It is, instead, a distinction that denotes "the basic personal postures of men, some of who [*sic*] confess and others of whom do not confess that Christ Jesus is Lord . . . ." The fact that the church is separated from the world is not meant to underwrite an ethic of self-righteousness . . . . Both church and world remain under the judgment of the Kingdom of God. . . . Those of us who attempt to live faithfully to that Kingdom are acutely aware how deeply our lives remain held to and by the world.[192]

---

[189] Hauerwas, "The Retarded and the Criteria for the Human," in Ibid., 129.

[190] In Hauerwas' tradition, and in the tradition of the author of this book.

[191] See Stanley Hauerwas, "The Church and the Mentally Handicapped: A Continuing Challenge to the Imagination" in Ibid., 53–62.

[192] Stanley Hauerwas, "The Gesture of a Truthful Story," in Ibid., 72–73.

> We cannot know the truth until we have been transformed by the story. We cannot know Jesus without becoming his disciples.... Such a community cannot help but stand in sharp contrast with the world.... it is a community that takes as its task the initiation of people into the story in a manner that forms and shapes their lives in a decisive and distinctive way. Put bluntly, the church is in the world to mark us. The church, therefore, aims not at autonomy [of the individual] but faithfulness.[193]

For Hauerwas, the great failure of the church in the modern age has been the attempt to be "relevant" and "successful" in the eyes of the world, and as the world would define those terms.

> Too often, in an effort to appear socially relevant, the church has accepted the world's agenda about what "real" politics involves. Thus calls for us to serve the world responsibly have too often resulted in the church simply saying to the world what the world already knows.... I am suggesting that we must be a patient people, as well as a courageous people, who have the skills to think through the current illusions about social justice and peace. We must be the kind of community that can draw on the character of convictions that expose the sentimentalities of the world—not the least of which is the assumption that nation-states have the right to qualify our loyalty as members of the church.[194]

Theology that spurs us to social action as an end in itself is a truncated theology: "liturgy is not a motive for social action. Liturgy is social action. Through liturgy we are shaped rightly to live the story of God, to become a part of that story .... The church is

---

[193] Ibid., 73–74.
[194] Ibid., 75.

nothing less than the sign of God's salvation in the world."[195] Jesus was certainly concerned about the weakest and most disadvantaged, and the church as the beachhead of the kingdom must do the same as a sign to and a rebuke of the world. Hauerwas notes that often teaching and discipling have

> ... naturally taken the form of encouraging greater study of the Scripture and theology, the assumption being that we will be better Christians if we simply know more. While I have nothing against the study of Scripture and theology, I think our emphasis in that respect has tended to make us forget that the way we learn the story is by learning such gestures as simple as how to kneel. More troubling, such emphasis excludes in a decisive manner a whole group of people from participation in God's Kingdom. For what do you do with the mentally handicapped? . . . It is certainly true that the mentally handicapped may not be able to read the story, nor are they always able to "understand" the "meaning" of the story, nor do they know what the social implications of the story may entail. But what they do know is who the story is embodied [sic] through the essential gestures of the church. They know the story through the care they receive, and they help the church understand the story that forms such care.... they feel and are formed by the liturgy that places us as characters in God's grand project of the creation and redemption of the world.[196]

Hauerwas does not naively suggest that those with severe cognitive disabilities are untouched by sin. Their redemption will come in the same way as anyone's will come: through the grace of God. But the channels of that grace are unbounded, and may not be what we

---

[195] Ibid., 77.
[196] Ibid., 79.

might term the "ordinary means of grace." "Nor am I suggesting that the mentally handicapped are somehow naturally ready to be formed by the story. They are no fewer sinners than any of the rest of us. Their desires require training no less than our desires. Faithfulness is not a natural task for the mentally handicapped or for us. We equally must be trained to face the world, as it is not what we would like it to be."[197] Above all, "The church as God's gesture in and for the world must be the people who manifest our conviction that we do not live on the world's time, but in God's time. I suspect we do that best when we show ourselves to be a people who have the time to care for one another even when some of us happen to be mentally handicapped."[198]

Hauerwas has been criticized for using insensitive language (he often speaks and writes of "the retarded"), and at times in a zeal to defend those with disabilities seems to laud disability itself. However, he has been a stalwart proponent of the dignity and humanity of those with cognitive disabilities.

While showing appreciation and respect for the work of Hauerwas regarding those with cognitive disabilities, John Swinton is nonetheless critical of an ambiguity in Hauerwas' thinking with regard to how those with cognitive disabilities fit into society.[199] "If [cognitive] disability is a gift that leads us to understand our true state as human beings, then why does Hauerwas seem to support the suggestion that we should do all we can to prevent disability? If people with intellectual disabilities are gifts . . . why should we not rejoice that they are born 'retarded' rather than 'normal'?"[200] Swinton notes that Hauerwas makes a distinction between "us" (the non-intellectually impaired) and "them" (those with cognitive disabilities), but in an unexpected way:

---

[197] Ibid.

[198] Ibid., 80.

[199] See Ibid.

[200] John Swinton, "The Importance of Being a Creature: Stanley Hauerwas on Disability," *Disability in the Christian Tradition, A Reader*, ed. Brian Brock and John Swinton (Grand Rapids, MI: Eerdmans, 2012), 520.

At one level his suggestion has positive force. No longer can we assume that the image of God is somehow owned by those who claim the status of "normal." In this sense, Hauerwas' idea is provocative and constructive. However, the problem is this: If God's face is the face of "the retarded," then where is the face of the "non-retarded?" Are disabled people to be equated with the "holy innocents" specially blessed by God? If so, then ... [this] suggests that "they" are like God and "we" are not![201]

Though not giving attribution to Barth, Swinton's approach to what makes for the *imago Dei* is found in relationship: "The proposition that human beings are by nature relational is a theme that runs like a golden thread throughout the Bible and Christian tradition.... Human beings are made in the image of God, and in and through their relationships they reveal something of the nature and shape of that image."[202] But relationships with those who have profound cognitive disabilities are not typical. Such relationships are not "balanced," as those with such cognitive impairments cannot reciprocate in kind. Furthermore, such people will never be "productive citizens." Such considerations challenge western notions of what it means to be a "person." Swinton notes, "To exclude or devalue a person on the basis of their dependency is to misunderstand the nature of human existence ...."[203]

Furthermore, the glory of the incarnation is not only in that God became man, but that Jesus demonstrated what it means to love our fellow man in the midst of a fallen world: "Jesus' friendships were always *intentional* and *personal*, primarily aimed at regaining the dignity and personhood of those whom society had rejected and depersonalized.... people with profound learning disabilities are

---

[201] Ibid., 523.
[202] John Swinton and Esther McIntosh, "Persons in Relation: The Care of Persons with Learning Disabilities," *Theology Today* 57, 2 (2000): 175.
[203] Ibid., 181.

forced to stand on the margins of western society. In this sense, they are the very people for whom Jesus came."[204] Swinton believes that those with severe cognitive disabilities enable a process of "transvaluation," that is, a way of valuing relationships differently: "most of our relationships are contingent on some kind of benefit they will bring to ourselves. If our relationships no longer yield this benefit, we have a tendency to move on to forms of relationship that give us what we want."[205] With the weakness of the incarnation in mind, Swinton maintains that those with disabilities ". . . remind us of dimensions of God which have been hidden by our culture's preference for such things as power, strength, and intellectual prowess."[206]

Swinton is critical of the (other) "disability theologians" for not taking sin seriously. "One thing that is noticeably underplayed in the theologies of Hauerwas and [Hans] Reinders is the impact of sin. The issues of church, sanctification, and redemption are a strong theme, but the fallenness of this world and the vulnerability of people with disabilities to the consequences of sin and fallenness do not feature as highly in their theologies."[207] But Swinton seems only to consider one dimension of sin and the fallenness of the world with respect to disabilities, i.e., sin against people with disabilities. He does not give any consideration to the idea that disabilities exist precisely because of sin's entrance into the world and its consequent fallenness.

The disability doctrine of Nancy Eisland employs a Liberation Theology paradigm, and thus comes from a Disabilities Studies perspective which ". . . sits broadly within a Marxist materialist paradigm."[208] Eisland, who was herself disabled due to a congenital

---

[204] Ibid., 183.

[205] John Swinton, "The Body of Christ has Down's Syndrome: Theological Reflections on Vulnerability, Disability, and Graceful Communities," *The Journal of Pastoral Theology* 13, 2 (Fall, 2003): 69.

[206] Ibid., 71.

[207] John Swinton, "Who is the God we Worship? Theologies of Disability; Challenges and New Possibilities," *International Journal of Practical Theology* 14 (2011): 299.

[208] Ibid., 278. Swinton's specific criticism of Eisland's theology is found on

bone defect, taught at the Candler School of Theology until her death in 2009. The premise of her theology of disability is that while disabled people are different, there is nothing "wrong" with them. Because creation is "very good," and because she completely discounts any notion of the fall as the source of evil in the world, disabilities cannot be bad. Her hamartiology is radically divergent from that of historically orthodox Christianity. Eisland contends that "To be human is to sin,"[209] that is, sinfulness is simply a part of the human condition as created by God.

Eisland's theology was developed out of an "epiphany" she had in which she beheld God in a wheelchair, "Not an omnipotent, self-sufficient God, but neither a pitiable suffering servant. In this moment I beheld God as a survivor, unpitying and forthright. . . . Here was God for me."[210]

Drawing on socialist inspired notions of equality as a reduction to the lowest common denominator, Eisland refers to those without disabilities as "the temporarily able-bodied," and envisions an eschaton in which everyone is disabled. She believes, in fact, that it is precisely in disability that the image of God is to be found:

> Our bodies participate in the *Imago Dei*, not in spite of our impairments and contingencies, but through them. . . . What is the significance of the resurrected Christ's display of impaired hands and feet and side? Are they to be subsumed under the image of Christ, death conqueror? Or should the disability of Christ [due to the irreparable wounds and resultant disability of crucifixion] be understood as the truth of the incarnation and the promise of the resurrection?"[211]

---

pages 281–86.
[209] Nancy L. Eisland, *The Disabled God* (Nashville, TN: Abingdon Press, 1994), 70.
[210] Ibid., 89.
[211] Ibid., 101.

Literature Review

Thus, "Jesus Christ, the disabled God, is not a romanticized notion of 'overcomer' God. Instead here is God as survivor."[212] "In presenting his impaired hands and feet to his startled friends, the resurrected Jesus is revealed as the disabled God. . . . [He] calls his frightened companions to recognize in the marks of impairment their own connection with God, their own salvation. In doing so, this disabled God is also the revealer of a new humanity."[213]

For Eisland, there is no consideration of the fact that a significant part of Jesus' earthly ministry was the healing of those with disabilities. She "reimages" the Christ of the Gospels from possessing a "spiritual body" in his resurrection, in which all of the demerits due to sin's entrance into the world have been done away with, into a Christ who is risen in disability as the pattern for humanity. All humanity will thus ultimately be disabled. Without giving credence to the fall, and not wanting to reject God, she concludes that it is traditional theology that she (and we all) must reject. She notes that people will find the image of Christ as the disabled God disconcerting if they are invested in a traditional Christian theology. "For people with disabilities who have grasped divine healing as the only liberatory image the traditional church has offered, relinquishing belief in an all-powerful God who could heal, if he would, is painful. Yet who is this god whose attention we cannot get, whose inability to respond to our pain causes still more pain? This god is surely not Emmanuel—God with us."[214]

Although Eisland states that ". . . the paucity of theological exploration of . . . intellectual disabilities is scandalous,"[215] she herself never addresses the issue. Coming from a Disabilities Rights perspective which emphasizes increasing self-direction and actualization, her theology is in fact exclusive of such people. Although

---

[212] Ibid., 102.
[213] Ibid., 100.
[214] Ibid., 105.
[215] Ibid., 28.

at junctures she has lucid and helpful insights,[216] in the main her departure from historic orthodoxy in order to embrace a Marxist inspired paradigm of struggle, coupled with an eschatological future which seems contrary to the Scriptures, and which many people would not find encouraging, makes her work of limited value.

Hans Reinders is a theologian and professor of ethics and mental disability at the Free University of Amsterdam. Like other "disability theologians," Reinders has sought to think through the theological implications of disability (specifically, those with severe cognitive disabilities). In contemplating the work of Jean Vanier, Reinders notes that the theology of l'Arche is largely *post facto*: "L'Arche is lived rather than thought of, so that when in Vanier's work we encounter a profound Christian vision, it is important to realize that it is only in hindsight that this vision emerged."[217] Reinders highlights the fact that l'Arche was founded on Christian compassion first; any theological insight came later.

Reinder's most influential book on the topic to date has been *Receiving the Gift of Friendship*. As mentioned in Chapter One of this work, Reinders explains that he had early believed that the doctrine of the *imago Dei* would provide an easy answer (at least from and for the church) to those who questioned the fundamental humanity of those with severe cognitive disabilities, but came to the conclusion that the "common sense view" of the *imago* as identified with the intellect caused him to abandon the doctrine as an avenue for finding worth in those with severe disabilities.

Reinder's contribution lies specifically in his willingness to consider the hardest cases. While those with cognitive disabilities who live in l'Arche communities are able to contribute in some way

---

[216] For example, she notes, "The persistent thread within the Christian tradition has been that disability denotes an unusual relationship with God and that the person with disabilities is either divinely blessed or damned, the defiled evildoer or the spiritual superhero." Ibid., 70.

[217] Hans Reinders, "Jean Vanier's Theological Realism," *Disability in the Christian Tradition: A Reader*, Brock and Swinton, 470.

to the community (and must be, in order to be "welcomed," i.e., formally invited to be a part of the community), Reinders considers the humanity of those with conditions like lissencephaly, anencephaly, and other conditions that often leave individuals able only to breath, eat, and eliminate waste. The thesis of the book is that only when we have truly received God's friendship will we be able to offer selfless friendship to those with severe cognitive disabilities, a friendship based not on reciprocity, but on the recognition of a common humanity.

Reinders' work contains many profound insights, but like so many of the "disability theologians" he has not really taken adequate account of the fall as the ultimate reason for disability. The struggle is palpable as he intuitively recognizes the evil of disability and the "very good" of creation and tries to reconcile them without recourse to sin's entrance into the world. His conclusion is that disability is not the tragic result of sin in the world, but simply the way God has made some people. He quotes the father of a disabled child with approbation: "Any artificial attempt to split my child from his disability is dishonest, dissociatively psychotic, or without any knowledge of my child. It is like saying, 'I like your child; it's just his body, mind and spirit that I don't like.' David's disability is global. It is part of him just as much as his species or gender."[218]

The impetus for Reinder's argument is his desire to dissuade the practice of aborting children who are discovered to have disabilities while still in the womb. Because abortion is at this point in time seen in much of western society as a *therapeutic* practice for dealing with disabilities discovered *in utero*,[219] Reinders concludes that in specific human beings disability and personality are inseparable if not indistinguishable.

---

[218] Hans Reinders, *The Future of the Disabled in Liberal Society: An Ethical Analysis* (Indiana: University of Notre Dame, 2000), 51.

[219] Erroneously, Reinders believes. He points out that oncology doctors fight cancer, not people with cancer. Yet there is no treatment for intellectually

> ... let us consider the case of James who is a young man with fragile X [syndrome]. Suppose we put this question to James' parents: If your son could be cured would you not prefer to have him without fragile X? What could James' parents say by way of response? Not much, I am afraid. A reasonable answer would be that the question is not only hypothetical, but also false. Of course they would want to have James without fragile X, except for the fact that he would then no longer be James. James is who he is because of fragile X syndrome.[220]

The clear implication of this is that disability is a part of who the person is. Reinders only considers those with cognitive disabilities caused *in utero*, however. This approach begs the question of those who have cognitive disabilities because they have at some point suffered a traumatic brain injury; are their disabilities a part of who the person is? And what of those who have physical disabilities? Should parents of children born with palatoschisis (cleft palate), for example, consent to the surgery to repair the deformity, or would doing so be indicative that they do not want their "actual" child? If a child suffered some cognitive disability as a result of post gestational illness and the disability could be treated or reversed, should the parents refuse such treatment because to have the child treated would be to reject their "actual" child? Following Reinders' line of reasoning, in all of these cases such questions would be "false" because the disabling condition and the personality of the people in question are indistinguishable from one another.

For many theologians addressing the issue of disability (and particularly severe cognitive disability) who have been influenced by the theologies of Schleiermacher on the one hand, or Barth on the

---

disabling conditions discovered in the womb, and so the "therapeutic" course of action is most often a suggestion to terminate the life of the child. See *The Future of the Disabled*, 55–58 for his discussion.

[220] Reinders, *The Future of the Disabled*, 60.

other, the evil of disability in the present world is not that there are disabilities from which people suffer. Rather the evil of disability is to be found in that people who are not disabled think that the "something wrong" is to be found in the disabilities themselves, rather than in the *valuation* of disabilities as "something wrong."

Reinders has advanced the discussion of the theology of cognitive disability because he has considered the hardest and most extreme cases. However, his lack of serious consideration of sin's effect on the physical world (including genetic malformation leading to cognitive disability) leads him to conflate the disability with the disabled person.

Michael Beates is a notable exception to most of the other "disability theologians." Standing in a more historically orthodox Protestant tradition, Beates came to the theological study of disabilities when his eldest daughter, Jessica, was diagnosed in infancy with multiple disabilities. Since 2000 he has served on the International Board of Directors of Joni and Friends.

Beates believes that God is sovereignly active over the disabilities that people have. He points out that in response to Moses' objections to go to pharaoh because he was "slow of speech and tongue" (Gen. 4:10), God declared "Who has made man's mouth? Who makes him mute, or deaf, or seeing, or blind? Is it not I, the LORD?" (Ex. 4:11). Beates comments, "Consider what God is saying here. Be careful not to miss the full impact of this! If you are like me, when you begin to let this statement settle, you exclaim, 'What?' In this startling response, God not only does not deny responsibility for conditions we normally consider disabilities . . . ; rather, to our surprise, God takes credit for them! God says these things are from him and made by him. This is a hard statement! And we must accept it and learn from it."[221]

Yet for Beates, disability is not simply "the way things are" but

---

[221] Michael S. Beates, *Disability & the Gospel: How God Uses Our Brokenness to Display His Grace* (Wheaton, IL: Crossway, 2012), 29.

are the result of a catastrophic event. "Paul speaks about the fallen nature of the whole creation."[222] ". . . humanity has been created *imago Dei*, 'in the image of God,' but with the advent of sin, that image has in some fashion been marred."[223] "With the fall came not only a rupture in our relationship and dwelling with God, but our bodies and all creation 'fell' as well."[224] The fall of man is thus at the root of disability: ". . . fellowship [with God] was broken at the fall. The result is that mankind is not simply broken relationally with God. . . . our brokenness profoundly effects every area of life."[225] "Physical brokenness [including that which causes cognitive disabilities] reminds us we are finite, that the world is not as it should be."[226]

Beates believes that the redemption that Christ came to bring includes healing for those with disabilities. In diametric opposition to Nancy Eisland, who believes that the eschaton will be populated by universally disabled people worshiping a disabled God, Beates is confident that in the eschaton disability will be done away with. Referring to Romans 8, he writes, "Paul says we also await the redemption of our bodies. The impact here is that just as all people need spiritual redemption, so we all need physical redemption as well."[227] He sees disability of all kinds (including the spiritual disabilities now suffered by able-bodied and minded people) as being a part of the "former things" that "pass away" (Rev. 21:4):

> The first active ramification of this fully realized dwelling [of God with man] is that God promises to wipe away tears and pronounces the end of death, mourning, crying, and pain. . . . this consistent thread [of the promise of redemption from

---

[222] Ibid., 62.
[223] Ibid., 72.
[224] Ibid., 73.
[225] Ibid., 80.
[226] Ibid., 81.
[227] Ibid., 62.

Genesis to Revelation] gives hope to those who see themselves as they really are [i.e., broken and needing salvation]. Because we know the ending of the story—the assurance of victory, redemption, and restoration—we can delight in and enjoy God, even in the midst of suffering or chronic disability and the myriad ways we are broken and weak. We have a future.[228]

The bulk of Beates' work is devoted to how God displays his strength through weakness, and practical issues of integrating into the body of Christ those with disabilities because "those parts of the body that seem to be weaker are indispensable, and the parts that we think are less honorable we treat with special honor" (1 Cor. 12:22–23).[229] He deals in various places with the history of *imago Dei* doctrine,[230] a topic dealt with in Chapter One.

Professional theologians are not the only Christians who have dealt with the effects of cognitive disability in their own family and have reflected theologically upon it. Greg Lucas is a graduate of Boyce College who works as a police officer in West Virginia. His adopted son Jake was born six weeks prematurely. After the adoption Jake was diagnosed with severe cognitive, developmental, and behavioral disabilities. In his book *Wrestling with an Angel*, Lucas chronicles the story of life with Jake and how God used his relationship with his son to mortify his own sin and see his utter dependence on Christ. He writes, "When people ask me how I became a follower of Jesus, I always tell them that a two-year-old, non-verbal, mentally disabled, autistic boy led me straight to the cross and since then has been used to display God's grace in the most amazing ways."[231]

Throughout the book Lucas has some profound insights that are

---

[228] Ibid., 69.
[229] See Ibid., 59–82.
[230] See Ibid., 26–33, 95–99, 113–24.
[231] Greg Lucas, *Wrestling with an Angel: A Story of Love, Disability, and the Lessons of Grace* (n.l.: Cruciform Press, 2010), 72.

set in the context of and derived from a historically orthodox expression of the Christian faith. Lucas clearly attributes disabilities to the fall: "We . . . live in a fallen, sin-stained world. Even the best things here are merely silhouettes of what God has in store for us on that day when sin is no more."[232] But rather than seeing the world through the lens of "us" (those without disabilities) versus "them" (those with disabilities), Lucas perceives that living in a fallen world means that we all suffer from disabilities of one kind or another. "Much like my son, I have been disabled all my life. My disability affects everything I do. Scripture diagnoses this disability as sin. Not individual acts of sin, but a sin nature, sin residing within my heart. It causes me to reject love and embrace fear. It plagues me with a slumber that makes me strangely satisfied to lie in my own filth and not be disturbed."[233]

A consistent theme throughout the book, and one that is contrary to Reinder's approach and understanding, is Lucas' hope and belief that final redemption will consist in part in the removal of all disability for the redeemed. "I stare at Jake for several minutes, imagining what he would look like or be like without his afflictions and handicaps. For a brief moment I am given a picture of my son without his disabilities. It is a wonderful gift from a gracious God."[234] He reveals his heart for his son when he writes, "One of the longest patterns of recurring intercessory prayer in my life has been directed at a single goal: that my son might be able to speak. If I could heal just one aspect of his condition, if I could give just one gift to address his physical ailment, it would be the gift of speech."[235] ". . . one of my greatest yearnings on earth is to have a deep conversation with Jake. This is just one of the things that, for me, will make heaven especially sweet."[236] Throughout the course of his maturation, Jake has been able to acquire five words. Reflecting on this, Lucas writes,

[232] Ibid., 60.
[233] Ibid., 23.
[234] Ibid., 29.
[235] Ibid., 53.
[236] Ibid., 55.

I think the appetizer is meant to increase our desire for the main course.... My heavenly Father ... has answered all my prayers for Jake—with glimpses of the greatness to come. He has granted a foretaste of his glory by revealing the shadow of his coming blessings.... I dream of a day when Jake and I sit quietly and stare into each other's eyes for a long precious moment. Broad smiles flash across our faces in silent communication of overwhelming joy. It's a smile shared only by the close bond of affection of fathers and sons. Then the silence is broken by Jake's voice. "Dad, there are so many things I have wanted to tell you." "I know son, I know." This is *the* answer to my prayer. And it will be worth the wait.[237]

For some who write about cognitive disability there is an assumption that all those with severe cognitive disabilities will be redeemed. Depending on the theological tradition, this may be attributed to an inability to reach a cognitive "age of accountability," a belief that cognitively disabled people are not implicated in Adam's sin, or because of the pity of God for those who cannot understand the Gospel enough to respond to it (or at least not in ways that can be observed by other people).

Lucas himself comes from a Calvinistic Baptist background, and so while he does not have the comfort that covenant baptism can afford the parents of children with disabilities, yet he embraces the mystery of God's will with a distinct hopefulness:

> The more I try to comprehend the sovereignty of God in salvation, the more I am astounded by his grace. Even the faith to believe the gospel is a gift given to those who deserve only his just wrath.... Through this gospel we obtain eternal life in order to experience His glory for all eternity. All of

[237] Ibid., 60–61.

this is obtained by grace through faith.... But how is this applied in the life of an individual who cannot respond in faith or who does not have the ability to comprehend the basic truth of the gospel? ... Many Christians approach this sticky theological topic with their feelings, bypassing biblical study in the fear that truth may not be as comforting as their emotions. We want to believe that ... mentally disabled people are basically innocent in the eyes of God. ... This rationalization feels good and makes sense to our hearts.... But is this biblically accurate? ... What I really mean is, what about those of us who love people like Jake? What are *we* supposed to believe? When it comes to such crucial theological questions, I have found that feelings are a weak salve to the hurts of my heart.... At what IQ level does God begin to require someone to respond in faith to His gospel in order to be saved? How much faith is enough faith? ... Yes, there is mystery. But there is enough sturdy truth in God's Word to keep me afloat.... This hope rests, not in self-sufficiency, but in the power of God's rescuing grace, in the power of a strength sufficient to breathe life into dead bones, a strength that can cover my sin with the cleansing life-blood of God's Son. So the bad news is that we are all born guilty. But the good news, especially for people like Jake, is that we are all born helpless, too. In ourselves we are, every one of us, powerless to understand, comprehend, or respond to God's plan of salvation.... If I am going to be saved, if Jake is going to be saved ... we all have precisely the same need. We must be *raised* from spiritual death, *given* a new heart that loves and desires God, *given* a new mind that treasures the gospel, and *given* saving faith in the sacrificial death of Christ for our sins.... They are all passive verbs.... Maybe now you are starting to see why I can have a realistic hope for Jake's salvation.... in the grand picture of God's rescue, Jake is no different than me.... In God's design, helplessness is not the same as hopelessness. To loosely paraphrase Augustine, *God gives what God requires.* . . . And this is my comfort for my son.[238]

Lucas' study of Scripture, his son, and his response to his situation has given him keen theological insights into the catastrophic effects of sin upon all people, and a steadfast hope in a loving and graceful God.

Although not seminary trained, Stephanie Hubach has also contributed significant and meaningful theological reflection on intellectual disability. She is a member of First Presbyterian Church (PCA) of Ephrata, Pennsylvania where she serves as Director of Disabilities Ministries. Her position there is not due to professional training but personal experience. In 1992 her son Timothy was born and immediately diagnosed with Down syndrome.

Like Beates and Lucas, Hubach sees disabilities not as an aspect of creation but as a result of the fall of mankind. She weaves into her anthropology the *imago Dei* and the doctrine of the fall in this way: ". . . the image of God . . . can be likened to a mirror that reflects God's glory . . . Unmarred at creation, what an incredible and awesome reflection that must have been! In a world now impacted by the fall, each person's mirror is cracked, yet all the pieces still remain. . . . Our struggle enters in because we find it much easier to identify the cracks in the mirror, and so we miss the image entirely."[239] Hubach too indicates that disability is universal, although some disabilities are more observable than others: "Our brokenness and neediness as humans is universal. How it manifests itself is variable. It is *same lake, different boat*."[240] This phrase ". . . reflects the truth that, as human beings, we share a common story, but the details of our experiences and our life circumstances

---

[238] Ibid., 43–50.
[239] Stephanie O. Hubach, *Same Lake Different Boat: Coming Alongside People Touched with Disabilities* (Phillipsburg, NJ: P&R Publishing, 2006), 46.
[240] Ibid., 40.

may vary significantly. We are *essentially* the same but *experientially* different."[241]

The paradigm by which we view disability affects our understanding of it. Hubach delineates what she believes to be two flawed views and one correct view. The first flawed view she terms the Historical View: disability is an *abnormal* part of life in a *normal* world. "Throughout the ages, people with disabilities have typically been, and continue to be, seen as aberrations.... [It] is focused almost exclusively on the distinctive, negative characteristics of the diagnosis, and very little on the shared, valuable personhood of the individual."[242]

The second flawed view she identifies as the Postmodern View: disability is a *normal* part of a *normal* world. "For some time now, disability advocates have been thoroughly annoyed by the 'abnormal' label slapped on those with disabling conditions." Thus, for example, Down syndrome is "not a deficiency . . . now is the time to recognize and celebrate disability." Hubach maintains, "The new language confuses everything and solves nothing. . . . If disability is something to be celebrated, then why don't more people attempt to acquire traumatic brain injuries? . . . the 'normal part of a normal world' perspective is absurd."[243]

Hubach maintains that the biblical view is that disability is a *normal* part of an *abnormal* world. Only "When we recognize that disability is a *normal* part of life in an *abnormal* world, can we begin to make sense of it—and ourselves."[244]

> Human beings were God's crowning act of creation. While fashioned as creatures, people were designed to intrinsically embody his likeness. This means that mankind has a myriad of finite possibilities that reflect God's infinite reality. These include the ability to love, to create, to rule, to relate, to design,

---

[241] Ibid., 37.
[242] Ibid., 24–25.
[243] Ibid., 25–27.
[244] Ibid., 27.

to reason, and so much more. . . . But then tragedy struck. . . . the fall of mankind occurred—adversely impacting every aspect of creation. . . . This marring of creation permeated not only the spiritual, but also the physical, the intellectual, the emotional, the psychological, and the social. . . . Does this mean that everything in human experience is *ruined* by the fall? Absolutely not. But it does mean that everything in human experience is *affected* by the fall. On every level of every dimension of the human experience there is a mixture of both the blessedness of creation and the brokenness of the fall. . . . For some people, the effects of brokenness are more noticeable or more dramatically experienced in one part of life over another. . . . However, all of us face the slow, incremental process of inching toward death on a daily basis. . . . Disability is essentially a more noticeable form of brokenness that is common to the human experience.[245]

For Hubach the redemption of Christ ultimately will bring about the healing for those with disabilities. Alluding to Tim Keller's book *Ministries of Mercy* she states, "Christ came to bring the kingdom of God back to earth. . . . The kingdom of God is the renewal of the whole earth through supernatural forces. As things are brought back under Christ's rule and authority, they are restored to health, beauty, and freedom."[246] The kingdom will come ultimately through healing, which ". . . implies a reversal of circumstances. But when reversal is not experienced, does that mean that the kingdom is not present even in part?"[247] In the in-between time of Christ's advent and his parousia, Hubach maintains that the kingdom may come in *help* which implies assistance, and *hope* which implies reminding that there will be a complete reversal of the circumstances of disability.[248]

---

[245] Ibid., 27–29.
[246] Ibid., 69.
[247] Ibid., 74.
[248] Ibid., 75.

A legitimate criticism may be leveled against Hubach's paradigm of disability as being a normal part of an abnormal world. Although her approach takes sin seriously, seeing the world now as an abnormal deviation from the "very good" of its original creation, it is simply not so that disability is a *normal* part of this abnormal world. Disabilities, and especially cognitive disabilities, account for only a very small percentage of the human population. By the metric of either the original intrinsic goodness of creation, or by a simple accounting of the majority of the population, disability, and particularly cognitive disability is clearly an *abnormal* part of an abnormal world.

This observation, however, does not detract from Hubach's valuable insights. One of her most profound reflections is the conclusion that the image of God may be expressed through varying abilities, but the image does not find its definition there. The image of God is intrinsic to human life. "When the image of God is central to our understanding of humanity, it sends a powerful message about human value to the world around us. Our culture often measures personal value as a function of productivity. . . . In God's economy, however, human value is defined by the Creator himself though the imprint of his image on mankind. . . . Seeing the present reality of the image of God in each person gives us perspective on ourselves and others."[249]

A Brief Consideration of the Historical Adam Debate and Its Consequences

Questions about, and denial of the historicity of Adam are not new; they go back at least as far as Spinoza and Schleiermacher. What is new is that some scholars today who identify themselves as Evangelicals[250] are questioning or denying the historicity of Adam.

[249] Ibid., 49.
[250] The word "Evangelical" has gone through various transitions of meaning ranging from the evangelizing efforts of Christians in the North American colonies in the seventeenth century, to those who stood with and were at times

Concern over this fact was expressed by Anthony Hoekema almost three decades ago, particularly in regard to the doctrine of the *imago Dei*: "In recent years a number of theologians standing in what is generally called the Reformed tradition have advanced the view that Adam and Eve were not actual historical persons who once lived on this earth but symbols of man's divine origin and fall into sin. As these theologians see it, the narrative of the fall in Genesis 3 does not describe something that actually happened in history."[251] Hoekema was critical of theologians such as H. M. Kuitert who held that Adam was not a historical figure, but a teaching model.[252] Hoekema believed that "The denial of the historicity of Adam ... has devastating results for the doctrine of man" because it means that "there was no time when man was not a sinner," and thus sin is tied "inseparably to man's finiteness, man's creatureliness, man's humanity."[253] Hoekema muses over whether salvation is even possible if this is the case, for to be "saved" would mean that man is not rescued from what he had fallen into and become, but is saved from what he was created by God to be.

Unlike the "amateur theologians" (those ordinary Christians who have been providentially chosen as parents and care-givers of children with severe cognitive disabilities, and who have reflected theologically on the situation and condition of their loved ones[254]) most of the professional theologians who deal theologically with

---

identified with the Fundamentalists who were against the theologically liberalizing tendencies of the Modernist movement of the late nineteenth and early twentieth centuries. Given the breadth of views held today by those who self-identify as "Evangelicals" (not all within the scope of historical orthodoxy as set forth in the early ecumenical creeds), the term is in the early stages of losing all meaning.

[251] Hoekema, 112.

[252] See H. M. Kuitert, *Do You Understand What You Read?*, trans. Lewis B. Smedes (Grand Rapids, MI: Eerdmans, 1970), 40.

[253] Hoekema, 116–17.

[254] Greg Lucas, Laura Hendrickson, and Stephanie Hubach would be examples of such "amateurs."

cognitive disability do not consider the fall as an ultimate source of such disabilities. In their writings there is a conspicuous lacuna of how we are to understand why there are disabilities in a world that was created by God to be "very good." Their lack of consideration of a historical fall often leads them to conclude that the disabilities of such people are not "bad," but that such people are just different; to put it tersely, some people have brown hair, and some have lissencephaly. For some of them,[255] whatever redemption looks like it does not include being "freed" from their disabilities, because their disabilities are a part of who they are as God's creatures.

The purpose for wading into a sampling of the literature of this debate is narrowly focused on the issue of the *imago Dei*. Specifically, the first concern is with those who by denying a historical fall contribute to the notion that birth disabilities are an aspect of *creatio* rather than of *lapsus*, and thus constitute no defacement of the *imago Dei* and do not require remedy.

The second concern is with those who hold the traditional Christian view of a historical Adam, and the fall as a historical event. Some who are arguing this case in popular circles are reinvigorating the idea that the *imago* is to be found in some substantive component or aspect of humankind, most notably the intellect. They are thus potentially (if inadvertently) setting the stage to renew the church's failure to appreciate that the cognitively disabled are, as everyone, *ad imaginem Dei creavit*, and are setting up criteria for determining who is to be considered human.

Evangelical Sympathizers of Darwin

Arguably the first person to raise the possibility that Adam was not a historical figure for a broader Evangelical audience was Dr. Francis Collins, who is not a theologian but a physician. Collins was the head of the Human Genome Project which mapped the DNA sequence for the human genome, an accomplishment which

---

[255] Nancy Eisland would be an example.

has already contributed to an understanding of the cause and treatment of diseases with underlying genetic errors.

In his book *The Language of God*, Collins presents the winsome and compelling testimony of his journey from atheism to becoming a Christian through what apologists generally call the moral argument, an argument which came to him via interaction with some of his patients and the writings of C. S. Lewis.[256] After embarking on a brief apologetic miscellany Collins takes up "The great question of human existence," and concludes that theistic evolution (or what he terms biologos) is the best explanation for the appearance of mankind.[257] Collins maintains,

> ... once life arose, the process of evolution and natural selection permitted the development of biological diversity and complexity over very long periods of time. Once evolution got underway, no special supernatural intervention was required. Humans are a part of this process, sharing a common ancestor with the great apes. But humans are also unique in ways that defy evolutionary explanation and point to our spiritual nature. This includes the existence of the Moral Law.[258]

Collins denies the existence of a historical Adam, although he does not engage the theological implications or consequences of doing so. He believes that "studies of human variation, together with the fossil record, all point to an origin of modern humans approximately a hundred thousand years ago, most likely in East Africa. Genetic analysis suggests that approximately ten thousand ancestors gave rise to the entire population of 6 billion humans on the planet. How, then, does one blend these scientific observations with the story of Adam and Eve?"[259] He answers this question,

---

[256] Francis S. Collins, *The Language of God* (New York: Free Press, 2006), 11–32.
[257] Ibid., 197–243.
[258] Ibid., 200.
[259] Ibid., 207.

> Many sacred texts do indeed carry the clear marks of eyewitness history, and as believers we must hold fast to those truths. Others, such as the stories of . . . Adam and Eve frankly do not carry the same historical ring. . . . I do not believe that the God who created all the universe, who communes with His people through prayer and spiritual insight, would expect us to deny the obvious truths of the natural world that science has revealed to us, in order to prove our love for Him. In that context, I find theistic evolution . . . to be by far the most scientifically consistent and spiritually satisfying of the alternatives.[260]

Collins' denial of a historical Adam would imply a denial of a historical fall, leading to the almost inescapable conclusion that cognitive disabilities (many of which are caused by genetic errors) are integral to creation as "very good," and man as being made in the "image of God."

The influence of Collins on the general Evangelical population was modest. It has been popularized, however, by Peter Enns, who served as Senior Fellow of Biblical Studies for Collins' BioLogos Foundation from 2008 until 2011. The approach of Enns in *The Evolution of Adam* has been compared to that of Kuitert, but it bears a greater similarity to the approach of Alan Richardson in his work *An Introduction to the Theology of the New Testament* published a half-century ago.

Accepting Darwin's contention that mankind is the product of a slow evolutionary process, Enns states, "If evolution is correct, one can no longer accept, in any true sense of the word 'historical,' the instantaneous and special creation of humanity described in Genesis, specifically 1:26–31 and 2:7, 22."[261] He is critical of those

---

[260] Ibid., 209–10.
[261] Peter Enns, *The Evolution of Adam* (Grand Rapids, MI: Brazos Press, 2012), xiv.

who would try to harmonize the biblical and evolutionary explanations for human origins: "some assert that there was a point in the evolutionary chain where God elevated two hominids (or a group of hominids) to the status of image-bearer of God (Gen. 1:26–27). . . .[But] this hybrid of modern and ancient accounts of human origins is hardly what the Bible depicts: two humans created specially by God."[262]

For Enns, the Adam texts in both Testaments function as pour quoi stories, *post facto* mythical explanations for an observable phenomenon.[263] The Adam account in Genesis 1 and 2, according to Enns, should not be read as an explanation of the origin of mankind, but as a story to explain the creation, disobedience, and exile of Israel. "Adam in primordial times plays out Israel's national life. He is proto-Israel . . . . This does not mean, however, that a[n actual] historical Adam was a template for Israel's national life. Rather, Israel's drama . . . is placed in primordial time. In doing so, Israel claims that it has been God's special people all along, from the very beginning."[264]

The use of Adam for theological purposes in the New Testament is found almost exclusively in the Pauline literature.[265] Enns states, "At the outset we should admit that Adam is a vital theological and *historical* figure for Paul. Without question, Adam plays a significant theological role for Paul, but Adam's theological significance cannot be distanced from Paul's assumption that he was the first man created by God."[266] Enns maintains that Paul was simply

---

[262] Ibid., xiv—xv.

[263] A more modern example of such stories is found in Kipling's "Just So Stories." See Rudyard Kipling, *The Works of Rudyard Kipling Complete & Unabridged* (London: Octopus Books Limited, 1984), 257–364.

[264] Enns, 66.

[265] The two exceptions are Jude 1:14 (which uses Adam simply as a temporal locator) and Luke 3:38. Luke undoubtedly is making a theological point in referring to "Adam, the son of God," but unlike Paul he does not elucidate his meaning and leaves it to his readers to draw out the significance.

[266] Enns, 120.

wrong in this assumption: "the scientific evidence we have for human origins and the literary evidence we have for the nature of ancient stories or origins are so overwhelmingly persuasive that belief in a first human, such as Paul understood him, is not a viable option."[267]

Enns understands Paul's use of the Adam story as a means of explaining the universality of sin and death, and the reconciliation of Jews and Gentiles into one body though faith in Christ. Regarding the first proposition, he states, "Even without a first man, death and sin are still universal realities that mark the human condition . . . even without attributing their cause to Adam, sin and death are with us, and we cannot free ourselves from them. They remain foes vanquished by Christ's death and resurrection."[268] Thus, although Adam is not actually the cause of sin and death in the world, "For many people, Adam has been a powerful explanation for addressing the question of human existence: what makes us who we are; why we do what we do; why our time on earth is short, with pain and suffering always at our side."[269]

According to Enns, Paul also invokes Adam to demonstrate a shared common ancestry between Jews and Gentiles, thus undermining the foundation of any dividing wall between the two: "the very fact that Paul appeals to Adam at all reflects a larger and pressing theological concern about the unity of the body of Christ, made up of Jew and Gentile alike. Paul's goal is to show that what binds these two utterly distinct groups together is their participation in a universal humanity marked by sin and death and their shared need of the same universally offered redemption. Paul's Adam serves that goal."[270]

Although Enn's approach has been enthusiastically embraced by some evangelicals, the implications for the doctrine of the *imago Dei* largely have not been considered. Richard Gaffin has pointed out that Enns' approach "precludes the fall as taught in Scripture. It

[267] Ibid., 122.
[268] Ibid., 124–25.
[269] Ibid., 126.
[270] Ibid., 127.

replaces the historical before-and-after of creation and fall with their side-by-side inseparability. Sin [and presumably its consequences] is not a matter of human *fallenness* but of human *givenness*."²⁷¹

If Enns and others who hold his views are correct, severe cognitive disability is not really disability at all. It is not a condition to be remedied. It simply is the way some people are created, and should be considered "very good."

In his book *Did Adam and Eve Really Exist?* Old Testament scholar C. John Collins seeks to make a case for a historical Adam. He notes that "a major goal of the Christian story is to enable those who believe it to make sense of the world . . . if we deny that all people have a common source that was originally good but through which sin came into the world then sin becomes God's fault, or even something God could not avoid. In either case there is little reason to believe that relief is headed our way."²⁷² Apart from a historical Adam, we have no historical fall. "The notions of sin as an alien invader that affects all people, and of atonement as God's way of dealing with guilt and pollution that comes from this defiling influence, depend on the story of the original family and their original disobedience."²⁷³

In recounting a personal tragedy of the unexpected death of a friend's 37-year-old mentally handicapped son, Collins says, "I realized that a person would grieve differently depending on what he thought about the introduction of sin into our world"; a belief in a historical Adam and therefore a consequent historical fall allows us to see that ". . . something in the world is not right, and we need God's help."²⁷⁴ Collins was asked to conduct the funeral, at which he spoke these words:

---

²⁷¹ Richard Gaffin, "Translator's Forward" in J. P. Versteeg, *Adam in the New Testament: Teaching Model or First Historical Man?*, 2nd ed., trans. Richard B. Gaffin Jr. (Phillipsburg, NJ: P&R Publishing, 2012), xiii.

²⁷² C. John Collins, *Did Adam and Eve Really Exist? Who They Were and Why You Should Care* (Wheaton, IL: Crossway, 2011), 133–34.

²⁷³ Ibid., 134.

²⁷⁴ Ibid., 135.

When we feel this grief, we are feeling that it's just not right for this to happen. We don't want our loved ones to suffer. . . . The Bible tells us that these feelings we have are *right*. Death and suffering are intruders in God's good world; they don't belong here. And the story of Adam and Eve, the first human beings, tells us how these evil things came in: When these, the parents of us all, disobeyed God, they opened the door for all manner of sin and evil, not only for themselves but for all of us. . . . But the Bible story does not end there: instead it tells us about how God wants to help us, to heal us of what is wrong with us.[275]

Representatives of the Intelligent Design Movement

Francis Collins has mischaracterized the Intelligent Design movement as a "god of the gaps theory" which "portrays the Almighty as a clumsy Creator, having to intervene at regular intervals to fix the inadequacies of his own initial plan for generating the complexity of life."[276] In fact, those who have been associated with the movement do not promote a particular theology and are not necessarily Christians or religious.[277]

Many involved in the I.D. movement are Christians, however. Because those in this movement are interacting with scientists and science-minded people, and not theologians, their approach to what "makes us human" moves us in a direction that may in fact be deleterious for the inclusion of those with severe cognitive disabilities. Charles Sherlock has noted, "Some seek to define what it means to

---

[275] Ibid., 136.

[276] Francis Collins, 193–94.

[277] An example of such an Intelligent Design advocate is David Berklinski, who is ethnically Jewish but religiously non-practicing. In his book provocatively titled *The Devil's Delusion Atheism and Its Scientific Pretensions* (New York: Crown Forum, 2008), Berlinski presents no theological position, but is critical of what might be termed an "evolution of the gaps theory," arguing that when certain scientists cannot determine the mechanism of biological development, they simply invoke "evolution" as an unquestionable panacea.

be human by way of contrast with the animals; at a popular level, reaction to Darwin's postulation of human descent from apes revived these sorts of notions."[278] An example of just this sort of argument is found in Ann Gauger who writes, "What distinguishes us from the great apes[?] What are our distinguishing characteristics? There are significant anatomical differences, of course. . . . More importantly, there are whole realms of intellect and experience that make us unique as humans. Abstract thought, art, music, and language: these things separate us from lower animals fundamentally, not just in degree but in kind."[279] Although Gauger is not addressing exceptions, statements such as these beg the question, "What are we to make of those humans who are incapable of abstract thought, art, music, and language?"

Fazale Rana, who holds a Ph.D. in chemistry from Ohio University, in common with Gauger concludes that "humans [are] qualitatively different from animals, including great apes and hominids. This distinction does not primarily refer to physical differences. . . . humans and all other animals . . . share at least some biochemical, genetic, physiological, and anatomical similarities." However, Rana is more explicitly theological: "One main distinction, however, separates human beings from animals: only people bear the image of God." Going on to explain what the image of God consists in, Rana writes, "People use their minds to reason and contemplate the future. People create, imitating their Creator. People . . . worship the Creator as God."[280]

Both of these approaches influence the understanding of the *imago Dei*. The approach of Francis Collins and Peter Enns makes sin and the consequences of the fall (including cognitive disability) a part of creation, and therefore not a thing to be remedied, or perhaps

---

[278] Sherlock, 74.

[279] Ann Gauger, "Science and Human Origins" in *Science and Human Origins* (Seattle: Discovery Institute Press, 15–30), 21.

[280] Fazale Rana, *Who Was Adam?* (Colorado Springs, CO: NavPress, 2005), 248.

worse, to be understood in a Gnostic way that would make the "very good" creation a *malum in se* from which Christ came to deliver us.[281] The approach of Guager and Rana seeks empirical evidence for what makes man differ from the animals, observing higher cognitive function as that difference, and (in the case of Rana explicitly) locates the *imago Dei* there. This begs the question of what to make of human beings who do not have the capacity for higher cognitive function, and tends toward criteria for defining humankind.

Writers like Gauger and Rana may maintain that the image of God is to be understood in terms of human potential and not merely in actuality, i.e., they may maintain that the higher rational, relational, or aesthetic functions are something that animals are incapable of even if they reach their full potential,[282] while a profoundly cognitively disabled human being would still have the potential to realize these abilities, even if only in the eschaton. Without addressing this specifically, however, their statements can be interpreted to establish a criterion-based valuation of humanity.

Conclusions

Reflection on the *imago Dei* doctrine since Karl Barth has drawn less upon the influence of Plato and Aristotle than did ancient, Medieval, and even Reformation theologians, and more on exegesis, other texts of the ancient Near East, and a more global theological

---

[281] This approach also raises serious christological questions. If sin is simply a part of the human condition, how can the incarnation be maintained without either denying that Christ was without sin (*contra* Heb. 4:15), or resorting to a gnostic docetism, or conceiving of Christ as an apollinarian *tertium quid*?

[282] Charles Yang, professor of linguistics at Pennsylvania State University, has recently demonstrated that the linguistic capability of young children is markedly superior to that of Nim Chimsky, a chimpanzee who in the 1970s was taught sign language. See Penn News, "Penn Research Shows that Young Children have Grammar and Chimpanzees Don't," Pennsylvania State University, http://www.upenn.edu/pennnews/news/penn-research-shows-young-children-have-grammar-and-chimpanzees-don-t (accessed September 23, 2013).

reflection. The insights of recent theologians have tended toward a more inclusive consideration of the *imago Dei*, although there are still remnants of criteria and hierarchy that surface in their writings.

"Disability theology" is still in its infancy, particularly with regard to the consideration of those with severe cognitive disabilities. Early work in this field did not begin with a theological framework for addressing intellectual disability, but simply reflected on the theological implications of the responsibility of the church and humanity in general toward such people. Some of the more recent work has been done by theologians who discount, deny, or downplay the effects of sin's entrance into the world. While certain of their insights have been helpful, in the main, most of these theologians have tended to confuse the disability with the person. Celebrating the disabling condition rather than the person, they struggle to harmonize the obvious "bad" arising from disability with the "very good" of creation.

The recent historical Adam debate in Evangelicalism may at first not seem to have much to do with the question under consideration, but those who deny a historical Adam and a consequent historical fall add to the struggle of how disability fits into a "very good" creation. In the past, American Evangelicalism would have appealed to the fall of man for the answer, but writers like Francis Collins and Peter Enns have called this explanation into question. In response, popular arguments in support of the special creation of mankind have often resorted to the "common sense view" of the *imago Dei*. These arguments identify the *imago* substantively in the various expressions of the intellect, and in what separates man from the animals. In doing so criteria are established that may be construed to determine who may be considered a human person, an approach that would find approbation with ethicists like Peter Singer.

3

Exegesis of Pertinent Passages

In a 2001 article in *Tabletalk* magazine, R. C. Sproul discussed the error of both Roman Catholics and Reformers in condemning Copernicus' theory of a heliocentric solar system because they had baptized the old Ptolemaic geocentricism as the view taught in Scripture. Sproul wrote,

> Those who study the Bible are fallible students of the Scripture. That is, theologians are not infallible. They can and often do err in their understanding of Scripture.... When Biblical theology and scientific theory reach contradictory conclusions, there is one thing I know for sure: They cannot both be right. At least one party must be wrong.... When the two spheres collide, it is time for the philosophy of the second glance.[1]

Sproul's statement highlights the likelihood that the conclusions reached by exegesis of God's word may be in error when such exegesis is engaged in abstraction from consideration of God's world. The substantive understanding of the *imago Dei* as it was early conceived and expounded was reached at a time not only when classical Hellenistic thought exerted an influence on theological

---

[1] R. C. Sproul, "Galileo Redux" *Tabletalk* (July 2001): 61.

formulations, but also when theologians had little experience with those with severe cognitive disabilities. A lingering substantive understanding expressed by Protestant ministers in the modern church (see Appendix 3) tends to an understanding that excludes, or at the very least ignores, those with severe cognitive disabilities from participation in the *imago*, or includes them only by way of special exception. The substantive approach to the *imago* sets up a potential collision between the Christian instinct to care for and protect those who are disabled, and the theological conclusion of e.g., Martin Luther who believed that a boy with (likely) Pader-Willi syndrome was "a mass of flesh without a soul" who should be suffocated.

Work on the doctrine of the image of God by modern theologians has given rise to some profound insights, but few of these theologians have taken into conscious consideration those with severe intellectual disabilities. Some of the "disability theologians" have provided helpful insight regarding those with intellectual disabilities, but few of them have engaged directly with the *imago* doctrine. As mentioned earlier in this work, Hans Reinders believes that the *imago* doctrine has been a source of more problems than it has solved when considering those with severe intellectual disabilities.

Much of the modern theology with respect to those with cognitive disabilities might be better categorized as philosophy, since it often incorporates insights from the humanities but does not engage with the biblical text, or employs it only anecdotally. Of those writers who approach the issue from a more historically orthodox perspective, most of them are interfacing with very practical issues of ministry.

To be sure, practical outcomes are the goal of all Christian theology. Paul reminded Timothy that the goal of the apostolic instruction is love from a pure heart, a good conscience, and a sincere faith, and he warned him about those who engage in useless speculation which leads only to meaningless talk (1 Tim. 1:3–6). However, it is also the case that all Christian theology must be grounded in a careful understanding of the Scriptures.

Exegesis of Pertinent Passages

Formulations of the *imago Dei* doctrine are arrived at inductively. The relevant texts are read and a theological hypothesis is formulated. Different theologians may consider identical texts in a different light or different texts that others have not thought germane, and so present different hypotheses. When a corpus of theological literature in a given locus is established, later theologians often arrive at conclusions by means of abductive reasoning; that is, the theologian chooses among the competing hypotheses, or the theologian may endeavor to synthesize two or more of the approaches.

Theological formulations must be examined for compatibility not only with the teaching of Scripture, but for compatibility with the real life of the church. The personal Word did not maintain a sublime transcendence for mankind's salvation, but became flesh for it. A Christian theology that would serve such a Christ must be no less immanent and involved in the life of the church.

If an incompatibility is found with either the Scriptures or the real life experience of the church, or both, it is time for "the philosophy of the second glance" at the relevant texts in order to adjust the formulation of the doctrine so that it will better accord with the totality of the Scriptures and the life of the church.

The study both of the *imago* theology and of the understanding of the *imago Dei* by contemporary Protestant clergy presented in Appendix 3 leads to the conclusion that the doctrine is in need of reconsideration in light of the church's likely-to-increase experience with those who have severe intellectual disabilities. While there has been theological reflection regarding such people, there has not been much consideration with a view specifically to how such people participate in the *imago*. There has been even less serious exegesis of the germane biblical texts with consideration given to such people as a part of the contextual paradigm.

This chapter will undertake such exegesis as a foundation for a reconsideration of the *imago Dei* in light of those with severe cognitive disabilities. Because the texts in question have been the object of the church's study for a long time, it is not anticipated that much will be uncovered in the way of new technical information. However, using the concept of the hermeneutical spiral,[2] as a part of the contextual referent for this exegesis, typical people, those with intellectual disabilities, and those with severe intellectual disabilities will be kept in mind.

Making those with severe cognitive disabilities a part of the contextual referent for exegesis, however, is not a license for reading into the texts things that are not there. While the Scriptures speak to the entirety of the human condition, including the condition of those with severe cognitive disabilities, nowhere do the Scriptures directly address this condition. Words and syntax have meaning, and it is illegitimate to read disability into texts where there is none. But language is semiotic with words standing for concrete objects and abstract concepts. The existential context for these concepts and objects is the world in which we actually live, but until very recently the model of the world in which we live did not include those with severe cognitive disabilities for most theologians.

The exegetical methodology used here is biblical-theological. While specific texts are analyzed in their historical and linguistic settings as a primary exercise, consideration is also given to how other passages of Scripture may bear on the understanding of the passages in question. This methodology is born out of the belief that although there is a diversity of human authors in a plurality of historical settings, the Scriptures are the work of one Author, and what is said in one place must be considered in the light of not only linguistics and immediate historical setting but of the canon as a whole.

Exegesis of the text is foundational to doing theology. Without the binder of accurately understood biblical data, any theology

---

[2] See Harvey M. Conn, "Normativity, Relevance, and Relativism," *Inerrancy and Hermeneutic* (Grand Rapids, MI: Baker Book House, 1988), 185–309, esp. 194 ff. where he distinguishes his concept from that of Gadamer's "hermeneutical circle," a concept which goes back to Martin Heidegger. See Middleton's discussion in *The Liberating Image* (Grand Rapids, MI: Brazos, 2005) 37–40.

constructed is apt to be as brittle as a structure made of bricks without straw. For the weightiness of the doctrine, the number of texts that bear directly upon it is surprisingly small. For the purpose of this study seven passages will be considered, three in the Old Testament and four in the New Testament.

Old Testament

Genesis 1:26–27

Meredith Kline was incisive when he wrote, "If our objective is to discern what the biblical idea of the image of God is, it would appear necessary to abandon traditional dogmatic wineskins, go back to the beginning of Genesis, and start afresh."[3] The primary text for consideration of the doctrine of the *imago Dei* is Genesis 1:26–27. This text contains the first occurrence of the phrase "image of God" and all subsequent texts that deal with the doctrine (in language or in concept) allude back to it.

> Then God said, "Let Us make man in Our image, according to Our likeness; and let them rule over the fish of the sea and over the birds of the sky and over the cattle and over all the earth, and over every creeping thing that creeps on the earth." And God created man in His own image, in the image of God He created him; male and female He created them. (Gen. 1:26–27 NASB)

Important for our consideration of this passage are the nouns "image" (צֶלֶם) and "likeness" (דְּמוּת), and secondarily the prepositions "in" and "according to" (בְּ and כְּ respectively). It is also necessary to identify precisely whose image and likeness is in view, whether God alone or God and the heavenly court.

---

[3] Meredith G. Kline, *Images of the Spirit* (Eugene, OR: Wipf & Stock, reprinted 1999), 13.

Exegesis of Pertinent Passages

What exactly does it mean for man to be created "in the image of God?" BDB indicates that the word צֶלֶם means an "image, (something *cut out*, cf. פֶּסֶל); . . . images, esp. of heathen gods." Holladay notes that the word means a statue, an image or a model; HALOT indicates it is a cognate of the Akkadian Ṣalmu, a statue, figurine, image; in particular: "1. the statue of a god; the statue of a king; a figurine; a relief, bas-relief; a shape, likeness, or representation." TWOT states, "The word basically refers to a representation, a likeness . . ." but then goes on, "God's image obviously does not consist in man's body which was formed from earthly matter, but in his spiritual, intellectual, moral likeness to God from whom his animating breath came. . . . God is non-material, the creator (Deut. 4:15–19). This spiritual aspect of man has been damaged by the fall and is daily tarnished by sin. But it was seen in perfection in Christ and will be made perfect in us when salvation is complete (Heb. 2:6–15)."

The conclusion reached here by the contributors of TWOT seems to be the result, not of linguistic study, but of a systematic theological pre-conclusion. צֶלֶם occurs seventeen times in the Hebrew Scriptures (and in Aramaic cognates in Dan. 2 and 3). It is used specifically to refer to humans as the image of God (Gen. 1:26–27; 9:6), of the sonship of Seth to Adam (Gen. 5:3), and of golden three-dimensional representations of mice and tumors (1 Sam. 6:5, 11). The remainder of the uses refer to idols, visible representations of false gods (2 Kings 11:18; 2 Chr. 23:17; Ps. 39:7; 73:20; Ezek. 7:20; 16:17; 23:14; Amos 5:26). If we set aside the Genesis text as the one in need of explanation and look at the remainder of the texts, it is obvious that צֶלֶם functions to indicate images (most often three-dimensional images) that represent something unseen, either because it is not physically present at that location or because it is invisible (viz. pagan deities).

The use of the word in the Genesis 1 text would most naturally indicate that man as צֶלֶם אֱלֹהִים is a visible representation of the invisible God. Among modern writers there is both recognition of, and discomfort with this idea. Routledge notes, "The most usual use of the term 'image' (*ṣelem*) suggests physical resemblance.... However, we have already noted that there is a fundamental, ontological distinction between God and the created order and that it is impossible to make a physical representation of God."[4] Certainly it is clear from the Old Testament texts that *human beings* are prohibited from making images of God, but it does not follow that God may not or cannot make an image of himself, and this is precisely what the Genesis text taken at face value would seem to convey.

There are two significant differences between the image that God makes and the images that humans make. First, the image that God makes "stands in" for him, so to speak, in relationship to the rest of creation, but God does not worship his fashioned image, nor should the fashioned image be worshiped by other human beings (i.e., other fashioned images). By contrast, the images of God (or the gods) that human beings make are made for the express purpose of worshiping (cf. Rom. 1:23). Secondly, the image that God makes is a living image of the living God. By contrast, the images that human beings make are dead images. Psalm 115 captures the contrast: "But their idols[5] are silver and gold, made by the hands of men. They have mouths, but cannot speak, eyes, but they cannot see; they have ears, but cannot hear, noses, but they cannot smell; they have hands, but cannot feel, feet, but they cannot walk; nor can they utter a sound with their throats. Those who make them will be like them, and so will all who trust in them" (Ps. 115:4–8 NIV).

The word צֶלֶם indicates as a primary meaning a physical, visible representation. Its use in Genesis 1:26–27 is unique because unlike its use when other images are in view, it denotes a living צֶלֶם of the living God. Because in this text the word refers to a living image, the physicality of the word does not preclude the other attributes

---

[4] Robin Routledge, *Old Testament Theology: A Thematic Approach* (Downers Grove, IL: InterVarsity Press, 2008), 139.

[5] עָצָב. Not every צֶלֶם is an עָצָב (if the Genesis texts are taken into account), but every עָצָב is a צֶלֶם.

of human beings (intelligence, relationality, capacity for dominion, etc.). The very word, however, indicates that the physical aspect of man cannot be excluded from the image. The historically prevalent substantive understanding of the image of God in which we look for some component *within* man as constituting the image, is fundamentally at odds with the word צֶלֶם, and is a view that owes more to Plato than to the Pentateuch. Gerhard von Rad was correct when he wrote, "One does well to separate as little as possible the bodily and the spiritual: the whole man is created in the *imago* of God."[6]

The other significant word which appears in tandem with צֶלֶם is the word דְּמוּת. It is necessary for this study not only to examine the word itself, but to consider the relationship of the words to one another.[7] דְּמוּת occurs twenty-five times in the Hebrew Bible. Holladay defines the word as "pattern; form or shape; image;" HALOT as a "model, shape, or likeness." BDB explains the word as a "likeness, similitude of external appearance." Most of the uses are in the book of Ezekiel (thirteen), and most often the word is used in connection with a theophanic or apocalyptic vision. It is significant that Ezekiel never directly sees the heavenly country, the heavenly courtiers, or God himself, but always "something like" them, a "similitude" of them. TDOT notes that Ezekiel "can speak only in allusions and deliberately veiled statements."[8]

Randall Garr has argued that while the nouns צֶלֶם and דְּמוּת are not exactly synonyms, they "do share a basic semantic content and imply a basic comparison between humanity and divinity. They are both similative nouns; they both express multiple degrees of referential similitude, including the physical."[9] The semantic similarity is

---

[6] Gerhard von Rad, *Genesis, A Commentary* Revised ed. (Philadelphia: Westminster Press, 1973), 56.

[7] For a history of approaches to interpreting the relationship between these two words, see Gordon J. Wenham, *Genesis 1–15*, Word Biblical Commentary (Waco, TX: Word Books, 1987), 29–32.

[8] 3:258.

[9] W. Randall Garr, *In His Own Image and Likeness Humanity, Divinity, and*

evident in the Genesis text. In fact, while the LXX renders צֶלֶם as εἰκών, and דְּמוּת as ὁμοίωσις in Genesis 1, in the Genesis 5:1 text ("In the day when God created man, He made him in the *likeness* of God") where the word דְּמוּת is used, and for which we would expect the LXX translation ὁμοίωσις, the Greek text unexpectedly uses the word εἰκών.[10]

The phrase commonly translated "in our *image* and according to our *likeness*" is best understood as a hendiadys.[11] Both words are used in the texts (outside of the Genesis text in question and Ezekiel) to indicate a physical representation, with דְּמוּת at times indicating a pattern or perhaps even a model (cf. 2 Kings 16:10). As the terms continue to be employed in the book of Genesis with respect to man's relationship to God, the words are used interchangeably. Thus in 1:27 there is mention only of the image and not of the likeness: "God made man in his own image, in the image of God he made him; male and female he made them." Conversely in 5:1 there is mention only of the likeness and not of the image: "When God created man he made him in the likeness of God." That the author changes from one noun to the other without any apparent change in meaning adduces strong evidence for their co-referentiality.

Throughout the history of exegesis a great deal of attention has been given to the prepositions in Genesis 1:26–27. It has been suggested that there is a significant difference between man *being* the image of God, and man being *in* the image of God.[12]

In his exegetical treatment of this passage, Garr maintains that "כְּ and בְּ are clearly different. On the one hand, כְּ is a similiative-separative preposition. It expresses approximation, likeness, or similarity. . . . on

---

Monotheism (Boston: Brill, 2003), 166.

[10] בְּיוֹם בְּרֹא אֱלֹהִים אָדָם בִּדְמוּת אֱלֹהִים עָשָׂה אֹתוֹ, cf. ᾗ ἡμέρᾳ ἐποίησεν ὁ θεὸς τὸν Αδαμ κατ' εἰκόνα θεοῦ ἐποίησεν αὐτόν.

[11] See E. W. Bullinger, *Figures of Speech Used in the Bible* (Grand Rapids, MI: Baker, 1968), 657–59.

[12] See Philip Edgecombe Hughes, *The True Image* (Grand Rapids, MI: Eerdmans, 1989), 15–23.

Exegesis of Pertinent Passages

the other hand, בְּ is a locative-proximate preposition. It expresses location (with—) in a realm, whether spacial or non-spacial."[13]

In Genesis 1:26–27 it seems best to take the preposition as an instance of the *beth essentiae*[14] and translate it simply "as." An example of this use of בְּ is found in Exodus 6:3, "I appeared to Abraham, Isaac, and Jacob *as* El Shaddai" (בְּאֵל שַׁדָּי). Although deviating from centuries of translation practice, Clines is correct in translating the Genesis text, "Let us make man *as* our image."[15]

There is not a great deal of difference between the *beth essentiae* and common uses of the preposition כְּ, and the two at times are interchangeable. In fact, although Garr has argued that the prepositions are not synonymous, he states, "Nevertheless, on occasion these two prepositions seem to be interchangeable."[16] In Genesis 5:1 בְּ is used with דְּמוּת instead of כְּ (בִּדְמוּת אֱלֹהִים עָשָׂה אֹתוֹ). The ancient translators of this text also indicate that they understood these words to have identical meanings. The LXX uses the same preposition (κατά) in both places in translating both Hebrew prepositions (καὶ εἶπεν ὁ θεός ποιήσωμεν ἄνθρωπον κατ' εἰκόνα ἡμετέραν καὶ καθ' ὁμοίωσιν), and the Vulgate uses only a single occurrence of a preposition (*ad*) for both objects (*et ait faciamus hominem ad imaginem et similitudinem nostram*).

Garr believes that these phrases (בְּצַלְמֵנוּ and כִּדְמוּתֵנוּ) "jointly qualify their antecedent. They 'stand side by side' in asyndetic combination. In the Septuagint and Samaritan version [and, it might be noted, the Vulgate] they do not; they each supply a conjunction between the phrases, and thus suggest that the phrases are potentially

---

[13] Garr, 111.

[14] See Bruce K. Waltke and M. O'Connor, *An Introduction to Biblical Hebrew Syntax* (Winona Lake, IN: Eisenbrauns, 1990), §11.2.5.e, 198.

[15] See D. J. A. Clines, "The Image of God in Man" *Tyndale Bulletin* 19 (1986), 70–85. Translating the phrase this way would be similar to saying that Christ coming ἐν σαρκί (1 Jn. 4:2) could be paraphrased by saying that Christ came "*as* a man."

[16] Garr, 111.

unrelated constituents." But in the Hebrew text "God . . . specifies two similative characteristics or attributes of the human creature: one proximate ("image"), and the other distal ("likeness"). In one respect, then, humanity will intimately participate in divinity [image]; . . . In another respect, humanity will be separate and distinct [likeness]."[17]

These considerations lead to the conclusion that God created man *as* his image and likeness. Whatever nuances in meaning that distinguish "image" and "likeness," the point of reference is the same: the human being is the visible representation of the invisible God.

Although the doctrine has been referred to in the west as *imago Dei*, we must ask in whose image mankind is made; that is, who exactly does the noun אֱלֹהִים refer to in the phrases צֶלֶם אֱלֹהִים (Gen. 1:27) and דְּמוּת אֱלֹהִים (Gen. 5:1)? Although early Christian theologians understood the "let us . . ." of Genesis 1:26 to be an inter-trinitarian cohortative, some more modern writers have followed a rabbinic tradition in understanding this cohortative as divine speech directed toward the angelic court (e.g., Kline, Garr). Does the plural noun אֱלֹהִים refer to God and a heavenly angelic court; that is, is mankind made in the image of "the gods" (God and the heavenly court)? There are two indications that what is in view is man as the image of God, and not as the image of the gods.

The first is found in the history of translation and the understanding of the phrases צֶלֶם אֱלֹהִים and דְּמוּת אֱלֹהִים. Psalm 8 says of mankind "You have made him a little lower than *elohim*" (מֵאֱלֹהִים), which the LXX translates as παρ᾽ ἀγγέλους. This indicates that the word אֱלֹהִים was indeed understood in some cases to include the angelic beings in its semantic domain. But the word is not so understood by the ancient translators of the Genesis texts. Both Genesis 1:27 and (somewhat unexpectedly) 5:1 are rendered with the phrase εἰκόνα θεοῦ. Neither of these passages are rendered with either εἰκόνα ἀγγέλων or εἰκόνα θεῶν. The second indication is found in the canonical context of the understanding of man in the

---

[17] Ibid., 113–14.

image of God. In 1 Corinthians 11:7 man[18] is said to be the εἰκὼν θεοῦ; in James 3:9 mankind[19] is said to be made καθ' ὁμοίωσιν θεοῦ. In neither of these cases are angels in view, least of all as a pattern for humanity.

In no instance in which the *imago* doctrine is elucidated is there ever an indication that mankind is made in the image or likeness of the angels. Angels, whatever resemblance they may bear to the divine, are not presented as the pattern for human beings. It is perhaps because mankind bears the divine image and angels do not that angels, once fallen, do not appear capable of being saved (Heb. 2:16; 1 Peter 1:10–12), and are inferior to the Son who in his incarnation is the "exact representation of God's nature" (Heb. 1:4). By contrast, angels are ministering spirits sent out for the sake of those who will inherit salvation (Heb. 1:14), by which inheritors of salvation they will be judged (1 Cor. 6:3).

Genesis 3:1–5

Genesis 3 is an often overlooked passage when considering the meaning of mankind made as the image of God. It records the elements that Paul would later use to construct a doctrine of the fall of mankind. The importance of the passage for our consideration, however, is not to be found in mankind's fall from communion with God, nor in the fall's effect upon the *imago*. Rather, it is to be found obliquely in the temptation of the woman by the serpent: "For God knows that in the day you eat from [the tree of the knowledge of good and evil] your eyes will be opened, and you will be like God, knowing good and evil" (Gen. 3:5 NASB). The phrase specifically to be considered is וִהְיִיתֶם כֵּאלֹהִים, "and you will become like God."

---

[18] Ἀνήρ; Paul here is making an argument based upon the creation order, not expositing an *imago* doctrine. To conclude from this text that woman is not the image of God would be to read into this text something that is outside of its purview.

[19] Ἄνθρωπος should be understood severally, i.e., while the reference is to humanity, each person individually is in view.

Exegesis of Pertinent Passages

The translation "you will become like gods" which is sometimes suggested, is unwarranted. The noun אֱלֹהִים occurs forty-one times in the Genesis text before its use in 3:5, and in every one of them it refers to one and the same God who created the heavens and the earth, and made mankind as his own image.[20]

Theologians since the second century have pondered how human beings who were created without sin could have been tempted to sin. The text of Genesis 3:5 provides insight, specifically in that the temptation was in the form of a suggestion that they would become like God. Were they not already like God by virtue of being created as his image and likeness? This text hints that while they were created to be God's likeness, the potential of that likeness was not fully realized, and the serpent seized upon their perception of this fact in order to tempt them to disobey God and realize their potential by rebellion.

The intuition of the Patristic theologians that there was something potential, incomplete, and future-oriented about man as the image of God as he came forth from the hand of the Creator has undergirding from this passage. To diabolically paraphrase the apostle John, the serpent's enticement amounted to, "Now you are the image of God, but it has not yet appeared what you shall be. But if you eat this fruit, you shall be like him, for you will perceive good and evil as it is."

Bridge Texts: Genesis 9:6 and James 3:9

What is the status of mankind with respect to the image of God after the fall of man? Is the image and likeness of God retained? Is the image retained but the likeness lost, as many of the patristic

---

[20] See the discussion on Gen 1:26–27. Kline, 22–23 *Images of the Spirit*, Garr, 17–21 and others maintain that the "Let us ..." of Gen 1:26 is a hortative declaration to a heavenly court of angelic beings. It is notable that while man may not make images of God in whose image he is made (e.g., 1 Kings 12:28, cf. 2 Kings 10:29), there is no such prohibition against making images of the angelic court (Ex. 25:18; 26:1) unless they are made as פְסִלִים (cf. Deut. 5:8).

writers believed? As we have already seen, Luther believed that the image of God was lost to fallen man: "I am afraid that since the loss of this image through sin we cannot understand it to any extent."[21] Genesis 9:6 and James 3:9 bear materially on the question.

Genesis 9:6 stands out from the surrounding text for its poetic parallelism. The statement is a primordial prohibition of murder. The fact that it comes after the fall of mankind makes it particularly significant. The NIV renders the text, "Whoever sheds the blood of man, by man shall his blood be shed; for in the image of God has God made man."

The same phrase is used here that is used in Genesis 1:27, בְּצֶלֶם אֱלֹהִים, although here the verb עָשָׂה is used instead of בָּרָא. The difference in verbs with the same phrase at these two different points in history is noteworthy. "The word [bārâ] occurs with great frequency in the Genesis account of creation, which is the first great act of God in history. The significant interchange between the words bārâ 'create' and 'āśâ [make] is of great interest. The word bārâ carries the thought of the initiation of the object involved. It always connotes what only God can do and frequently emphasizes the absolute newness of the object created."[22]

This observation is consistent with the uses of the two words in their respective texts. Genesis 1:26–27 depicts mankind as a special initial creation of God, whereas Genesis 9:6 indicates mankind made by God through the ordinary means of procreation. The verb is fientive[23]

---

[21] Martin Luther, "Lectures on Genesis Chapters 1–5" reprinted in Hueser, "Luther and Disability" in Brian Brock and John Swinton, *Disability in the Christian Tradition: A Reader* (Grand Rapids, MI: Eerdmans, 2012), 212.

[22] TWOT. A case can be made for עָשָׂה and בָּרָא being used synonymously in Gen 1. The hortative "Let us make" of v. 26 is realized in the phrase "so God created" in v. 27. However, Gen 2:3 gives indication that בָּרָא is in concept antecedent of and in order to עָשָׂה: "And God blessed the seventh day and hallowed it, for on it he rested from all his work *which God had created to make*" אֲשֶׁר־בָּרָא אֱלֹהִים לַעֲשׂוֹת . . . , where לְ indicates purpose of action, HALOT (7).

[23] See Ronald J. Williams, *Williams' Hebrew Syntax*, 3rd ed. (Toronto:

(a subtlety picked up on by the NIV translators in their rendering of the verb in the past perfect tense) which further indicates the active, on-going nature of the making of mankind as the image of God.

Genesis 9:6 specifies that the reason for the prohibition of the unjust taking of human life is that mankind is and continues to be, even after the fall, made as the image of God. But what of God's likeness? Has it been lost, as the patristic writers maintained? James 3:9 sheds important light on the answer to this question.

Speaking of the powerful and incongruous use of the tongue, James states almost incidentally, "With it we bless our Lord and Father; and with it we curse men, who have been made in the likeness of God" (NASB). The phrasing of James (τοὺς ἀνθρώπους τοὺς καθ' ὁμοίωσιν θεοῦ γεγονότας) is taken from Genesis 1:26 of the LXX (ποιήσωμεν ἄνθρωπον . . . ἡμετέραν . . . καθ' ὁμοίωσιν). James is not here referring to Adam in his state of innocence, but to people (note the plural) known to the readers, contemporaries of whom he says they are made "in the likeness of God."

Taken together, these passages show that human beings, not only before the fall, but since the fall, are the image of God *and* the likeness of God. This is not to say that the image is undamaged. On the contrary, the universal conclusion of orthodox Christianity is that every faculty of body and soul has been damaged by the fall. But this damage does not undo the fact that mankind has been created as the image and likeness of God. Archeologists who come upon an image of Baal, no matter how damaged it is, will recognize it as an image of Baal. They will not conclude, "This used to be an image of Baal."

New Testament

That the image of God has been damaged by sin is the inescapable conclusion of the New Testament passages which speak of

---

University of Toronto Press, 2007), § 134, 57, and Waltke and O'Connor, § 22.1.1, 363–64.

the renewal of the image of God in Christ. Most significantly, in the New Testament Christ is the image of God (2 Cor. 4:4) to whom his redeemed people are being and will be conformed (Rom. 8:29; 2 Cor. 3:17–18).

To say that Christ is the image of God, however, raises a significant question: *when* is the Son of God the image of God? Has the Son always (*ad intra*) been the image of God? This is the approach of Hughes, who writes, "... the Second Person of the Trinity is the Image of God in which man was created.... Thus as the eternal Son he is the Image, and as the incarnate Son he is in the image."[24]

Keeping in mind our study of the Hebrew prepositions of Genesis 1:26–27, Hughes' emphasis and conclusion is questionable. More significantly, however, the Greek εἰκών, based in the New Testament as it is on the Hebrew צֶלֶם, is by its definition a *visible* representation. It is and only can be of the *incarnate* Son that Paul writes, "He is the image of the invisible God [in his incarnation], the firstborn of all creation [in his resurrection, cf. 1:18]" (Col. 1:15). In every passage of the New Testament, the Son who shows forth the Father is always the incarnate Son.[25]

1 Corinthians 15:45–49

Chapter 15 of 1 Corinthians contrasts the first Adam (who was made as the image of God, and whose image his progeny bear, Gen. 5:3; 1 Cor. 15:49a) with the last Adam (who in his incarnation is the image of God, 2 Cor. 4:4, and whose image his progeny will bear, 1 Cor. 15:49b). In this chapter Paul engages in a polemic against

---

[24] Hughes, 235.

[25] Even in the case of Heb. 1:3, "[The Son] is the radiance of [God's] glory and the exact representation of his nature." *Contra* Kline, the context clearly sets the statement within the incarnation. The word is used of the Son of God, not in eternity, but in "the last days" (1:2), i.e., the time of his incarnation, including his "making purification for sin" and his "sitting down at the right hand of the majesty on high" (1:3); and it is paired with χαρακτήρ which in every case outside of the NT refers to a visible, physical image and representation except when used metaphorically (as e.g., 4 Macc 15:2).

those who say there will be no resurrection. He avers that the resurrection of Jesus is the indispensable fact of the Christian faith, the one upon which the veracity of its efficacy entirely rests: "If Christ has not been raised, your faith is useless; you are still in your sins" (1 Cor. 15:17). So closely is Christ bound to redeemed humanity, however, that "if the dead are not raised not even Christ has been raised" (1 Cor. 15:16).

In a very real sense, the church does not await the resurrection. The resurrection has already begun in the resurrection of Jesus. What the church waits for is the conclusion of the resurrection. And while the conclusion of the resurrection will be general, encompassing both the redeemed and the lost (Dan. 12:2, John 5:29), Paul has in view here those who will be conformed to Christ, the second Man and last Adam. The text reads, "So also it is written, 'The first man, Adam, became a living soul.' The last Adam became a life-giving spirit. However, the spiritual is not first, but the natural; then the spiritual. The first man is from the earth, earthy; the second man is from heaven. As is the earthy, so also are those who are earthy; and as is the heavenly, so also are those who are heavenly. And just as we have borne the image of the earthy, we shall also bear the image of the heavenly" (1 Cor. 15:45–49 NASB).

It is noteworthy that Christ is presented here as the "second Man." As Paul sets out the parallel, there is no one between the first Man (Adam) and the second Man (Christ). Christ is also the "last Adam;" there will be no one who comes after him. All of humanity is thus encompassed in either Adam or Christ (1 Cor. 15:22).[26]

It is significant that Paul uses *imago* language here ("just as we have born the image of the [man of] dust, we shall also bear the image of the heavenly [man]"). God had created Adam in the likeness of God (Gen. 5:1), and Adam had begotten Seth in his image (Gen. 5:3). In a similar way, Christ is not eternally "the heavenly

---

[26] For a full treatment of this, see Geehardus Vos, *The Pauline Eschatology* (Phillipsburg, NJ: Presbyterian & Reformed, 1986).

man." He is a man (or better, *the* man) only after his incarnation. In his resurrection he continues to be human, but his humanity is now permanently transfigured. He is the firstborn of all creation (Col. 1:15), the start of the new creation.

It is precisely because Christ has ascended into heaven and sits at the right hand of God that he is now "the heavenly man" who in John's vision is expressed in language similar to that of Ezekiel ("... and in the middle of the lampstands *one like* a son of man [ὅμοιον υἱὸν ἀνθρώπου], Rev. 1:13). As Adam had begotten offspring in his image, so Christ begets offspring (Isa. 53:10; Heb. 2:13) in his image. But the begetting that Christ does is not a this-creation begetting. Adam could beget children because God had breathed into his nostrils the breath of life and Adam became a living soul (1 Cor. 15:45; Gen. 2:7 נֶפֶשׁ חַיָּה). Like the other "living souls" (Gen. 1:20, 21, 24), mankind was given the mandate to be fruitful and multiply (Gen. 1:22–28) and so bring forth others "after their kind" (Gen. 1:21, 24, 25). In Paul's comparison Christ similarly begets children because in his resurrection he became a life-creating Spirit.[27]

In the New Testament, and particularly in the Pauline literature, κύριος refers most often to the incarnate Christ, so it is surprising to read the statement "Now the Lord is the Spirit" (ὁ δὲ κύριος τὸ πνεῦμά ἐστιν, 2 Cor. 3:17). The glorified Lord cannot be

---

[27] By saying that Christ became the life-giving Spirit, the apostle is not indicating a modalistic transmutation from one Person of the Trinity into another. However, in the mystery of the Godhead there is a circumincession of the Persons such that the acts or even the properties of one can be said to belong to the others. Thus, John can say that "the Spirit was not yet, for Jesus had not yet been glorified" (οὔπω γὰρ ἦν πνεῦμα, ὅτι Ἰησοῦς οὐδέπω ἐδοξάσθη; John 7:39). He does not by this deny the existence of the Holy Spirit before the glorification of Christ, but rather indicates that the Spirit of the *crucified, risen, ascended and permanently transfigured Christ* was "not yet." In the same Gospel beginning in chapter 14 Jesus tells his disciples that he will leave them but that the Holy Spirit will come. Yet in the very context of speaking of his leaving and the Spirit's coming, he says, "I will not leave you as orphans; *I* will come to you" (John 14:18).

separated from the Spirit, and as we behold his glory we are "transformed into the same image" (2 Cor. 3:18). Thus, just as the children of Adam are begotten by him (γεννάω in the LXX, Gen. 5:3), so the children of Christ are re-begotten "by the washing of regeneration (παλιγγενεσία) and [the] renewal of the Holy Spirit" (Titus 3:5).

Adam is the "dusty" (χοϊκός) image of God who even in his state of sinless innocence did not realize all of the potential of the *imago Dei*. In his sin the *imago* was defaced in every faculty of body and soul, but not lost. He who is the (unrealized, and now defaced and damaged) image of God begets a son in his image (Gen. 5:3).

In parallel contrast, Christ in his incarnation is the image of the invisible God. This is because "in him dwells all the fullness of the Deity *bodily*" (Col. 2:9). The somatic aspect is not incidental. But in the bodily *imago* of his incarnation Christ bore the demerits that accrued to Adam after his rebellion. Thus "God sent his own Son in the likeness of sinful flesh" (Rom. 8:3, cf. Phil. 2:7). By his resurrection Jesus not only overcomes the demerits that had defaced the *imago* (Rom. 6:10), but in his glorification he fulfills the latent potential of the *imago Dei* that was unrealized in Adam.

It is thus that when human beings are begotten again by the living and abiding word of God (1 Peter 1:23), it is to a living hope through the resurrection of Jesus Christ (1 Peter 1:3), and it is his *glorified* image that they will bear (1 Cor. 15:49). In Christ there is no mere repairing of what was defaced in Adam, no mere restoration to the condition before the fall. There is rather a full realization of the *imago Dei* which was never actualized in Adam. Christ gains for those he represents more than Adam lost for those he represents.

Colossians 3:9–10

The occasion for Paul's letter to the Colossians seems to have been the reports of danger of the church being led astray by a philosophy that was at odds with the gospel, a philosophy which led not only to heterodoxy, but heteropraxy in their personal lives.

The letter contains some key concepts that bear on 3:9–10 and

Exegesis of Pertinent Passages

the doctrine of the image of God. It speaks of God having "rescued us from the domain of darkness, and transferring us into the kingdom of his beloved Son" (1:13), and of that Son as "the image of the invisible God, the firstborn of all creation" (1:15). It reminds them of the mystery of "Christ in you, the hope of glory" (1:27), that in Christ "all of the fullness of Deity dwells in bodily form" (2:9), and that they should keep seeking the things having to do with Christ, so that when Christ is revealed "you also will appear with him in glory" (3:4). In language similar to that of Romans 6, it tells them to consider the members of their bodies dead to sinful practices: "Do not lie to each other, since you have taken off your old self with its practices and have put on the new self, which is being renewed in knowledge in the image of its Creator" (Col. 3:9–10 NIV).

The very mundane sounding admonition ("do not lie to each other") is supported by a deeply profound statement. The NIV (and most modern translations) is misleading in rendering the phrase "old self." The RSV "old nature" is better, but still misses the very significant point. The phrase is literally "the old man" (τὸν παλαιὸν ἄνθρωπον). The *imago* language used in conjunction with it leads to the conclusion that "the old man" is not one's self, but is in fact Adam.

If this is so, then "the new (τὸν νέον[28]) man" is a reference to Christ. While Paul can speak of putting on Christ as an imperative (cf. Rom. 13:14) he does not do so here. The aorist participles for "taking off" and "putting on" indicate something that has already been done.[29]

Perhaps modern translators are uncomfortable with rendering the phrases "the old man" and "the new man" because they believe it will indicate that Christ is now "being renewed according to the image of God." Paul, however, is not speaking about Christ

---

[28] The adjective is an antonymous substantive. "Man" does not appear with it, but if the first part of the sentence is translated as "old man," "new man" is the only proper translation.

[29] See F. Blass and A. DeBrunner, *A Greek Grammar of the New Testament and Other Early Christian Literature* (Chicago: University of Chicago Press,

Exegesis of Pertinent Passages

in himself, individually or abstractly considered, but rather Christ as united with his people, or perhaps it would be better to say his people in him. In Christ they are already a new creation; the old is passed away, the new has already come (2 Cor. 5:27). And yet these renewed people continue to engage in acts of rebellion which they are exhorted to stop; how can this be?

The tension of what the redeemed already are in Christ but have not yet fully become is summed up by the apostle John (1 John 3:2). He writes, "Beloved, already we are the children of God...;" we have already been renewed and have been made a part of the new creation of which Jesus by his resurrection is the first fruits. "... but it has not yet appeared what we shall be." There is an already-not yet character to our being in the eschatological image of God, and thus the redeemed are being renewed in Christ[30] in knowledge in the image of his Creator.[31]

2 Peter 1:4

The statement that Christ's redeemed people will be "partakers of the divine nature" in 2 Peter 1:4 is startling to many Western Christians. Since the patristic period the doctrine of theosis has not been much emphasized in the West. The disquieting statement of Athanasius that Christ "was made man in order that we might be made God," coupled with the Reformed insistence upon the Creator-creature distinction, and a reaffirmation of Chalcedonian orthodoxy expressed in the Westminster Standards[32] all are indicative of the reasons that the doctrine is viewed with suspicious in the West.

1961), §339, 174–75.

[30] Ἀνακαινόω, a word that seems to be of Paul's own coining.

[31] For a full treatment of the already—not yet character of the kingdom of God and the redeemed people of God, see Herman Ridderbos, *The Coming of the Kingdom* (Philadelphia: Presbyterian & Reformed, 1962).

[32] "The Son of God, the second person in the Trinity, being very and eternal God, of one substance and equal with the Father, did, when the fulness of time was come, take upon Him man's nature, with all the essential properties, and common infirmities thereof, yet without sin; being conceived by the power of

Exegesis of Pertinent Passages

The theosis doctrine will be analyzed in the following chapter, but 2 Peter 1:3–4 is a significant text for the purpose of this study: "His divine power has given us everything we need for life and godliness through our knowledge of him who called us by his own glory and goodness. Through these he has given us his very great and precious promises, so that through them you may participate in the divine nature and escape the corruption in the world caused by evil desires" (NIV).

At issue is what it means to "participate in the divine nature." The noun κοινωνός means "a partaker," or "a participant" (e.g., 1 Cor. 10:18, 20; 2 Cor. 1:7; 1 Peter 5:1). Although the word can convey the idea of being a participant *with*, sometimes leaving what is participated *in* unexpressed (e.g., Luke 5:10), that idea usually requires a correlative in the dative case. In instances in which the correlative is in the genitive case (as it is in this passage), it usually indicates what one is a participant *in*.[33]

What the recipients of 2 Peter are participants in is the θείας φύσεως. While many lexica give the gloss "nature" or "natural" for the word φύσις, BDAG indicates the word can mean "The natural character of an entity; *natural characteristic or disposition* [italics added]." Although much of Thayer's lexical work is out of date, his definition of φύσις is helpful: ". . . *the sum of innate properties and powers by which one person differs from others*, distinctive native peculiarities."[34] The word is used ten times in the New Testament outside of this passage. In about half of them the word could be translated "natural," i.e., having to do with the environment or inclinations of created things. In the other half of the passages, the word refers to distinctive and peculiar native properties.

---

the Holy Ghost, in the womb of the virgin Mary, of her substance. So that two whole, perfect, and distinct natures, the Godhead and the manhood, were inseparably joined together in one person, without conversion, composition, or confusion. Which person is very God, and very man, yet one Christ, the only Mediator between God and man." WCF 8:2.

[33] See BDAG 1.a.b.
[34] TGELNT.

The nature that is in view is described by the word θεῖος, a word that is used only in 2 Peter (twice) and the book of Acts (17:29), but which had wide use outside of the New Testament. Liddell-Scott indicates the word refers to the divine, at times even meaning the divine being or Deity. What exactly this means is the subject of our inquiry, but it is clear from the passage that becoming a participant in the divine nature is a result of the exercise of divine power, and the knowledge of God who called us, by which he has given us his great and precious promises (v. 3). Being partakers of the divine nature is a condition yet to be fulfilled (note the subjunctive mood), and is subsequent to escaping the corruption that is in the world (note the aorist participle), an escape that is already initiated in the redemption of Christ but is not yet completed (cf. Jude 5).

The use of the word in Acts 17:29 is instructive. Preaching the gospel to the Athenians in the Areopagus, Paul, whose spirit had been provoked by the many idols in the city (17:26), said, "Therefore since we are God's offspring, we should not think that the divine being (or divine nature, θεῖος) is like gold or silver or stone—an image made by man's design and skill" (NIV).

Two things are notable here. The first is Paul's statement "*we are God's offspring,*" the "we" being inclusive. The grammatical structure indicates (and virtually all translations reflect) that being God's offspring is as descriptive of the idolatrous Athenians who are in the process of rejecting Paul's message as it is of Paul himself. Paul's statement to the Athenians is universal. All people are the γένος τοῦ θεοῦ.

While "offspring" is a possible gloss, BDAG indicates the word can mean "entities united by common traits, *class, kind*;" Friberg indicates that the word can convey the meaning "a distinctive species of something; *kind, class* (1 Cor. 12:10)."[35] As noted previously, Catherine Beckerleg, considering only the Genesis text, raised the intriguing possibility that man is "God's kind." She notes

---

[35] ALGNT.

that in the Genesis 1 account, all living thing are created "after their kind."

> Clearly the author is emphasizing the creation and reproduction of each species *according to its own distinctive type or class*.... [This] implies that just as the plants and animals were created according to their own type, man was made, at some level, according to *Elohim's kind*.... It seems that being created in the image and likeness of God is both comparable to being created "according to God's kind," yet distinct from it.... Yet at some level, man belongs to the divine class or species, that is, humanity's kind or type is God.[36]

In the LXX of the Genesis 1 text, in all ten occurrences of the phrase "after its [or their] kind," the Hebrew phrase is translated in the Greek as κατὰ γένος. It is therefore notable that Paul says that he and the Athenians (and by inference, all people) are γένος τοῦ θεοῦ.

The second prominent thing to note is how the text portrays the Athenians' understanding of the divine, an understanding indicative of the disruption that man's sin has brought into his relationship with God. Paul indicates that the Athenians believed that the likeness (cf. ὅμοιος) of the divine nature can be stamped (cf. χάραγμα) on gold and silver and stone by the design and skill of man. This idolatry is not only a repudiation of who God is, but it is a repudiation of who God created man to be. As mentioned earlier, that man is prohibited from making images of God does not mean that God is prohibited from making images of himself.

The sin of idol-making is, among other things, the sin of human debasement. By making man in his own image, God in the very act of creation established man in an elevated position. When

---

[36] Catherine Leigh Beckerleg, "The 'Image of God' in Eden: The Creation of Mankind in Genesis 2:5–3:24 in Light of the *mis pî pît pî* and *wpt-r* Rituals in Mesopotamia and Ancient Egypt" (Ph.D. diss., Harvard University, 2009), 181–82.

people make images of God or the gods, however, they are by that activity laying the groundwork for their own degradation, for "those who make them will become like them" (Ps. 135:18). By making tame and controllable gods, mankind hopes to elevate himself, but in fact he succeeds in doing just the opposite. In exchanging the glory of the incorruptible God for corruptible images, they establish a groundwork that inevitably leads to every kind of debasement and evil (see Rom. 1:18–32).

But man, who was created as "God's kind," is redeemed by Christ for better things, specifically to become "participants in the divine nature." If the LXX translation of Psalm 8, which is employed by the writer to the Hebrews (2:7–9), is to be understood such that man's inferiority to the angels is temporary (the temporal use of βραχύς[37]), it would indicate that the angels are destined to be subject to man, an idea supported by Paul in 1 Corinthians 6:3 ("Do you not know that we will judge angels?").

Richard Bauckham has pointed out the historical context of the phrase "partakers of the divine nature." He notes that Hellenistic Judaism in the first century had a theosis doctrine, but one which did not envision "any kind of pantheistic absorption into God. They do not intend to blur the distinction between God and his creatures;" but because man is "created in God's image, [he] is capable of resembling God in his immortality and incorruption."[38]

Given the canonical context of 2 Peter 1:4, it may be hyperbole to say that "Christ became man in order that man might become God," but it is not extravagant hyperbole. The historic doctrine of the incarnation is that "The Son of God, the second person in the Trinity, being very and eternal God, of one substance and equal with the Father, did, when the fulness of time was come, take upon Him man's nature, with all the essential properties . . . thereof."[39] Peter's

[37] BDAG, 2.

[38] Richard K. Bauckham, *Jude, 2 Peter*, Word Biblical Commentary (Waco, TX: Word Books, 1983), 180f.

[39] WCF, 8.2.

statement that God's redeemed people are to be "partakers of the divine nature" is the complement to that doctrine.

This does not mean that man will be transmuted into God, or that there will be a hypostatic union of the divine nature and the human nature in human beings. What it does mean, however, is that mankind in his redemption and as "new creation" is destined to fulfill the potential which was never realized in the first creation, to be greater than the angels and to be "the spitting image" of God, i.e., to look and be as much like God as is creaturely possible.

Conclusion

Stepping back to take a bird's eye view of this biblical-theological exegetical endeavor, the following exegetical conclusions are summarized: From the words used in Genesis 1, it is apparent that the image of God is something that is fundamentally physical. This does not mean that man's body alone is the image of God, but rather that man, created as a psycho-somatic unity, man *qua* man, constitutes the image of God.

It was noted that "image" and "likeness" are co-referentials, and that while it is possible to distinguish between image and likeness, it is not possible in the Genesis passage to divide out and separate the image of God from the likeness of God. Further, man is not made according to a previous image, but is himself created *as* God's image. In most English translations, the Hebrew preposition has been rendered with a gloss, or the LXX has been followed. The preposition is an instance of *beth essentiae* indicating that the image of God is what man was created *as*. Yet even if the common translation of being made *in* the image of God is retained, it affords no basis for a substantive understanding of the *imago Dei*. There is a vast difference between saying that man is made *in the image of God*, and saying that the image of God is something *in man*. The Genesis text indicates that neither the image of God nor the likeness of God is some *donum superadditum* to an already existent creature (chronologically or logically considered).⁴⁰ The image of God rather is simply *what man is as he was created.*

The Genesis 3 text indicates that the theological instincts of the early church fathers which caused them to look for something latent, potential, and unfilled in man were not without warrant. Because of this instinct some of the patristic writers read back into the text an unjustified division between the image and the likeness. The temptation by the serpent, however, that mankind (who had been created in the image and likeness of God) could "become like God" suggests not only that there was an unrealized potential in mankind, but that mankind was cognizant of this unrealized potential, a potential which they were led to believe could be obtained through their own rebellious efforts. Thus the image of God seems to be something which at the very time of man's creation was an already-not yet, a present possession that nevertheless had an eschatological and telic orientation.

The Genesis 1 and 5 texts demonstrate that the image and likeness of God are a hendiadys. The texts of Genesis 9:6 and James 3:9 further indicate that man since the fall is still both the image and the likeness of God. Genesis 9 prohibits murder specifically on the basis that man is made as the image of God. This is not merely a historical statement regarding Adam. It was noted that the word rendered "create" for God's activity which produced Adam (Gen. 1:27) indicates the initial and special creative act of God. By contrast, in Genesis 9:6 God is said to have "made" man, a different verb the meaning of which does not indicate an initial and special creative act, but is consistent with God continuing to make man

---

⁴⁰ In Roman Catholic theology, the *donum superadditum* plays a mediating role between the baser (animal) instincts of man, and his higher, angelic aspirations. The *donum superadditum* is thus not unlike Freud's *ego*, which mediates between the baser impulses of the *id* and the higher aspirations of the *superego*, except that in Roman Catholic understanding, mankind is created as essentially dis-integrated, and the harmonizing element is added as an "alien" factor, and is lost in the Fall.

through the ordinary means of human procreation. Thus there is an affirmation that mankind as a whole and each person as an individual since Adam, in whom all are fallen, are still the image of God by constitution.

James 3:9 shows something similar with respect to the likeness of God. In the Genesis 9 text, murder is prohibited on the basis that man is the image of God. In the James text, the incongruity is noted between blessing God and cursing men, who are made in the likeness of God. According to James, the men who are cursed by the readers are their contemporaries, indicating that fallen man is yet God's likeness.

The first Corinthian epistle (15:45–49) presents Christ as the second Man and the last Adam. Although *imago* language is not used here of Christ explicitly, it is implicit in drawing a paralleling contrast between Christ and Adam, the first Man who was made in the image of God. Just as Adam had begotten a son in his image (Gen. 5:3), Christ's redeemed people will bear his image (1 Cor. 15:49). The image, however, is not merely the image of the incarnate Christ, but in this passage it is the image of the incarnate, resurrected, and permanently transfigured Christ. Adam as the image of God, even before his sin, was a "dusty" (i.e., earthy) image, and Seth was that same "dusty" image even apart from the consideration of sin. What Christ's people are destined for is not merely restoration to Adam's "dusty" but pristine condition, but to something distinctly superior. The resurrection of Jesus guarantees not only removal of sin, but the attaining to something that Adam did not have even in his innocence: "As is the dusty one, so also are those who are dusty; but as is the heavenly one, so also are those who are heavenly. And just as we have borne the image of the dusty one, we shall also bear the image of the heavenly one" (1 Cor. 15:48–49).

Noting that images are always physical and visible representations of things that are invisible (either by nature, or because they are not at that moment present), exception was taken to the idea that Christ was the image of God before his incarnation. Being the "image of the invisible God" (Col. 1:15) speaks necessarily of the incarnation (cf. Heb. 10:5). In his state of humiliation, Christ, the man without sin, was the *imago Dei* in its latent potential. In his state of exaltation, however, Christ is the eschatological *imago Dei* in its glorious fullness.

For Christ's people to have "put off the old man" (Col. 3:9) is to have put off Adam, not Adam as the creation of God, but Adam in his rebellion which is at the root of our sinful practices. To "put on the new man" is to have put on Christ, and to be "renewed to true knowledge according to the image of the one who created him" (Col. 3:10). This is not merely a restoration to an adamic innocence, but the bearing of the *imago Dei* as it has been fully realized in the risen Christ. It is in light of this reality that the Colossians are not to lie, because they are being renewed in the one who is himself now the eschatological image of God, the God who cannot lie (Titus 1:2, Heb. 6:18).

The embryonic potential in Adam as he came forth from the hand of God has been actualized in Jesus Christ, the incarnate and resurrected Son of God. 2 Peter 1:4 indicates that "in him" people—people who are broken, wounded, and disabled because of the sin of the first Man—will escape the corruption (i.e., the decay-prone dustiness) of the world and be made partakers of the divine nature. This does not mean that creatures will become the Creator, for in one sense God has no likeness (Isa. 40:25; 46:5). But it does mean that the purpose of God will not be thwarted, and that the latent potential of man to be the most God-like of all creatures which was never realized in Adam, and having now been realized in Christ, the God-man, will be realized in all those who are vitally united to him.

4

A Reconsideration of the *Imago Dei*

In his book *The View from the Center of the Universe*, physicist Joel Primack takes issue with the thesis of Thomas Kuhn that science advances by paradigm shifts in which old ideas are radically displaced by new ones.[1] Primack argues that it is rather the case that old, true theories fit into new paradigms which produce new, more accurate theories, which new theories incorporate rather than reject older ones. Thus, Primack argues, Einstein's theory of general and special relativity is not a repudiation of Newtonian physics, but an expansion and clarification of it.[2] Primack represents this idea graphically:

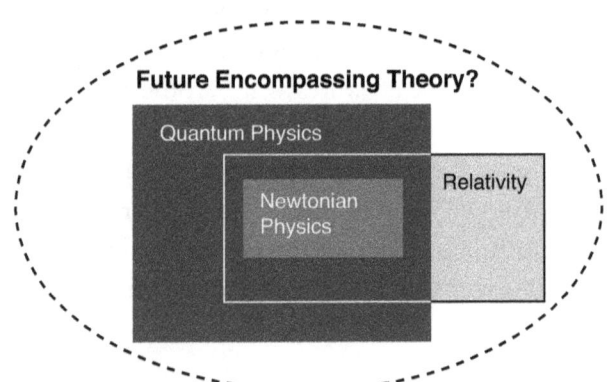

[1] Thomas S. Kuhn, *The Structure of Scientific Revolutions* (Chicago: University of Chicago Press, 1962).
[2] Joel R. Primack and Nancy Ellen Abrams, *The View from the Center of the Universe* (New York: Riverhead Books, 2006), 23–33.

A Reconsideration of the *Imago Dei*

The goal of this chapter is to reconsider the *imago Dei* doctrine based on the data arrived at by the exegesis of the previous chapter, consciously utilizing as a contextual referent those with severe cognitive disabilities. While interacting critically with the approaches of theologians past and present, their broad theological constructs will not be intentionally repudiated. The insights of theologians from the patristic, medieval, Reformation, and modern periods will not be jettisoned, but incorporated into a new paradigm.

Barth's relational understanding of the *imago Dei*, as well as the functional understanding that began in the patristic period and was expanded in the Reformation era, have thoughtful insights. The weakness with these approaches is not their perspectives on the *imago Dei* per se, but in absolutizing any one of them to the exclusion of all others, and an attempt to find in them the *essence* of the *imago Dei*.

Even the substantive approach of the patristic writers, which is exegetically the weakest of the approaches to the doctrine, is not without merit. However, even if one translates the Genesis 1 passage, "So God made man in his own image" (rather than "God made man as his own image"), man being made in the image of God, and the image of God being made in man, are two different things. Their exegesis aside, however, the theological instinct of the patristic theologians was insightful: although there is something broken about the image since the fall, even in man's state of sinless innocence there was some unrealized potential to man as the *imago Dei*.

The doctrine of humanity as it has been set forth by modern disability theologians has been rife with difficulty due to the theological framework and presuppositions of their considerations. To the degree that they have considered mankind *vis-à-vis* disability, they have tended to look at humanity in light of creation only and discount humanity in light of the effects of the fall. To be sure, as the exegetical study has shown, there is something consistent about mankind as the *imago Dei* throughout human history, both pre-lapsum and post-lapsum, but a satisfyingly redemptive understanding of the *imago* will be elusive unless the doctrine is considered through the great epochs of creation, fall, and redemption.

The *Imago Dei* in Creation

The biblical creation account indicates that man is more than an intelligent animal. Unquestionably mankind bears a similarity to the other terrestrial creatures. Observation reveals a homology between the structure and design of organs and the body as a whole which mankind shares with other creatures. The Genesis text underscores this similarity. As schooling fish and aquatic life are "living souls" (1:20; נֶפֶשׁ חַיָּה); as the great monsters of the deep are "living souls" (1:21); and as cattle, lizards, and all terrestrial creatures are "living souls" (1:24); so human beings are "living souls" (2:7). And just as God blessed the great sea monsters, and every living creature that moves, with which the waters swarmed, and every winged bird on the fifth creative day and said to them "Be fruitful and multiply" (1:22), he gave this same directive to mankind (1:28).

Yet for all of the homological and linguistic/taxonomic similarities, of mankind alone is there recorded a conciliar deliberation, and a determination by God to create man (אָדָם) as his own image (1:26, 27). It should be noted that man is not only fashioned on the last creative day (1:31), but his creation was also the last creative act. The creature thus decreed to be *imago Dei* is the apex of creation. God, it seems, reserved the greatest creaturely status for the last creature. Mankind is the eschatological figure of protology.

Many modern Hebraists believe that the conciliar deliberation ("Let us make man in our image . . . .") is one of God addressing the heavenly council of angels. The small bit of information the Scriptures provide would indeed indicate that the angelic beings already existed at the time of the terrestrial creation. In the Genesis account there is no explicit mention of the celestial creation.[3] The serpent

---

[3] "In the beginning God created the heavens and the earth" (Gen 1:1) is a

A Reconsideration of the *Imago Dei*

(Gen. 3:1ff) is later identified in Scripture with Satan (Rev. 20:1; 2 Cor. 11:3; cf. Rev. 20, viz. John 8:44; cf. Matt. 3:7; 12:34; 23:33) who stands among "the sons of God," i.e., angels (Job 1:6). Job 38:1–7 indicates that the angels were already in existence before the first creative day of Genesis ("Where were you when I laid the foundation of the earth . . . when the morning stars sang together and all the sons of God sang for joy?")

If the recorded creation order indicates a connection between mankind's being created last and the exalted status of being made *imago Dei*, and if angels were created before the terrestrial creation, this suggests something about the ultimate place and status of angels vis-à-vis mankind in the created order. The reasons for rejecting that God's conciliar speech is addressed to angels were pointed out in the last chapter. Mankind is never said to be made as the image of angels. He is made as the image of God (Gen. 1:27; "as his image," בצלמו; not "as their image," בצלמם).

The precise way in which mankind is the image of God has been a subject of discussion in the Christian community for two millennia. The suggestions for answering this question have not been entirely satisfying. Perhaps the question can be better approached by asking "*When* does mankind become the image of God?" The obvious answer is at his creation. Such an answer is not a tautology. If Genesis 2 is taken as supplemental information and perspective on Genesis 1 rather than as a contradictory creation account, the answer emerges that man is the image of God the moment God breathes the breath of life into his nostrils and he becomes a "living soul" (2:7). The fact that being created in the image of God (Gen. 1:27) is bound up with being a living soul is indicated by the fact that immediately after man's creation as the image of God, he is given directives that presuppose life: be fruitful and multiply, take

---

merism denoting the totality of creation. The verse is best taken as a summary statement, with the latter half (the creation of the earth) explicated in the rest of the chapter.

stewardship of the earth, benevolently rule the other "living souls" (Gen. 1:28).

As pointed out in the previous chapter, mankind is forbidden from making images of God, but this does not preclude God from making an image of himself. One of the salient differences between the images that man makes and the image that God makes is that man-made images (idols) are non-living. The *imago Dei* is by definition a living soul (*animae vivae*) because God is *Deus vivens*. Augustine believed that everything that *is* reflects the Creator, who is "the being" (ὁ ὤν, Ex. 3:14) and the source of all that is. Furthermore, creaturely being is hierarchical with inanimate creation occupying a lower station than animate creatures. As such, mankind as the divine image bears homological and functional similarities to the animals and intellectual and dynamic similarities to the angels, but the *imago Dei* is not found in the similarities with either. These similarities are neither the source of, nor do they exhaust what it means for man to be the image of God. The source of the *imago* is God alone. The commonality that humans exhibit with other creatures is incidental of the fact that all are creatures of the Creator. The similarities are not constitutive of the *imago*.

The word צֶלֶם will not allow the exclusion of man's body from the *imago Dei*; in fact, as demonstrated in the last chapter, the word veritably requires the body of man. But the pre-animate body of man is not itself the image of God. The phrase is properly applied only to the human being once he or she is a psycho-somatic unity.

The *imago Dei* is what man *qua* man is constituted. There are no constituting criteria for the *imago* other than being made a living human being. Much of the past and present *imago* theology proposes or presupposes that the *imago Dei* is to be identified with some substantive component, some function, or some ability. This approach has continued to exert influence in the church because there is a great deal of truth to such observations and reflections.

The miscalculation has been in understanding and expressing these aspects as *constituting* the *imago Dei* rather than seeing these aspects as *consequential* of man's being made as the image of God. There is undoubtedly some correspondence between the *imago* and the intellect, the *imago* and the task and function given to mankind, the *imago* and human interpersonal relationships. But it is a mistake to think of any of these things as constitutive of the *imago Dei*. To do so is to establish criteria by which to determine which human beings may be deemed to have this privileged relationship to God. It is, in fact, close to the Gnostic error which believed that only some human beings had "the spark of the divine," evidenced by their ability to grasp a certain (in their case mystical) *gnosis*. Other human beings who did not have "the spark of the divine" were incapable of attaining the *gnosis* and thus were considered to be mere animals.[4]

While there can be no question that rationality is a part of the original human constitution, even in the similarity with the rest of the terrestrial creation there is differentiation that indicates intellect. Thus while the text says of the animals, "God blessed them and said, 'Be fruitful and multiply, and fill the waters of the seas, and let the birds increase on the earth" (Gen. 1:22), of mankind the text says, "God blessed them and God said *to them*, 'Be fruitful and multiply, and fill the earth ...'" (Gen. 1:28). With respect to animal fecundity, God makes a pronouncement of decretive fiat. But with respect to human beings, he speaks *to them*, an act that presupposes receptive language and volitional obedience and cooperation.

Man's intellect is seen not merely in his receptive capacity for language, but also in his expressive capacity for language. His ruling

---

[4] Bart D. Ehrman, *Lost Christianities: Christian Scriptures and the Battles Over Authentication Part 1 Course Guidebook* (Chantilly, VA: The Teaching Company, 2002), 21: "The knowledge [*gnosis*] is secret; it is not for everyone because not everyone has the spark [of the divine]. Some people were pure animals. Others had some possibility of an afterlife through faith and good works (the normal Christians). Only some had the possibility of a fantastic afterlife, in the return to the realm of God whence they came (the Gnostics)." Though Ehrman cites no source, he is likely referring to "The Tripartite Tractate." See James M. Robinson, General ed., *The Nag Hammadi Library* (San Francisco: Harper Collins, 1988), 94–100.

over the fish of the sea, and the birds of the air, and over every living creature that moves along the ground, is evidenced in man's taxonomic activity: he is given the assignment of naming the animals (Gen. 2:19–20), an activity which not only expresses mastery over the things named but indicates intelligence. It is evident that the naming is not arbitrary and irrational, for it is in the cataloging that Adam recognizes the lack of any creature suitable for his partnership (Gen. 2:20b).

There is the closest connection between those abilities that are associated with the intellect and the *imago Dei*, but *contra* Basil,[5] the intellect is not the human being, and thus is not the *imago Dei*. If it were, we would have to conclude with Thomas Aquinas that angels are more nearly the image of God than man is, a proposition that can be arrived at only by taking a train of logic off the track of sound exegesis of the Scriptures. Intellect and the *imago Dei* are closely bound to one another, but they are not indistinguishable, nor inseparable. The textual sequence is indicative of the relationship: God self-deliberates to make man as his image (Gen. 1:26), God creates man as his image (Gen. 1:27) with the result that man is imbued with intellectual ability that makes him able to relate to God obediently, cooperatively, linguistically, and personally. Human beings are not the image of God because they possess intelligence as a criterion for that status; rather, human beings possess intelligence because they are constituted the *imago Dei* by virtue of their creation. The former rests entirely on the latter.

Likewise the functional approach to the *imago Dei* is insightful and helpful but only if it is understood that man's functional ability rests on his being the image of God. His functional ability is not the criterion that constitutes him as the image of God. While the task

---

[5] "But you will ask, 'Why does it [Gen 1:26] not speak of the rational part?' It says that the human being is according to the image of God, but the rational part is the human being." St. Basil the Great, *On the Human Condition*, trans. Nonna Verna Harrison (Crestwood, NY: St. Vladimir's Seminary Press, 2005), 35–36.

of ruling over the creatures is touched upon by some of the patristic writers, it becomes more prominent during the Reformation period. The Westminster divines coordinate the image of God with the familiar Reformation triad of knowledge, righteousness, and holiness, and add to it "with dominion over the creatures."[6] There is an undeniable textual connection between God's determination to create man as the image of God and the task of dominion: "Then God said, 'Let us make man as our image, as our likeness, *and let them rule over* [the animals].'"

Douglas Hall has championed the functional understanding of the *imago Dei* with a caution that mankind's dominion requires a responsible stewardship that Christians have not always understood or exercised. Although Hall gives credence to other approaches to the *imago Dei*, he concludes, "... it would appear to be irresponsible exegetically to dissociate the *imago Dei* entirely from the concept of human dominion."[7]

It seems evident from the text, however, that this capacity and ability for dominion is a consequent of man's being made as the image of God. Capacity and ability do not constitute man as the image of God: "Then God said, 'Let us make man as our image, as our likeness, *and let them rule* (וְיִרְדּוּ) over [the animals].'" The *waw* here is conjunctive-sequential.[8] Man is not constituted the image of God as a result of ability or function. His ability and function are

---

[6] WSC, 10.

[7] Douglas J. Hall, *Imaging God: Dominion as Stewardship* (Grand Rapids, MI: Eerdmans, 1986), 71.

[8] Bruce K. Waltke & M. O'Connor (*An Introduction to Biblical Hebrew Syntax*, [Winona Lake, IN: Eisenbrauns, 1990]) use Gen 1:26 as an example of a simple conjunctive *waw*, one of the purposes of which is to connect an imperative [*sic*. The verb is actually jussive] and a cohortative, § 39.2.5. This use of *waw* "serves to join two clauses which describe interrelated or overlapping situations not otherwise logically related." But is it really so that there is no logical relationship intended between God's determination to make man as his image and the task given to man to exercise dominion? The use of *waw* here seems to better fit the description of conjunctive-sequential *waw*, § 39.2.2.

the consequent, not the antecedent to being created as the image of God.

Barth believed that past theologians had speculated too much about what constituted the image of God and thought rather that what constitutes the *imago* lay on the surface of the text: "So God created man as his own image, as the image of God he created him; *male and female he created them.*" The image of God was to be found in the "I-Thou" relationship reflected in the differentiation of the human sexes which he saw as a reflection of the unity and diversity of God himself. The Christian doctrine of the Trinity indicates that though God is the creator of all things, and is thus antecedent to all things, yet there was never a time when God was alone. God is *ab intra* God-in-relationship. Thus Barth believed that the *imago Dei* was to be found, not in an analogy of being, but rather in an analogy of relationship.

Barth's perspective has been hugely influential, and textually there does seem to be a connection between the sameness and differentiation of humanity *vis-à-vis* the image of God. Recall Anthony Hoekema's consideration of how peculiar it is that man is a created person. Archetypical personality is uncreated; personality has its origin in God. God is personal or, better, tri-personal. An inanimate creation, and even created animals, are not mysterious. But a *created person* is a mystery, since creation indicates dependence, and personality independence.[9] Personality, it would seem (when it is considered that the Triune God is the exemplar of it), requires relationship. For Barth, this constitutes the *imago Dei*: "In all His future utterances and actions God will acknowledge that He has created man male and female, and in this way in His own image and likeness."[10] Barth is careful to say that the *imago Dei* does not consist in any

---

[9] Anthony A. Hoekema, *Created in God's Image* (Grand Rapids, MI: Eerdmans, 1986) 5–10.

[10] Karl Barth, *Church Dogmatics*, trans. O. Bussey and H. Knight, (Peabody, MA: Hendrickson, 2010), 3.1: 187.

action or state, but is simply man himself as he is created by God.[11] But he understands the image of God particularly in the relational differentiation of mankind into male and female.

There is undoubtedly a connection between the *imago Dei* and personal relationship. It is evident from the covenantal structure of the Scriptures[12] that God is interested in community and not merely in individuals. The insight of Barth has been an important consideration in the development of the *imago* doctrine. But does the essence of the *imago Dei* simply lay on the surface of the text as Barth maintains? Berkouwer did not believe so. He wrote, "Even though Barth is convinced that the text gives us a 'well-nigh definitive statement,' it is not unreasonable to ask whether this is actually the case."[13]

One difficulty with Barth's approach is that it may give the impression that the *imago Dei* is what humanity collectively, and not the individual, is constituted. Although Russell Hinter struggles to maintain that ". . . it is the individual man, male and female, who is made unto the image and likeness of God,"[14] he ties together themes from Augustine and Barth in a polemic against modern individualism that leads him to ask and affirmatively answer whether "social entities [notably marriage] [can] be said to exist in the image of God."[15] Responding to Hinter's essay, Gilbert Meilaender notes that Hinter complicates rather than clarifies matters.[16]

---

[11] Ibid., 184, "It is not a quality of man. Hence there is no point asking in which of man's peculiar attributes and attitudes it consists. It does not consist in anything that man is or does. It consists and man himself consists as the creature of God. He would not be a man if he were not the image of God. He is the image of God in the fact that he is a man."

[12] See Meredith G. Kline, *The Structure of Biblical Authority*, 2nd ed. (South Hamilton, MA: Meredith G. Kline, 1989).

[13] G. C. Berkouwer, *Man, the Image of God*, trans. Dirk W. Jellema (Grand Rapids, MI: Eerdmans, 1962), 72–73.

[14] F. Russell Hinter, "*Imago Dei* in Catholic Theology," in *Imago Dei: Human Dignity in Ecumenical Perspective*, ed. Thomas Albert Howard (Washington, DC: The Catholic University Press, 2013), 42.

[15] Hinter, 43.

[16] Gilbert C. Meilaender, afterword to *Imago Dei: Human Dignity in*

The biblical texts in fact indicate that *imago Dei* applies to the individual, not just to humanity. It is because of this fact that "gender-inclusive language" can be difficult when dealing with the *imago* doctrine.[17] The 2011 edition of the New International Version translates Genesis 1:27, "So God created *mankind* in his own image, in the image of God he created *them*; male and female he created them." While it is true that אָדָם can refer collectively to "mankind, people," it is inaccurate to translate the text this way here. God is said to have created, not אָדָם, "mankind," but הָאָדָם, "*the* man" in his own image.[18] This is underscored in 1 Corinthians 11:7 in which "man" (ἀνήρ) is said to be "the image and glory of God." This is in no way an exclusion of women (or woman) from participation in the *imago Dei*, nor could such a notion be entertained without ignoring the context of the Genesis account: "So God created the man in his own image, in the image of God he created him, *male and female he created*

Ecumenical Perspective, ed. Thomas Albert Howard (Washington, DC: The Catholic University Press, 2013), 117.

[17] For an excellent discussion of the difficulty by one who is a proponent of gender-inclusive language, see Charles Sherlock, *The Doctrine of Humanity* (Downers Grove, IL: InterVarsity Press, 1996), 239–46.

[18] *Contra* C. Ben Mitchell, "The Audacity of the *imago Dei*" in *Imago Dei: Human Dignity in Ecumenical Perspective*, ed. Thomas Albert Howard (Washington, DC: The Catholic University Press, 2013), 84. "When *Adâm* is used with the definite article, typically the text is referring to "humankind" (as in Gen. 1:27). When the noun is used without the definite article, Adam, the man, is usually in view." In the conciliar deliberation of Gen 1:26 the noun is anarthrous (נַעֲשֶׂה אָדָם), indicating that "Adam, the man, is in view" (Mitchell). In Gen 1:27 where the creation event is reported the article is employed (אֶת־הָאָדָם) "to indicate definiteness when the object or person has already been mentioned (Ronald J. Williams, *Hebrew Syntax: An Outline* [Toronto: University of Toronto Press, 1986], §83); it "is employed when the object or person is definite in the thought of the narrator" (Williams, §84); see also HALOT B.1, 3. While the article can be used in other contexts to express generic class (Williams §92, HALOT B.6) the grammatical context of Gen 1:26–27 does not allow that usage. For a full treatment of the Hebrew definite article see Peter Bekins, "Non-prototypical Uses of the Definite Article in Biblical Hebrew," *Journal of Semitic Studies* 58, 2 (Autumn 2013): 225–40.

them." But what these passages indicate is that man—each individual human being of either gender—is constituted the *imago Dei.*

Barth's relational approach to the *imago* is backwards in the same way the substantive and functional approaches are. Personal and gender differentiation and relationality are not antecedent to and constitutive of the *imago Dei.* Rather, the fact that each individual person is constituted as *imago Dei* is the basis for personal differentiation and relationship. Sherlock captured this idea: ". . . consider someone on a desert island. He or she is still a human being, made in the image of God. But being isolated from others . . . , it makes sense to say that this person is in danger of becoming 'dehumanized.' The structures which long for fulfillment in relations with . . . others . . . remain; but their weakness is perhaps rather worse than their absence."[19]

Human beings as the pinnacle of creation and as *imago Dei* were, along with the rest of creation, the objects of the divine benediction: "And God saw all that He had made, and behold, it was very good" (Gen. 1:31). At the creation of mankind, although human intellect did not constitute the *imago Dei*, there was nothing to impede or damage the expression of the *imago* in man's intellect, for at the creation there were no physical or noetic effects of sin to blight that intellect. Had man not disobeyed God, had he continued in that state of benediction, we may soundly conclude that man would never have heard the malediction of "very bad;" there would be no defects of body or mind, such as palatoschisis or Angelman syndrome. Although human functionality does not constitute the *imago Dei*, there would be no curse upon creation (upon not only the ground, but upon man's body as well) that would frustrate the outworking of the *imago* in such a way as to render his work futile, and no defect of soul that would produce selfishness, ruthless ambition, or indolence. Although human relationships do not constitute the *imago Dei*, there would be no disruption in the outworking of

---

[19] Sherlock, 44.

the *imago* in those relationships that are present now due to sin; no spousal abuse, no adultery, and no child molestation.

Every day in the reality in which we presently live, people experience the "very bad" of the fall: parents receive dreaded news of spina bifida and Down syndrome; workers receive dreaded news of job terminations and significant failures; men and women receive dreaded news of adultery. They receive such news, not with joy, and not with indifference, but they receive all of these things as "very bad" news, a fact which indicates that something has changed, that something is wrong. What that "something" is, and how it has affected individuals *vis-à-vis* the *imago Dei* will be the subject of the next section of this chapter. But before turning to the *imago Dei* in the fall, we will consider that while God's good creation was complete by the sixth creative day and thus received God's benediction, the Scriptures hint that the good creation of God was not yet consummated.

Many of the patristic writers distinguished between the image and the likeness of God in that the former is what man has by virtue of his creation, and the latter is what he was to become as he grew in similarity to God. As already mentioned, the words employed in the Hebrew Bible will not bear the weight of this distinction, but the patristic writers had good theological instinct. In studying the temptation by the serpent in Genesis 3:1–5, it becomes apparent that there was a perception on the part of the primordial pair that their likeness to God was lacking. The temptation amounted to a shortcut to attain a status that they were called to obtain through obedience.

Colossians 1:15 indicates that in his incarnation Christ is the visible image of the invisible God. He is also the firstborn of all creation, which is a reference to his resurrection (cf. Col. 1:18). Christ did not "come back from the dead," but in his resurrection he is himself the start of the eschatological creation for which Adam had the potential, but never attained. Although *imago* language is not used in 1 Corinthians 15, it is evident there that Christ by his death and resurrection gained for himself and those he represents more than Adam lost by his disobedience.

This unrealized potential has often been overlooked in modern western theology, because other theological considerations have pushed it to the side. In the 1940s, for example, a controversy erupted between Gordon Clark and Cornelius Van Til over epistemology. Clark's approach to man's knowledge seemed to Van Til to be a blurring of the Creator-creature distinction. When Van Til wrote *The Defense of the Faith* more than a decade later, the controversy with Clark led him to address the image of God doctrine in such a way as to intimate (though not to explicitly state) that there was no lack in man at the time of his creation with respect to knowledge: "Man is created *in God's image*. He is therefore like God in everything in which a creature can be like God. . . . Man was not created with comprehensive knowledge. Man was finite and his finitude was originally no burden to him. Neither could man ever expect to attain to comprehensive knowledge in the future."[20] It would be hard to contradict Van Til's point here that man's knowledge is not and will never be identical to God's knowledge. But his manner of stating it may easily lead to the conclusion that if man had not disobeyed God he would have remained essentially as he was.

Among theologians on the cusp of or in the modern era, however, there was often an instinct that what Adam had by virtue of his creation had not been brought to its full completion. Hodge writes, "With regard to immortality, it is certain that if man had not sinned he would not have died. But whether that immortality which would then have been the destiny of his body, would have been the result of its original organization, or whether after its period of probation it would have undergone a change to adapt it to its everlasting condition, is a matter of subsequent consideration."[21] Later Hodge answers this question by indicating his understanding that Adam would have gained the elevated status which is now realized

---

[20] Cornelius Van Til, *The Defense of the Faith* (Phillipsburg, NJ: Presbyterian & Reformed, 1967), 13–14.

[21] Charles Hodge, *Systematic Theology* (Grand Rapids, MI: Eerdmans, reprinted 1982), 2:92.

in Christ: "... if the Apostle, when he says we have borne the image of the earthly are, like the body of Adam as originally constituted, then his [i.e., Adam's] body, no less than ours required to be changed to fit it for immortality."[22]

Louis Berkhof (a contemporary of Van Til) also intimates that Adam in his creation had not yet reached the potential he would have if he had sustained the probation. He writes "If Adam stood the test, this life would be retained not only, but would cease to be amissible, and would therefore be lifted to a higher plane."[23]

Sometimes modern theologians who are not addressing the question of the destiny of mankind had Adam not sinned shed light on the issue while considering other loci. In his book *The Meaning of Sex*, Dennis Hollinger takes up the question "Where is history going?" and answers it by saying, "... the Christian worldview embodies a consummation in which all things are made new by God."[24] Expositing the teaching of Jesus in Luke 20:34–36, Hollinger writes, "If sex is a good gift of God from creation, why is marital sex not a part of the final eschaton? ... Jesus is not teaching that we will be asexual in heaven, but rather without marriage. His reference to the angels does not mean that we will be angelic beings without bodies, but rather that we, like the angels, will no longer die. And if we no longer die in our eternal state, *then there is no longer a need for procreation, one of the major purposes of God's good gift* [italics added]"[25]

It is evident that human sexuality and procreation were a part of God's design in man's innocence from the mandate to "be fruitful and multiply" immediately after the creation of man (male and female) as the image of God and before the fall. The time of man's innocence was one in which death was not yet a part of human

---

[22] Ibid., 116.

[23] Louis Berkhof, *Systematic Theology, New Combined Edition* (Grand Rapids, MI: Eerdmans, 1996), 213–14.

[24] Dennis P. Hollinger, *The Meaning of Sex* (Grand Rapids, MI: Baker Academic, 2009), 89.

[25] Ibid., 90.

experience (Gen. 2:17; Rom. 5:12). It thus stands to reason that if human death was not a part of God's original design, then it was not God's plan for human sexuality to continue forever. It is reasonable to conclude that while God's creation was complete in the making of mankind, it was not yet brought to its consummation. Though speaking of redemption in Christ, Hollinger's conclusion is just as applicable to an earth of undying humans that had reached its population capacity: "The ultimate intimacy and communion with God will fulfill all that we have longed for sexually in this world. The final consummation does not render sex suspect; it simply reminds us what sex is: a good, but finite, gift of God."[26]

Although I am not sympathetic to J. Richard Middleton's open theistic perspective,[27] some of his insights into the *imago* doctrine are astute. Middleton argues that "There are two important literary clues for understanding Genesis 1 not as an alternative creation story to Genesis 2 . . . , but as a prelude to the rest of the Genesis narrative . . . ."[28] The first clue is that there is no "morning and evening" of the seventh creative day, indicating that the day has not reached a conclusion. The second is that God gives mankind the role of vice regency. Taken together, Middleton believes that this indicates that whereas God's work has ceased, man's activity has just begun. The *imago Dei* is thus not static, but dynamic, and may be increased or diminished in expression in proportion to man's obedience or disobedience. Middleton's arguments lead to the conclusion that the *imago* prompts movement. By the actions of the first created pair, that image must be more or less evidenced. It cannot remain in stasis.

---

[26] Ibid., 92.

[27] J. Richard Middleton, *The Liberating Image: The* Imago Dei *in Genesis 1* (Grand Rapids, MI: Brazos, 2005), 294. He speaks of God "taking a risk" with regard to the task he entrusts to human beings, and withdrawing "to see what develops." In footnote 70 on that page, Middleton indicates that he formulated his ideas independently of Clark Pinnock, but after learning of Pinnock's view he has become sympathetic to it.

[28] Ibid., 290–91.

The image of God is expressed in numerous abilities and attributes that mankind shares in common with angels and animals. It is expressed in qualities and aspects such as man's intellect, his work, and his relationships, including the most intimate of relationships. None of these, however, *constitute* the image of God; all of them are rather *consequent* of the image of God.

Although the Scriptures never say that "life was promised to Adam, and in him to his posterity, upon condition of perfect and personal obedience,"[29] the church has reasonably concluded that Adam had such a promise from passages such as Genesis 2:17; 2:9; and 3:23–24. In the same way, we may conclude from passages such as Genesis 3:18; 3:15; 1 Corinthians 15 and others, that although the work of creation was completed it was not consummated. Had Adam sustained the probation, although it would be impossible to say precisely what the contours would look like, mankind would have begun the journey toward consummation.

As the federal head of humanity, Adam's disobedience inflicted twin evils on the human race. Modern Protestant Christianity has tended to focus only on one of those evils: mankind's fall from his original state before God. The ancient church (and today the Eastern Church) acknowledges both of the evils: not only did Adam lose for himself and his posterity what he had in his state of original righteousness, but he failed to embrace and enter into that condition by which mankind would have gained the consummation of all that is "very good."

The *Imago Dei* in the Fall

"The problem of evil" is frequently traced to the third century B.C. materialist philosopher Epicurus. The Epicurean Paradox is often presented in words like these: "Is God willing to prevent evil, but unable to do so? Then he is not omnipotent. Is he able, but not

---

[29] WCF, 7.2.

willing? Then he is malevolent. Is he both willing and able? Then why is there evil? Is he neither willing nor able? Then why call him 'God?'"

Questions of theodicy aside, the Epicurean Paradox demonstrates that the recognition that there is evil in the world is universal. The belief that evil constitutes a problem is universal to all but the most consistent materialists. Yet even they tend to lose their "objective" acceptance of evil if evil befalls them or their loved ones.

Philosophers distinguish between two kinds of evil in the world. Moral evil is that evil which is deliberately and malevolently caused or carried out by moral agents, notably other human beings. Surd (or natural) evil is an evil that comes about by "the nature of things" through such phenomena as natural disasters. The universal recognition of evil as well as the *problem* of evil indicates a recognition that something is not as it was designed or intended to be. A cup that leaks is recognized to have a problem because it does not fulfill its designed purpose.

Since its inception Christianity has attributed the source of the evil experienced by mankind to the fall, which brought a subsequent curse not only upon man as a "living soul" (Gen. 3:19b) but upon his labor (Gen. 3:18–19a) and his environment itself (Gen. 3:17). While Romans 5:12–14 traces every instance of moral evil back to a solidarity with Adam through whom sin entered the world, it is significant to note that the categories of the curse listed above are most naturally subsumed under the rubric of surd evil. While death can certainly come about through the specific sinful acts of people (e.g., abuse, neglect, and violence, toward self or others), even when care is taken to preserve human life, accident, disease, or old age will eventually return all people to the dust. While laziness can be the cause of a poor crop (cf. Prov. 6:6–11), so can locusts, hail, and too much or too little rain. And while people can by greed or malice poison and damage the environment, so can volcanic eruptions, earthquakes, and tsunamis. It is notable that Christian theology has typically understood, not just moral evil, but *all* evil that touches humanity as rooted in the fall of mankind.

A Reconsideration of the *Imago Dei*

In Chapter Three it was argued that the image of God has not been lost in man as a result of the fall. Theologians who affirm the continuity of the *imago* after the fall, however, often struggle to make sense of how this is so and frequently default to "loss" language. Such a struggle is seen in Jochem Douma. Affirming that man in his fallen and pre-redeemed condition is still the image of God, he nonetheless writes, "Can we say that unbelievers are still the image of God? We must answer that question in the negative, even though our 'no' is not without qualification. . . . It is not always so easy to strike the proper balance in our perspective about man as the image of God."[30] Douma's struggle stems specifically from the reality of moral evil, the conscious rebellious acts against God. Does moral evil demonstrate a loss of the *imago Dei*? I would argue that it no more demonstrates a loss of the *imago* than does surd evil.

The reflection of God has been badly defaced in the fall. To the degree that the image of God is reflected in relationships, that reflection is distorted. Man's most intimate relationships with God (Gen. 3:8–11) and others (Gen. 3:7, 12) are damaged. His relationship to the rest of creation is also damaged (Gen. 3:17–19). To the degree that the image of God is reflected in functionality, that reflection is now distorted by tyranny and exploitation. Mankind's uniqueness as a living image is now vitiated in that death becomes a part of his reality (Gen. 3:19; Rom. 5:12). To the degree that the image of God is reflected in the intellect, that too is damaged by both surd and moral evil, in a universal, though not an even, distribution. Thus a person with Down syndrome may be unable to carry out some or all of the tasks assigned to Adam because of the surd effects of the fall upon his ability to think. By contrast, a Stephen Hawking may be able to perceive with his mind realities that are beyond the reach of the mean of humanity, but may employ his intellect to suppress the

---

[30] J. Douma, *The Ten Commandments: Manual for the Christian Life*, trans. Nelson D. Kloosterman (Phillipsburg, NJ: Presbyterian and Reformed, 1996), 51, 53.

truth in unrighteousness, to exchange the truth for a lie and worship creation rather than the Creator (Rom. 1:18–25).[31]

It bears repeating that man is not the image of God because he possesses certain attributes or abilities. The attributes and abilities are not the criteria or cause of the *imago* but are the consequences of the *imago*. Because God created man as his image, damage or defacement of that image does not translate him into a non-image. A defaced image of Baal with feet and cephalic protuberance broken off does not cease to be an image of Baal; it is an image of Baal with the feet and cephalic protuberance broken off. Similarly, those qualities which we may recognize in humanity as being a reflection of the divine are not constitutive of the image, but are consequent of it. Cultic statues have the tell-tale cephalic protuberance because they are images of Baal; they are not images of Baal because they have a cephalic protuberance.

All of those moral qualities which we may recognize as "very good" certainly are reflective of the image of God. But even when people do "very bad" things they still reflect the image of God, though in a perverted and distorted way. C. S. Lewis noted, "You can be good for the mere sake of goodness: you cannot be bad for the mere sake of badness. . . . badness cannot succeed even in being bad in the same way that goodness is good. Goodness is, so to speak, itself: badness is only spoiled goodness. . . . All the things which enable a bad man to be effectively bad are in themselves good things—resolution, cleverness, good looks, existence itself."[32]

Suicide bombers waging jihad are only able to carry out their missions because of an evil courage. Courage itself, however, is a good attribute, and so even in perpetrating evil they cannot but help express something of God's image, no matter how perverted in form it may be. It is precisely because moral evil is both a declension from

---

[31] See Stephen Hawking and Leonard Mladinow, *The Grand Design* (New York: Random House, 2010). The book is deceptively titled, its thesis being that there is no design because there is no God.

[32] C. S. Lewis, *Mere Christianity* (New York: Harper Collins: reprinted 2000), 44–45.

A Reconsideration of the *Imago Dei*

and a parasite on the good that the Scriptures affirm that even fallen man continues to be the image of God.

Moral evil is not the only evil that resulted from the fall. Surd or natural evil also exists. Because a sense of justice is artifactual of the *imago Dei* and because people's fallen hearts are more sensitive to the sins of others than to their own, there is a desire (at the least) to see instances of surd evil as a poetic justice. There is a certain satisfaction to stories of the villain who, killing others to steal their gold, is dragged to the bottom of the sea by it. Thus there can be a tendency to see all surd evil as a direct result of a moral evil. This was the attitude of Jesus' disciples in John 9:1–2: "As he went along, he saw a man blind from birth. His disciples asked him, 'Rabbi, who sinned, this man or his parents, that he was born blind?'" It is because of attitudes such as this that people tended to hide away (or worse) their intellectually disabled children for fear that others would believe that they must have done something extraordinarily bad to "deserve that." Jesus, however, was quick to point out that the man's disability was not due to the sin of the man or his parents, but would serve to glorify God (John 9:3).

Today we congratulate ourselves that we are more enlightened. Western society in general recognizes that intellectual disability is seldom anyone's "fault." The problem, however, is that in maintaining this, modern society does not recognize intellectual disability (or any disability) as a fault at all. Disabilities are not seen as an evil, not even as a surd evil. People who have disabilities are simply "different." This attempt, evident both inside[33] and outside[34] of the Christian

---

[33] See Rakesh Vajpai, "Sequenom Playing God… Well, Not Yet," The Blessing Called Down Syndrome, entry posted October 1, 2009, http://downstrisomy.blogspot.com/ (accessed September 7, 2013); and Amy Julia Becker, "Three Reasons Why We May Not Want to Cure Down Syndrome," Patheos, entry posted July 24, 2013, http://www.patheos.com/blogs/thinplaces/2013/07/three-reasons-why-we-might-not-want-to-cure-down-syndrome/ (accessed September 7, 2013).

[34] See Friedel Taube, "'Not Stupid Just Different': Raising Awareness of Down Syndrome," Deutsche Welle, http://www.dw.de/not-stupid

community, which seeks to "celebrate people with disabilities" often degenerates into a celebration of the disabilities themselves. Such perspectives draw upon the Disabilities Rights Movement, which in turn is rooted (intentionally or otherwise) in a hierarchy of human value discussed in Chapter One. Although in even the Christian iteration of this movement the *imago Dei* is not considered, a certain substantivism is: people with intellectual disabilities are seen as valuable because of the "contribution they can make to society,"[35] a notion that calls into question the viability of the lives of human beings such as Oliver de Vinck and Kelly who cannot make such contributions.

Much as we may want to pretend otherwise, the fact that there is on-going research and treatment regimens and interventions prescribed for those diagnosed with cognitive disabilities indicates the recognition, not that something is merely different, but that something is *wrong*. We do not intervene and treat people for mere differences such as the color of one's hair, eyes, or skin. To use the stark language of Stephanie Hubach, the notion that there is nothing "wrong" with the condition of intellectually disabled people, but that they are simply different, and a "normal part of a normal world" is "absurd."[36]

Although their goal is ultimately born of a concern for the valuation of people with disabilities, attempts by theologians such as Nancy Eisland and Hans Reinders to "normalize" disability are not helpful. Their approach denies parents, the church, and society at large the expression of an intuited fact in the case of those challenged with disabilities: something is wrong.

-just-different-raising-awareness-of-down-syndrome/a-16825825 (accessed September 7, 2013).

[35] See e.g., Ellen Seidman, "What People with Down Syndrome Bring to the World: Everything," Parents, http://www.parents.com/blogs/to-the-max/2012/10/01/down-syndrome/what-people-with-down-syndrome-bring-to-the-world-everything/ (accessed September 7, 2013).

[36] Stephanie O. Hubach, *Same Lake Different Boat: Coming Alongside People Touched by Disability* (Philipsburg, NJ: P&R Publishing, 2006), 27.

A Reconsideration of the *Imago Dei*

During his earthly ministry Jesus healed the sick and disabled. That parents brought their children to Jesus for healing required their recognition that something was wrong, not merely that their children were different. The fifth chapter of John's Gospel records an interaction between Jesus and a man who suffered from a debilitating disease for thirty-eight years, a disease that robbed him of his ability to walk. Jesus' question to the man was penetrating: "Do you want to become well (ὑγιής; sound, whole, healthy)?" (John 5:6). Given the thesis and conclusions of Nancy Eisland's book *The Disabled God*, the correct response would have been for the man to tell Jesus that there was no unwellness about his condition; he was simply different from other people.

Calvin believed that shifting the blame for evil to God's original creative plan was a culpable act of calling evil good. Although he was dealing primarily with moral evil, his observations are applicable to the surd evil that comes upon people living in a fallen world: ". . . the whole man is overwhelmed—as by a deluge—from head to foot, so that no part is immune from sin. . . . Now away with those persons who dare write God's name upon their faults . . . . They perversely search out God's handiwork in their own pollution, when they ought rather to have sought it in the unimpaired and uncorrupted nature of Adam."[37]

Intellectual (nor any) disability does not negate the image of God. Intellectual ability is the outcome of being made as the image of God. Cognitive disability may result from traumatic brain injury, congenital chromosomal defect, or for other reasons. A broken image, however, is still an image. The brokenness of a human being does not change the fact that that person by virtue of being human is made as the image of God; nor are we compelled to assert that evil is actually good to maintain that this is true.

The Scriptures indicate not that some people are broken images, but that all people are broken images, though we are broken

---

[37] John Calvin, *Institutes of the Christian Religion*, trans. Ford Lewis Battles (Philadelphia: Westminster Press, 1960), 2.1:9–10.

in different ways. All are morally broken (cf. Gen. 8:21; Rom. 3:23; 5:12; Eph. 2:1–3), some more visibly than others. All too suffer from surd evil, though in a diversity of ways. The effects of the fall on mankind, whether moral or surd, may distort in various ways the reflection of God in man, but it does not and cannot diminish the fact that man is *imago Dei*. Human beings are constituted *imago Dei* by virtue of God's creation of them; they are not constituted *imago Dei* by virtue of some ability, attribute or criterion in them.

It is perhaps precisely because man is *imago Dei* that, having sinned, he is capable of being saved. The angels, for whatever similarity of appearance (e.g., John 20:12 cf. Luke 24:4) or ability they bear in common with mankind, are not constituted *ad imago Dei* (further indication that the *imago* is not found in appearance or ability). Angels seem to be members of classes rather than races,[38] and there seems to be for them no federal solidarity as there is for humanity (Rom. 5, 1 Cor. 15). Speaking in the context of the incarnation, the writer to the Hebrews avers that God gives help to the children of Abraham, but not to angels (Heb. 2:16). Angels who sin seem to be lost irretrievably; they are bound over and consigned to judgment (2 Peter 2:4). Unlike elect human beings who are all chosen for redemption from their fallen condition (cf. 1 Peter 1:1–2), it appears that "elect angels" (1 Tim. 5:21) were chosen not to rebel, rather than to be redeemed.

The most significant bearing upon man as the image of God is seen in God's undertaking to redeem man from his fallen condition. The Westminster Shorter Catechism states, "The only Redeemer of God's elect is the Lord Jesus Christ, who, being the eternal Son of God, became man, and so was, and continueth to be, God and man in two distinct natures, and one person, forever."[39] That God himself became a man, not for a season, but for *forever* is indicative of the fact that not only has God's image not been lost to man, but that it is God's aim to remedy its defaced condition.

---

[38] See e.g., Berkhof, 146.
[39] WSC, 21.

The *Imago Dei* in Redemption

The literary fact that the phrase "the image of God" disappears from pages of Scripture early in the Old Testament and is not invoked again until the New Testament reflects a redemptive-historical reality. As discussed in Chapter Three, the Son of God in his incarnation became the image of God, the physical and visible representation of the invisible God (cf. Col. 1:15). Christ is the eschatological Adam who is the *imago Dei* (2 Cor. 4:4) in whom the *imago Dei* will be not only restored but perfected.

It is significant to note that in the incarnation the Son of God entered into *this* fallen creation. While the Scriptures affirm that the man Jesus Christ was innocent of any moral evil (cf. John 8:46; 2 Cor. 5:21; Heb. 4:15; 7:26), unlike the innocent Adam, he was not immune to the surd evil that now pervades the creation and mankind's experience. It was not into a pristine Eden that he came, but into a cursed creation. The Westminster Confession of Faith notes, "The Son of God, the second person in the Trinity, being very and eternal God, of one substance and equal with the Father, did, when the fulness of time was come, take upon Him man's nature, with all the essential properties and *common infirmities thereof*, yet without sin [italics added]."[40] In his incarnation and before the resurrection, in what the writer to the Hebrews calls "the days of his flesh" (5:7), Jesus suffered all the natural evil that had accrued as the result of sin. Jesus knew hunger (Matt. 4), knew frustration (Luke 9:41), knew betrayal by a beloved friend (Matt. 26:48), and at the last knew death (Luke 23:46). The picture of the soldiers bringing down a crown of thorns upon his head (Mark 15:17) is an unmistakable sign: he, though morally innocent, bore all the evil that is the sum of the curse (cf. Gen. 3:18).

In his incarnation Jesus is the epitome of the image of God in this creation. In his resurrection he is the start of the new creation,

---

[40] WCF, 8.2.

and the apex of the image of God to which his people will be conformed. The redeemed will be conformed to the image of God's Son in their glorification (Rom. 8:29–30). As they have borne the image of Adam, the "dusty" man, so they will bear the image of Christ, the heavenly man (1 Cor. 15:49); with unveiled faces they are being transformed, and one day will be transformed into the same image of the glory of God (2 Cor. 3:18).

The implications of Christ as the image of God in the incarnation and the resurrection for the topic under consideration are profound. As already noted, the meaning of the word צֶלֶם will not allow the *imago Dei* to be confined to some substantive fragment of man, but must include the body of man. Yet the pre-animate body of Adam is not the image of God, for this image is constituted a living image. It is only once Adam becomes a "living soul" (Gen. 2:7)—once he becomes a "he" and not merely an "it"—that he is the *imago Dei*. The fact that man as a "living soul" is the image of God expresses itself in moral, intellectual, linguistic, functional, representative, and relational ways. But even in his fallen condition man remains the image and likeness of God. The image can be defaced and damaged, but it cannot be obliterated by either moral evil or surd evil.

Nancy Eisland's notion that disability is the very essence of the *imago Dei* is surely incorrect. But the incarnation and work of Christ indicate that no evil that accrues from the curse can eradicate the *imago Dei*. For Christ from the time of his incarnation is *the* image of God, and never ceases to be so.

Is Christ the image of God while he is in the tomb? We cannot answer "no" to that question without substantivizing the *imago Dei* as being something that is in Christ rather than Christ himself contrary to the meaning of צֶלֶם/εἰκών, and replicating something akin to the Apollinarian heresy. Yes, even in the grave Christ is the image of God. Adam's pre-animate body was not the image of God until he became a "living soul." In the incarnate Christ the image is indelible: once he became a living human soul in the womb of Mary he never ceased being the image of God, even in death.

Death is the ultimate disabling condition, and all disabilities are harbingers of death.[41] Yet from the time of his incarnation, Christ is the image of God. He is the image of God through the disfiguring scourging. He is the image of God though the quadriplegia of crucifixion. And he is the image of God in death, the ultimate cognitive disability. Human cognition is the mysterious interplay between the human ψυχή and neural synapses (the somatic aspect of the cognitive equation), and when "his spirit departs, he returns to the earth; in that very day his thoughts perish" (Ps. 146:4 NASB). Even so, Christ is still the image of God.

If the ultimate end of Christ, the *imago Dei*, is the grave, there is no hope, no good news. But the canonical Gospels all report his resurrection three days after his death, and the New Testament (both the covenant itself and the document) is built upon that foundation. Jesus maintains that his death and resurrection is what the entirety of the Old Testament is about (Luke 24:25–27, 44–47). In the death of Christ, the *imago Dei*, broken and distorted by an evil both intimately acquainted with and yet alien to him, was not obliterated. This fact, coupled with the biblical witness that fallen man is yet the *imago Dei*, places Christ in solidarity with all his people, no matter what they suffer. He truly has been "made like his brothers in all things" (Heb. 2:17).

Prominent among the major themes of the New Testament is that Christ, having been made like us, his people shall be made like him. The process of becoming like him begins now. In Christ, who is the alpha of the new creation, his people are already "new creation" (καινὴ κτίσις, 2 Cor. 5:17) but have not yet reached their goal (Phil. 3:10–12). The apostle John says it this way: "Beloved, already we are children of God, and it has not yet appeared what we shall be. We

---

[41] Life expectancy for those with physical and intellectual disabilities is lower across the board than for the general population. See M. P. Barnes, *Life Expectancy for Those with Disabilities*, revised 9th version (Newcastle upon Tyne: International Centre for Neurorehabilitation and Neuropsychiatry, May 2007).

A Reconsideration of the *Imago Dei*

know that when he appears, we shall be like him, because we shall see Him just as he is" (1 John 3:2).

Nancy Eisland's hope was oriented to the *already*, and it is through this lens that she conceives of the *not yet*. She envisioned an eschaton in which disability is the norm. In order to do this she recognizes that a "revisioning" must take place, because the church has from earliest times symbolized Christ as a "conquering lord."[42] Drawing attention to the wounds of Christ, Eisland maintains that we must rather see the risen Christ now as the "disabled God."[43] The goal for Eisland is one in which the *imago Dei* is brought to its apex in disability. In the eschaton, the multitudes of the disabled redeemed will gather around the throne in worship of the disabled God.

This picture is completely at odds with what we find in the post-resurrection appearances, revelations, and descriptions of Jesus. Although the scars of crucifixion are yet present, there is nothing to indicate that Christ is in any way disabled. John's description of him in Revelation 1, and John's consequent reaction to the sight ("I fell at his feet as though dead"), hardly presents a picture of a disabled Christ.

Furthermore, in the incarnation the eschatological kingdom of God has broken into the present. In Christ the kingdom of God had drawn near (Matt. 4:17), and that kingdom is manifested in healing: "Jesus went throughout Galilee, teaching in their synagogues, proclaiming the good news of the kingdom, and healing every disease and sickness among the people" (Matt. 4:23). Although often no connection can be made between the disability one suffers and one's own moral culpability, all disability is the result of the fall, a contradiction of the "very good" of creation. The fact that Jesus in the proclamation of the kingdom of God brought physical as well as spiritual healing is indicative that reversal of the effects of the curse is a feature of the kingdom.

---

[42] Nancy Eisland, *The Disabled God: Toward a Liberation Theology of Disability* (Nashville, TN: Abingdon Press, 1994), 94.
[43] Ibid., 94.

In passages like Leviticus 21:16–23 physical disability disqualifies one from participation in the tabernacle worship. Nehemiah 8:1–3 could be read in such a way as to exclude those with cognitive disabilities. For Eisland such passages constitute a "dangerous" and "disabling theology."[44] Although such passages sound harsh to modern ears (as do many aspects of the Mosaic Law) they are seen in a new light in the coming of the kingdom of God. In the prefigurement of the Mosaic Law, disabled persons who bear visibly the effects of the fall are barred from the worship. But in the new creation, not disabled persons, but disability itself will be barred from the worship of God. The healing brought by Jesus in the proleptic coming of the kingdom anticipates the eschatological vision seen by John:

> And I saw a new heaven and a new earth; for the first heaven and the first earth passed away, and there is no longer any sea. And I saw the holy city, new Jerusalem, coming down out of heaven from God, made ready as a bride adorned for her husband. And I heard a loud voice from the throne, saying, "Behold, the dwelling of God is with men, and he shall dwell among them, and they shall be his people, and God himself shall be among them, and he shall wipe away every tear from their eyes; and there shall no longer be any death; there shall no longer be any mourning, or crying, or pain; the first things have passed away." And he who sits on the throne said, "Behold, I am making all things new." And he said, "Write, for these words are faithful and true." And he said to me, "It is done. I am the Alpha and the Omega, the beginning and the end. I will give to the one who thirsts from the spring of the water of life without cost. He who overcomes shall inherit these things, and I will be his God and he will be my son" (Rev. 21:1–7 NASB).

[44] Ibid., 70–75.

It is evident from the New Testament that the eschatological goal is not a mere restoration to Eden. Christ gained more than Adam lost. Instead of only the Garden, the redeemed gain a City. And the City itself is the holiest of places, its dimensions being proportioned analogously to the Holy of Holies (Rev. 21:16 cf. 1 Kings 6:20). In the eschaton, everything is made new (Rev. 21:5). Heaven and earth are new and occupy the same space and time, and on this new heaven-earth the City is located.

The redeemed, too, will be different. Sin and its consequences from which Christ came to deliver us will be done. The mourning, crying, and pain that arises from disability and every other evil will be a thing of the past. But the Scriptures also indicate that redeemed humanity will reach the apex of what Adam was created to become but fell before reaching.

In Chapter Three we looked at 2 Peter 1:4 and began to consider what it meant for human beings to become "partakers of the divine nature" in light of Beckerleg's insight that man was created after "God's kind." For many reasons the ancient theosis doctrine came to be muted in the west, and the Easternchurches came to be the self-professed custodians of it. Finlan and Kharlamov note, "In lay theology [in the west] the term is usually perceived as blasphemous or absurd."[45]

This perception has two origins. The first is a misunderstanding due to the translation "deification,"[46] a word which may convey to some a gnostic-like reabsorption into the Bythos or a Mormon-like polytheism. The second is in the poor representation of the doctrine by some of its proponents.

There is, to be sure, a danger in the way some modern writers in the Orthodox communion have cast the theosis doctrine. Although Christ is the eschatological Man, the one to whom redeemed humanity will be conformed, Genesis 9:6, James 3:9, and Acts

---

[45] Stephen Finlan and Vladimir Kharlamov, eds., *Theosis: Deification in Christian Theology* (Eugene, OR: Pickwick Publications, 2006), 8.

[46] "Divinization" may be a more accurate translation, but it is difficult to say that it would be received any better than "deification."

17:28–29 indicate that fallen man is yet the image and likeness of God by nature of creation. Statements such as "We have yet to become human … ,"[47] and the idea that people "… are not yet human beings; we are human becomings"[48] may prove unwise in a world in which people like Peter Singer and Steven Pinker already are questioning the humanity and personality of certain people and the dignity and right to life of any. Meilaender's criticism is well founded: "[Behr] is prepared … to say, 'We have yet to become human.' I suspect that readers might both understand what he means by this and find it puzzling. We are, after all, talking about human beings, not dogs. … [I]f we focus on the *imago* as our destiny in Christ [only], how would this connect to the idea of human dignity [now]?" He writes, "[W]e must be able to talk not only about destiny but also about nature."[49]

The theosis doctrine is, in fact, inseparable from the *imago* and incarnation doctrines. "Behind the doctrine of deification there lies the idea that the human person is made according to the image and likeness of God the Holy Trinity."[50] It is because man is made as the image of God that the incarnation does and can take place, and it is Christ in his resurrection and glorification to which redeemed mankind will be conformed (Phil. 3:10–11; Rom. 8:29). The goal is not one of mere restoration to the pre-fallen condition of Adam, but rather to "… transform our lowly bodies so that they will be like his glorious body" (Phil. 3:21 NIV). As the apostle John beheld the glorified Christ whose "… head and hair were white like white wool, like snow; and his eyes were like a flame of fire; and his feet were like burnished bronze, when it has been caused to glow in a furnace, and

---

[47] John Behr, "The Promise of the Image," in *Imago Dei: Human Dignity in Ecumenical Perspective*, ed. Thomas Albert Howard (Washington, DC: The Catholic University Press, 2013), 35.

[48] See Anthony M. Coniaris, *Achieving Your Potential in Christ: Theosis* (Minneapolis, MN: Light and Life Publishing, 1993), 5.

[49] Meilaender, 116.

[50] Timothy Ware, *The Orthodox Church*, new ed. (New York: Penguin Books, 1993), 231.

his voice was like the sound of many waters ... and his face was like the sun shining in its strength" (Rev. 1:14–26), so the redeemed are to reflect an identical but derivative glory: "[We are] not as Moses, who used to put a veil over his face that the sons of Israel might not look intently at the end of what was fading away.... But we all, with unveiled faces beholding as in a mirror the glory of the Lord, are being transformed into the same image from glory to glory, just as from the Lord, the Spirit" (2 Cor. 3:13, 18).

Though not emphasized in most modern Protestant circles, the theosis doctrine was not unknown to the Reformers. Myk Habets has written, "Theosis—the deification of the human person—can and must be seen to be compatible with Reformed theology.... According to Reformed scholars, union with Christ is at the heart of Reformed theology.... It is important to highlight that not only did the early church and Eastern Orthodox adopt the language of theosis, so did the Protestant Reformers."[51] Habets cites Calvin[52] and Jonathan Edwards[53] in their use of the theosis doctrine. He concludes that "The doctrine of theosis was not neglected in the Western tradition, not least within Reformed Theology. It has been there all along, if underdeveloped."[54]

Although the term itself is sparsely used in Protestant theology, theosis accurately stated could be the occasion for little dissent: "... the concept of deification [is] the transition from corruptibility, destruction, and death to immortality, new creation and eternal life."[55]

---

[51] Myk Habets, "Reforming Theosis" in *Theosis: Deification in Christian Theology*, vol. 1, ed. Stephen Finlan and Vladimir Kharlamov (Eugene, OR: Pickwick Publications, 2006), 146–47.

[52] "In one of his rare uses of the word 'deification,' Calvin writes, "We should notice that this is the purpose of the Gospel to make us sooner or later like God; indeed it is, so to speak, a kind of a deification" (citing Calvin's commentary on 2 Peter 1:4), 148.

[53] Ibid., 150.

[54] Ibid., 151.

[55] Vladimir Kharlamov, "The Emergence of the Deification Theme in the Apostolic Fathers" in Finlan and Kharlamov, 52.

Theosis presented accurately is never conceived of as absorption of the human person into the divine. The human person being a *person* always maintains his or her distinction: "The idea of deification must always be understood in the light of the distinction between God's essence and his energies. Union with God means union with the divine energies, not the divine essence."[56] Using an apophatic methodology, Kallistos Ware underscores that the theosis doctrine cannot be construed to mean that a hypostatic union between redeemed people and God takes place: ". . . there is between the divine and human natures of Christ . . . a 'hypostatic' or personal union: Godhead and manhood in Christ are so joined that they constitute, or belong to a single person. . . . the union between God and the saints is not of this kind. . . . In the Age to come God is 'all in all' (1 Cor. 15:28); yet 'Peter is Peter, Paul is Paul, Philip is Philip. Each one retains his own nature and personal identity . . . .'"[57]

Without using the word, the Presbyterian theologian John Murray captures the theosis doctrine: "When we think of the glory of God as the chief end and goal of sanctification, we must appreciate the extent to which God will be glorified in the glorification of his people. . . . it is only in relation to the redemption of the elect that the incarnation of the Son has meaning. The glorification of the elect is really one with the final glorification of him who himself is the embodiment of the glory of God."[58] Murray continues,

> The conformity [to the image of his Son] . . . includes conformity to the likeness of the body of Christ's glory (Phil. 3:21), and must, therefore, be conceived of as conformity of the

---

[56] Timothy Ware, *The Orthodox Church* (New York: Penguin Books, 1983), 232.

[57] Kallistos Ware, *The Orthodox Way*, rev. ed. (Crestwood, NY: St. Vladimir's Seminary Press, 1995), 125.

[58] John Murray, "The Goal of Sanctification" in *The Collected Writing of John Murray*, vol. 2, *Systematic Theology* (Carlisle, PA: Banner of Truth, 1977, 313–17), 314.

image of the Son incarnate. But the glorified Christ does not cease to be the eternal Son. Hence conformity to his image as incarnate and glorified is conformity to the image of him who is the eternal and only-begotten Son. This is the highest end conceivable for created things, the highest end conceivable not only by men but also by God himself. God himself could not contemplate or determine a higher destiny for his creatures.[59]

Meilaender's previously mentioned cautions are well-marked. The theosis doctrine could cause one to become future-focused in such a way as to make Christians "so heavenly minded that they are no earthly good." If care is not taken to underscore the essential human nature as created *ad imago Dei*, and so to see people in the present only as "potential human beings," Christians could become the allies of decidedly anti-Christian philosophies. Rightly conceived, however, the theosis doctrine is a repudiation of our tendency toward an arrogant superiority with respect to those who are severely cognitively disabled. It enables us not only to see the potential of God-likeness in them, but reminds us too that not only are we all implicated in the sin that brought all kinds of evil into the world, but that even in those abilities in which we can tend to take an untoward pride, we are not now what we can be and by the grace of Christ will be. The greatest glory of fallen man in a fallen world will pale in comparison to when the longed for "adoption as sons, the redemption of our bodies" (Rom. 8:23) is realized.

When I was a child, I remember being with my father and seeing a man who was a wood carver. As he was busy with a piece of wood, I looked in amazement at a duck he had carved. The detail of the image of the animal was exquisite. I thought to myself, "That looks like a *real* duck." The amazement must have shown on my face. "You like that?" he asked me; "That one's not done yet. Here's one that's done." The man produced a duck the detail of which was

---

[59] Ibid., 316.

unbelievable. The individual feathers were all finely filamented, tear ducts were in the corners of the eyes, and though the image was designed to sit flat, there were webbed feet pulled up under it. "That one's done," he said. The first duck was an astonishing work of art. The duck he showed me, however, looked as though Midas had touched a living duck, but instead of turning to gold it had turned to wood.

In his book *The Weight of Glory* C. S. Lewis wrote,

> . . . the cross comes before the crown, and tomorrow is a Monday morning. A cleft has opened in the pitiless walls of the world, and we are invited to follow our great Captain inside. The following Him is, of course, the essential point. That being so, it may be asked what practical use there is in the speculations which I have been indulging. I can think of at least one such use. It may be possible for each to think too much of his own potential glory hereafter; it is hardly possible for him to think too often or too deeply about that of his neighbour. The load, or weight, or burden of my neighbor's glory should be laid on my back, a load so heavy that only humility can carry it, and the backs of the proud will be broken. It is a serious thing to live in a society of possible gods and goddesses, to remember that the dullest and most uninteresting person you talk to may one day be a creature which, if you saw it now, you would be strongly tempted to worship . . . ."[60]

Cognitive Disability and the *Imago Dei*: Can It Be Restored *ad Imago Christi*?

There is a strong connection between sonship and image. Kline has noted, "Since the Spirit's act of creating man is . . . presented as the fathering of a son and the man-son is identified as the

---

[60] C. S. Lewis, *The Weight of Glory* (New York: Harper Collins, reprinted 1980), 45.

A Reconsideration of the *Imago Dei*

image-likeness of God, it is evident that image of God and son of God are mutually explanatory concepts. To be the image of God is to be the son of God."[61] This is significant when we take account of the fact that the opening of John's Gospel puts forth the idea that people are not now "naturally" children of God, a situation that Jesus came to remedy: "He came to his own, and those who were his own did not receive him. But as many as received him, to them he gave the right to *become* children of God, to those who believe in His name, who were born not of blood, nor of the will of the flesh, nor of the will of a man, but of God" (John 1:12–13, italics added). Before his rebellion Adam may have been a son of God (cf. Luke 3:38), but John indicates that our fallen condition in him means "children of God" is something we must now become, rather than something that we are.

And yet, even the Athenians in their active and immediate rebellion against the gospel message of amnesty and adoption are still "God's offspring," "God's *kind*" (γένος τοῦ θεοῦ, Acts 17:28–29). It is this ambiguity, this contradiction of the fallen world that prompted theologians like Luther to conclude that the image of God was lost, a conclusion that may be inescapable were it not for passages such as Genesis 9:6 and James 3:9.

Connecting all the data points in Scripture, we conclude that from the moment of conception human beings are constituted as "living souls" and are thus *imago Dei*. Whatever distortions of body or soul take place in their development *in utero* or *ex utero*, they are still the image of God. Because of sin in the world, all people bear distortions, some more notable and visible than others; but all are no less the image of God despite the distortions. *Imago Dei* is simply what man *qua* man is constituted.

The distortions, the "very bad" that intruded into the "very good" creation, are a result of man's sin. As already noted, sin and

---

[61] Meredith G. Kline, *Kingdom Prologue: Genesis Foundations for a Covenantal Worldview* (Overland Park, KS: Two Age Press, 2002), 45–46.

its consequences cannot be simplistically construed in a *quid pro quo* fashion; the evil that a person suffers is not due necessarily to that person's own sin, but may be due simply to the fact that "sin is in the world" (cf. Rom. 5:13). Although we may not legitimately conclude that those with extraordinary challenges in life are "getting what they deserve," nor can we legitimately contend that there are any completely "innocent" people. To borrow the words of the Westminster Confession of Faith (6.3) no one "descended by ordinary generation" is without sin.

This raises significant questions with regard to those who are severely cognitively disabled. If they are implicated in the guilt of Adam's sin and participants in its pollution, how can such people be saved, if salvation entails justification (Rom. 8:30), and justification comes by faith (Rom. 3:28), and faith requires a certain level of understanding? Is it possible for such people to "pursue holiness, without which no one will see the Lord" (Heb. 12:14)? Is it thinkable that such people could become "partakers of the divine nature, having escaped the corruption that is in the world by lust" (2 Peter 1:4)?

It is tempting to absolve those with severe cognitive disabilities from the guilt of Adam's sin. Are their lives not difficult enough without the thought that such people are "by nature children of wrath, even as the rest" (Eph. 2:3)? Yet the only way to excuse them from implication in Adam's sin is to replicate the Pelagian heresy in the hope that if the cognitive disability is severe enough, the person in question cannot follow the "bad example" of Adam. Yet it is *Adam* who is created in the image of God, and the fact that people after him bear that image appears to be dependent upon their connection to him (Gen. 1:26, cf. 5:3). While we may feel compelled out of pity to exempt certain people from Adam's sin, the Scriptures simply will not allow us to do so. Sin is the universal condition of fallen mankind (Rom. 3:23; 5:12; Gal. 3:22). If anyone can be justified before God "by nature," Christ need not have come.

A Reconsideration of the *Imago Dei*

Stanley Hauerwas has noted the absurdity of trying to maintain that those with cognitive disabilities are free from sin,[62] an absurdity that anyone who is spiritually astute and who has lived or worked with such people well understands. To be sure, sin is expressed through the vehicle of the body (cf. Rom. 6:13–19), including the brain, and those of diminished capacity may be concomitantly diminished in their ability to express their sin. But even in the case of a Kelly or an Oliver de Vinck, sin is present, a proposition the truth of which is not based upon observation of the person's behavior, but upon what the Scriptures teach about the universality of sin and the fact that "no one of all the living is righteous before [God]" (Ps. 143:2). To maintain that those with severe cognitive disabilities are without sin is to rob them of the dignity of being human, of being implicated with the rest of humanity in the first man's sin, and in need of a savior.

But how would God's salvation be mediated to people with the most severe cognitive disabilities? The Scriptures are clear that justification is a necessary element in the *ordo salutis* (Rom. 8:30), and that it is in being "justified by faith, [that] we have peace with God through our Lord Jesus Christ" (Rom. 5:1). Salvation is initiated in the life of a person by "the washing of regeneration and renewing by the Holy Spirit" (Titus 3:5), and in being "born again to a living hope through the resurrection of Jesus Christ from the dead" (1 Peter 1:3), by "seed that is not perishable, but imperishable, through the living and abiding word of God" (1 Peter 1:23).

There is thus a close connection in Scripture between faith and regeneration. How one conceives of the relationship between the two may seem to make little difference when considering typical people, but when considering those with severe cognitive disabilities, the relationship makes all the difference.

A soteriology that makes regeneration dependent upon faith provides little encouragement or hope for those with severe cognitive

---

[62] Hauerwas, "The Gesture of a Truthful Story" *Theology Today* 42, 2 (July 1985), 179.

disabilities. In the book *How to be Born Again*, Billy Graham lays out just such a soteriology, the very title of the book indicating that being born again is something that is within the control of human beings, and thus subject to a "how to" instruction. He states, "Any person who is willing to trust Jesus Christ as his personal Savior and Lord can receive the new birth now."[63]

This begs the question of what to make of those with cognitive disabilities. Graham's answer is that God has made the gospel message simple: "I could not help thinking how kind and understanding and compassionate God has been in choosing to reveal himself to man through simple childlike faith rather than the intellect. There would otherwise be no [chance] for little children or the mentally retarded or the brain damaged."[64] "Jesus made everything so simple, and we have made it so complicated. He spoke to the people in short sentences and everyday words, illustrating his messages with parables and stories."[65]

In making faith antecedent to regeneration, Graham stresses that faith is simply trust in a person (Jesus Christ) and is thus uncomplicated, and therefore gives opportunity to even "the mentally retarded" to be born again. But "the mentally retarded" Graham pictures apparently only include those with forms of cognitive disability such as Down syndrome which allow for some level of understanding and receptive and expressive language. The inescapable conclusion of Graham's soteriology is that people with conditions like lissencephaly or Angelman syndrome, who typically do not have a capacity to understand or express things linguistically, cannot be saved, because they cannot be born again, because they cannot have faith.

A more biblical soteriology sees faith as a response to God's grace that is enabled by regeneration, which in turn rests upon

---

[63] Billy Graham, *How to Be Born Again* (Nashville, TN: Thomas Nelson, 1989), 152.
[64] Ibid., 148.
[65] Ibid., 155.

election. The Scriptures teach that we are not merely weakened, but dead in our trespasses and sin (Eph. 2:1). Dead people cannot exercise faith or obey any command unless they first are made alive (cf. John 11:43–44). "Regeneration is an act of God.... It is not an act which, by argument and persuasion, or by moral power, he induces the sinner to perform.... It is God who regenerates. The soul is regenerated."[66] "God effects a change which is radical and all-pervasive, a change which cannot be explained in terms of any combination, permutation, or accumulation of human resources, a change which is nothing less than a new creation by him who calls the things that be not as though they were, who spake and it was done, who commanded and it stood fast. This, in a word, is regeneration."[67] "Regeneration is the beginning of all saving grace *in us*, and all saving grace in exercise on our part proceeds from the foundation of regeneration. We are not born again by faith or repentance or conversion. We repent and believe because we have been regenerated."[68] This more biblical soteriology provides hope of redemption for those with severe cognitive disabilities. If faith causes regeneration, then the salvation of those with severe cognitive impairment is either impossible, or must take place without regeneration (which, given the teaching of the New Testament, is also impossible). If, however, faith is enabled by regeneration, then it is possible for regeneration to take place, but for faith and/or its expression to be inhibited by somatic (including brain-related) maladies.

Regeneration takes place in the course of history, and is predicated upon God's election which takes place before the foundation of the world (Eph. 1:4). The term "election" is used so frequently in the Scriptures that it can hardly be denied. The question is, "What is election predicated upon?" Although there are those who have posited everything in individuals from superior morals to superior

[66] Charles Hodge, *Systematic Theology*, 3:31.
[67] John Murray, *Redemption Accomplished and Applied* (Grand Rapids, MI: Eerdmans, 1955), 96.
[68] Ibid., 103.

intellect as the foundation for election, Romans 9:11–20 stands in stark opposition to the idea that election is based upon anything within individual people:

> Yet, before the twins were born or had done anything good or bad—in order that God's purpose in election might stand: not by works but by him who calls—she was told, "The older will serve the younger." Just as it is written: "Jacob I loved, but Esau I hated." What then shall we say? Is God unjust? Not at all! For he says to Moses, "I will have mercy on whom I have mercy, and I will have compassion on whom I have compassion." It does not, therefore, depend on human desire or effort, but on God's mercy. For Scripture says to Pharaoh: "I raised you up for this very purpose, that I might display my power in you and that my name might be proclaimed in all the earth." Therefore God has mercy on whom he wants to have mercy, and he hardens whom he wants to harden. One of you will say to me: "Then why does God still blame us? For who is able to resist his will?" But who are you, O man, to talk back to God? (NIV)

There are three possible rubrics under which to understand those with cognitive disabilities *vis-à-vis* the doctrine of election. The first possibility is that no people with severe cognitive disabilities are among God's elect; the second is that all people with severe cognitive disabilities are among God's elect; and the third is that some of those with cognitive disabilities are among the elect, and others are not.

The possibility that no people with severe cognitive disabilities are among the elect seems unlikely when the revelation of God's character in Scripture is considered. Fear of Yahweh precludes cursing the deaf or putting a stumbling block before the blind (Lev. 19:14). God's people are called upon to affirm their own curse should they mislead someone who is blind (Deut. 27:18). Part of Job's self-justification before God was that he was "eyes to the blind, and feet to the lame" (Job 29:15). In promising redemption, God declares, "'In that day,' declares Yahweh, 'I will assemble the lame, and gather the outcasts, even those whom I have afflicted'" (Mic. 4:6). Among the great signs of the kingdom that Jesus performed, healing of the sick was prominent (e.g., Matt. 4:23–24). The concern that Jesus expresses for "the least of these" (Matt. 25:40–45)—those whom societies cast aside as being without value—would seem to indicate that God not merely tolerates the presence of those with severe cognitive disabilities, but has a special concern for them. Given such passages, it would be inconceivable that no persons with severe cognitive disabilities are among God's elect.

Are all those with severe cognitive disabilities numbered among God's elect? Given the character of God and his concern for those society rejects, it would hardly be surprising if this were so, but it would be impossible to say from the Scriptures that this is definitively the case. The words of the Westminster divines are both appropriately cautious and hopeful: "Elect infants, dying in infancy, are regenerated and saved by Christ through the Spirit, who worketh when, and where, and how He pleaseth. So also are all other elect persons, who are uncapable of being outwardly called by the ministry of the Word."[69]

The healing that Jesus brought in the days of his flesh was a sign of the eschatological healing which will banish every "very bad" from the midst of redeemed humanity. Not all whom Jesus healed physically were healed spiritually,[70] but this fact does not negate the *sign* of healing, any more than Simon's betrayal of his baptismal confession negated baptism itself as a sign and seal of the covenant of grace (Acts 8:9–24, cf. WCF 28.1, WLC 165, 177).

In examining the Gospels, we find that Jesus healed in three circumstances: he healed those who themselves sought him for

---

[69] WCF, 10.3.

[70] John 5:1–15 tells of a lame man whom Jesus healed, and who later subsequently sought out the religious leaders who were enemies of Jesus to betray him to them.

healing (e.g., Matt. 21:14; Mark 3:10; 5:25–30; Luke 5:15; 6:17–19; 8:47; 17:11–14); those whose healing was sought by others (e.g., Matt. 4:24; 8:5–16; 15:30; John 4:47 ff.); and those who did not seek healing from him, nor was healing sought by anyone for them, but who were healed by him out of his compassion (e.g., Matt. 14:14; 15:22 ff.; Luke 14:1–4; 22:51; John 5:6 ff.). If the physical healing that took place at the time of Jesus' earthly ministry is a sign of eschatological healing, the instances of those who were healed when no one was seeking healing from him provide a basis for hope for those who are outside of the church and are severely cognitively disabled.

The instances in the Gospels in which Jesus healed people at the request and through the faith of others (e.g., Mark 2:1–12) provide a well-grounded hope for the parents of children with severe cognitive disabilities born within the church, whose parents seek Jesus for the healing of their children. In stating this, I write from the perspective of my own tradition, which understands the children of believers to be members of the church, and thus the subjects of baptism.[71] The development of a covenant theology, including a covenantal understanding of baptism, blunted the harsh transcendence of the stark doctrine of election, and the declaration that God "has mercy on whom he desires, and he hardens whom He desires" (Rom. 9:18).[72]

Baptist ecclesiology does not include the children of believers, repentance and credible profession of faith being a necessary prerequisite for church membership.[73] Although this means that church

---

[71] *The Book of Church Order of the Orthodox Presbyterian Church* (Willow Grove, PA: The Orthodox Presbyterian Church, 2011), "The universal church visible consists of all those persons, in every nation, *together with their children*, who make profession of saving faith in the Lord Jesus Christ and promise submission to his commandments" (Form of Government 2.1, italics added); "Baptized children ordinarily shall be received as noncommunicant members when their parents are received as communicant members" (Directory for Public Worship IV.A.7).

[72] See Peter A. Lillback, *The Binding of God, Calvin's Role in the Development of Covenant Theology* (Grand Rapids, MI: Baker Academic, 2001).

[73] John Gill, *A Body of Doctrinal and Practical Divinity* (London: Whittingham

members' children who have the most severe cognitive disabilities cannot receive the sacrament (or ordinance) of baptism and can never become Baptist church members *de jure*, my observation has been that they often are regarded as church members *de facto*. In reading *Wrestling with an Angel* by Baptist layman Greg Lucas, one is left with the strong impression that he regards his severely cognitively disabled son Jake to be redeemed by Christ and in some sense a member of the church. One *Täufer* doctrinal statement notes, "Since Jesus Himself paid the debt for sin and not man, and since by virtue of His atonement alone even the saints are permitted to enter heaven; it should be clearly perceptible that the sins of the innocent and abnormal mind are likewise covered."[74]

The relationship of the sacraments to those with severe cognitive disabilities is tradition-dependent. Those who see the sacraments in

---

& Rowland, 1815), 622–23: "[Those who are members of a Gospel-church] should be persons of some competent knowledge of divine and spiritual things; who have knowledge not only of themselves, but of their lost estate by nature, and the way of salvation by Christ, in his Person as the Son of God; but have some knowledge of God in his nature, perfections, and works . . . ." John L. Dagg, *Manual of Theology and Church Order*, vol. 2 (Harrisonburg, VA: Gano Books, reprinted 1982), 128: "Only so far as this evidence of true discipleship appears, are we required, or even authorized, to exercise brotherly love [i.e., reception into church membership]." Augustus H. Strong, *Systematic Theology* (Old Tappan, NJ: Fleming H. Revel, 1907), 897–98, "They only can properly be members of the local church . . . who have become regenerate persons. . . . each regenerate man recognizes in every other a brother in Christ . . . ," a recognition which comes through expressions of faith and repentance. Samuel E. Waldron, *A Modern Exposition of the 1689 Baptist Confession of Faith* (Durham: Evangelical Press, 1989), 318–19: "A further implication [of church membership] is that baptized disciples who leave one church for another ought not to be and ought not to expect to be gullibly or automatically received by another local church. They ought to willingly provide that church with proof of their discipleship by verbally relating their experience of Christ, letters of recommendation from their former church and their manifest good conduct and submission to the Lord and his church."

[74] *Doctrinal Treatise, Old German Baptist Brethren*, 3rd ed. (Covington, OH: The Vindicator, 1970), 13. "The innocent" here referring to infant children who lack a developed understanding and cognitive ability. In the context the term clearly does not mean "without sin."

an *ex opere operato* light (such as Roman Catholics[75] and Protestants who embrace the Federal Vision movement[76]) will include severely intellectually disabled persons in both the sacraments of baptism and the Lord's Supper.

Baptists would typically exclude the most severely cognitively disabled persons, who can make no expression of their faith, from participation in both sacraments (ordinance), and from a *de jure* membership in the church. However, as already noted, this hardly means that Baptists necessarily believe that such people cannot be saved.

In my own tradition, which follows the Westminster Standards, the children of believers are received by covenant baptism into the membership of the church whether or not they have disabilities. However, participation in the Lord's Supper requires public profession of faith and covenantal separation from their parents.[77] Thus to participate,

> It is required of them that receive the sacrament of the Lord's Supper, that, during the time of the administration of it, with all holy reverence and attention they wait upon God in that ordinance, diligently observe the sacramental elements and actions, heedfully discern the Lord's body, and affectionately meditate on his death and sufferings, and thereby stir up themselves to a vigorous exercise of their graces; in judging themselves, and sorrowing for sin; in earnest hungering and thirsting after Christ, feeding on him by faith, receiving of

---

[75] See Archdiocese of Baltimore, "Sacramental Preparations for Persons with Disabilities," http://www.archbalt.org/evangelization/disabilities-ministry/sacramental-preparation.cfm (accessed September 26, 2013).

[76] See Alan D. Strange, "Understanding the Federal Vision," *New Horizons of the Orthodox Presbyterian Church*, February 2007, http://www.opc.org/nh.html?article_id=478 (accessed September 26, 2013).

[77] Book of Church Order of the Orthodox Presbyterian Church, IV.A.8.: "Noncommunicant members of the congregation may be received into communicant membership only by confession of faith."

his fulness, trusting in his merits, rejoicing in his love, giving thanks for his grace; in renewing of their covenant with God, and love to all the saints[78]

My daughter, who meets the consensus criteria for Angleman syndrome, is not capable of meeting these requirements. But it is conceivable that someone with Down syndrome may exhibit such understanding, if simply. Although such questions are typically left to individual sessions,[79] I suspect that most sessions, while not omitting any of these criteria, would take into account the person's ability to exhibit these things to the level of their intellectual capacity. Although I am not personally acquainted with any such cases, I do not believe that a person with intellectual disabilities who is able to make a simple but sincere profession of faith commensurate with his or her abilities would be restricted from communicant membership. The Lord's Supper is not understood in my tradition to be the privileged practice of the theological and intellectual elite.

Although among Protestants only baptism and the Lord's Supper are understood to be sacraments, the New Testament provides another sign of God's grace that can and should be applied to those with severe cognitive disabilities without contradicting the ecclesiastical traditions of any. James 5:14–15 teaches, "Is anyone among you sick? Let them call the elders of the church to pray over them and anoint them with oil in the name of the Lord. And the prayer offered in faith will make the sick person well; the Lord will raise them up. If they have sinned, they will be forgiven" (NIV).

As my wife and I came to realize the extent of our daughter Rebecca's disabilities, we called upon our presbytery (the ministers and elders of our regional church) to anoint her with oil and pray for her healing. Their performance of that biblical sign on May 1, 2004 has brought a great deal of comfort to our family. Beyond our relief,

---

[78] WLC, 174.
[79] The pastors and elders of a particular local congregation.

however, did the presbytery's action accomplish anything? I believe the text cited provides the answer to that question.

Is anyone among you sick? The word ἀσθενέω is defined as meaning "to suffer some debilitating illness, *be sick*; to experience some personal incapacity or limitation, *be weak*."[80] This well described Rebecca's condition. She was plagued by seizures and was not achieving the developmental milestones associated with language or ambulation. We were cautioned by the doctors that she might not speak or walk. Following the provisions of this passage gave us opportunity to confess our faith in a good Creator and acknowledge a world gone awry due to sin. Rebecca was not merely different. Something was wrong. She was sick and weak, and engaging in this biblical ritual enabled us to seek Jesus for her healing in a way that was not private and hidden.

Let them call for the elders of the church. Although Rebecca herself could not call for the elders of the church, in the Gospels people sought out Jesus for the healing of others, and especially of their children (John 4:46–54; Mark 5:38–43). Thus, it seemed (and seems) appropriate that we on our daughter's behalf should seek out the elders of the church to minister to her in this way in the Lord's name.

And let them pray over them and anoint them with oil in the name of the Lord. Oil in the ancient Near East had numerous uses, including a medicinal use (cf. Luke 10:33–34).[81] Related to this use, it is used symbolically for healing in this passage. It must be stressed that its use here is semiotic. The elders are not being called upon to add the Hippocratic Oath to their vows of ordination. They are rather applying a symbol of the Lord's healing (cf. Mark 6:13).

And the prayer offered in faith will make the sick person well. This

---

[80] BDAG, 1. and 2.

[81] See J. A. Thompson, ed. *Handbook of Life in Bible Times* (Downers Grove, IL: InterVarsity Press, 1986), 274; Lawrence O. Richards, ed., *The Revell Bible Dictionary* (Old Tappan, NJ: Fleming H. Revell, 1990), 70–71; F. L Cross and E. A. Livingston, eds. *The Oxford Dictionary of the Christian Church*, 2nd ed. (Oxford: Oxford University Press, 1983), 60; Walter A. Ewell, ed. *Evangelical Dictionary of Theology* (Grand Rapids, MI: Baker Book House, 1984). 51–52

is a remarkable statement. In the passage, it is the elders who are praying, so the faith in view is the faith (fidelity in prayer) of the elders. The text states that the prayer *will save* (σώσει) the sick person. It is noteworthy that the word for "make well" here (σῴζω), while legitimately translated "to save or free from disease,"[82] is the same word that is used for God's work of saving from the transcendent danger of eternal death.[83] It is also to be noted that the verb is not in the subjunctive mood, indicating what may take place, but is a future indicative, indicating what will take place.

Has the Scripture promised more than can be delivered? When my wife and I called upon the elders of the church to anoint our daughter with oil, the possibility that she would never walk or speak was very real. Today she is able to walk very well. Did this come about because the elders, in faithful obedience to the Scriptures, followed the provisions of James 5:14–15? I will not deny that this is a possibility. But Rebecca's gait is abnormal, and she still does not speak. Is this all the healing we can expect?

The Lord will raise them up. If they have sinned, they will be forgiven. This is the crux of the passage. The word "to raise up" (ἐγείρω) may indeed mean "to raise up from sickness; to restore to health,"[84] but it frequently refers to *resurrection*.[85] The healing that is

---

[82] See BDAG, 1.c.

[83] See BDAG, 2.

[84] See BDAG, 8.

[85] DBAG, 6.: to cause to return to life, *raise up* (Mt 10:8; J 5:21; Ac 26:8; 2 Cor. 1:9; Of the raising of Jesus Ac 5:30; 10:40; 13:37; 1 Cor. 6:14; 15:15ff; 2 Cor. 4:14. More fully ἐ. τινὰ ἐκ νεκρῶν (mostly of Jesus' resurr.) J 12:1, 9, 17; Ac 3:15; 4:10; 13:30; Ro 4:24; 8:11; 10:9; Gal. 1:1; Eph. 1:20; Col. 2:12; 1 Th 1:10; Hb 11:19; 1 Pt 1:21;. to enter into or to be in a state of life as a result of being raised, *be raised, rise*, approaches ἀναστῆναι in mng. gen. νεκροὶ ἐγείρονται Mk 12:26; Lk 7:22; 20:37; 1 Cor. 15:15f, 29, 32, 35, 52. Of Lazarus ἐγερθήσεται J 11:12 v.l. σώματα … ἠγέρθησαν Mt 27:52; ἐγείρεται σῶμα πνευματικόν 1 Cor. 15:44; cp. 15:42f; τὸ σῶμα ἐγείρεται AcPlCor 2:27; cp. 2:26 (in imagery after 1 Cor. 15:37). ἐάν τις ἀπὸ νεκρῶν ἐγερθῇ Lk 16:30 v.l.; ἐάν τις ἐκ νεκρῶν ἐγερθῇ 16:31 P[75].—Of John the Baptist ἀπὸ τῶν νεκρῶν Mt 14:2; cp. ἐκ νεκρῶν Mk 6:14; Lk 9:7.—Of Christ: ἐκ νεκρῶν Mt 17:9; J

promised is without qualification and is an eschatological certainty. It may or may not have manifestations in this age. The healing that it speaks of ultimately has its reference in the age to come.

Although Protestants do not understand this passage sacramentally, this sign of healing, carried out in faith by my presbytery, and coupled with Rebecca's baptism has afforded my wife and me much comfort and confidence. It has bolstered a hope that she is numbered among the "little ones [who] to him belong; they are weak but he is strong."

Sola Gratia

At the time of the Protestant Reformation, five distinctive "alone" elements came to be emphasized: Scripture, faith, grace, Christ, and the glory of God. Of these, the most difficult for us to accept is that our salvation is *sola gratia*, by grace alone. This, of course, is not denied in concept by Christians, but it is often denied in fact. Having been instructed in the model of pastoral counseling taught by the Christian Counseling and Education Foundation, I would summarize their counseling model as: "the practice of helping people to stop living out of the impoverished slavery of trying to make themselves acceptable, and accept that God has made them acceptable in Christ."[86]

2:22; 21:14; Ro 6:4, 9; 7:4; 1 Cor. 15:12, 20 (cp. Just., D. 108, 2 ἐγηγέρθαι); 2 Ti 2:8. Also ἀπὸ τῶν νεκρῶν Mt 27:64; 28:7; ἀπὸ νεκρῶν ITr 9:2. Without this qualification τῇ τρίτῃ ἡμέρᾳ ἐγερθῆναι Mt 16:21; 17:23. καθὼς εἶπεν 28:6; ὄντως εἶπεν 26:34. διὰ τὴν δικαίωσιν ἡμῶν Ro 4:25; ὑπὲρ αὐτῶν (τῶν ζώντων) 2 Cor. 5:15. Abs. Mt 26:32; Mk 14:28; 16:6; Lk 24:6, 14 (v.l. ἐκ νεκρῶν); Ro 8:34 (v.l. ἐκ v.); 1 Cor. 15:13f, 16f.

[86] An example of the outworking of this can be found in books by CCEF staff such as Edward T. Welch, *What Do You Think of Me? Why Do I Care?* (Greensboro, NC: New Growth Press, 2011), and *Shame Interrupted* (Greensboro, NC: New Growth Press, 2012); and Paul David Tripp, *Instruments in the Redeemer's Hands* (Phillipsburg, NJ: P&R Publishing, 2002) and *Dangerous Calling Confronting the Unique Challenges of the Pastoral Ministry* (Wheaton,

A Reconsideration of the *Imago Dei*

Our difficulty with accepting that we stand before God by grace alone has a bearing on why we are so uncomfortable with those who are severely disabled. John Doud has noted that ". . . 'the healthy' tend to avoid those with disabilities whose scars, breakdowns, and obvious imperfections present stark reminders of human frailty, vulnerability, and mortality."[87] The presence of those with severe cognitive disabilities is a rebuke to our self-defined worth, and a reminder that God's salvation is *per solam gratiam*. As descendants of Adam, those with cognitive disabilities are, like all of us, made as the image of God. That image has been marred in many ways by sin's entrance into the world, but it cannot be obliterated. The image of God is simply what people are.

We so easily blind ourselves to our own moral faults that mar the *imago*. We are quite comfortable speaking of the *imago Dei* in terms of man's intellect, his ability or achievement, his intricate relationships. The presence of those with severe intellectual disabilities challenges us that the *imago Dei* is not something within us, not some capability we possess—our intellect, our linguistic capability, or our ability to create, or to exercise authority, or to relate as husband and wife. All of these aspects are results of our being made the image of God, not the substance of it or criteria for it. "Image" is a noun, not a verb. Although there is a certain validity in speaking of "imaging God" (Hoekema), the word "image" in both testaments is a noun, not a verb. To whatever degree people "image" or act out the image of God, they do so because "image of God" is foundationally what they are. Being is antecedent to doing. People are not the image of God because they image God in some way; they image God (to whatever extent they can or may) because they are the image of God.

Every person is *imago Dei*. And we are, every one of us, broken images. All Christians will assent to the truth of such a statement.

IL: Crossway, 2012).

[87] John Foster Doud, "Church Accessibility for Person with Disabilities: A Religious Imperative" (D.Min. Thesis, McCormick Theological Seminary, 1993), 25.

But while we may profess our belief that we are broken images, in our heart of hearts we doubt it.

Christ came to redeem a people for himself, to enable us to "put on the new man, which is being renewed in knowledge after the image of him that created him" (Col. 3:10). But this renewal comes about only by grace. The presence of those with severe cognitive disabilities within the church challenges us to acknowledge that just as the protological *imago Dei* comes about by God's condescending grace, so too the renewed eschatological *imago* is not of works, accomplishments, or abilities, lest any man should boast. It is the gift of God's grace. If in the course of the process of renewal, the state of our bodies (including our brains) allows for the profound theological insights of a Luther, or a Calvin, or an Edwards, then thanks be to God. But those gifts are the *outworking* of the image being renewed, not the substance of, or the criteria for the renewed image. Those whose intellects allow for profound insight into the revelation of God must say in the words of Peter *mutatis mutandis* those who are severely cognitively impaired, "We believe that we are saved through the grace of the Lord Jesus, in the same way as they also are" (Acts 15:11).

Those who bear the "very bad" of severe cognitive disabilities are nonetheless the image and likeness of God. Some of them are members of the church, visibly numbered among the redeemed and being restored in the image of their Creator. Their—*our* outer man may be wasting away, but their—*our* inner man is being renewed day by day (2 Cor. 4:16). Not of "them," but of *us* together it is said, "Beloved, now we are the children of God, and it has not yet appeared what we shall be; but we know that when he appears we shall be like him, for we will behold him just as he is" (1 John 3:2). He "will transform our lowly body to be like his glorious body, by the power that enables him also to subject all things to himself" (Phil. 3:21). And "just as we have borne the image of the man of dust," with all of its unrealized potential, and inestimable disabilities of body and soul due to sin's entrance into the world, "we shall also bear the image of the man of heaven" (1 Cor. 15:49).

5

Implications and Practical Applications

Throughout church history those with severe cognitive disabilities have largely been excluded from the contextual paradigm upon which *imago Dei* models have been predicated. The approaches to the *imago* doctrine have varied widely, from models of an actual or reified substance in man, to the functional tasks given to mankind by God and their concomitant abilities, to the intricacies of interpersonal relationships.

The analysis of the views of modern Protestant clergy in the U.S. (Appendix 3) suggests that many reflect these historical understandings of the *imago Dei*. In the sample as a whole the substantive understanding of the image of God was the plurality view, followed by the functional and then the relational views. The pattern held for most of the sample by ecclesiastical tradition and by level of theological education. Regarding the intellect, only one respondent explicitly indicated that the image of God is seen in "making visible the communicable attributes of the invisible God . . . irrespective of . . . disabilities (mental and physical)." A number of the respondents reflected the view of Basil that the image of God is in no way associated with the body and instead is found in the powers of reason. Nearly half (45%) of the respondents explicitly stated or strongly implied that the image of God was co-substantial with human intellect.

Implications and Practical Applications

To the extent that approaches to the *imago* doctrine have been criteria-based they have had the *de facto* effect of excluding those with the most severe cognitive disability from a theoretical participation in the *imago Dei*. As Reinders has indicated, few Christians would in fact exclude such people, but their inclusion is of necessity by way of special exception or anomaly. Anomalies, however, never really reside in the subject of consideration; they are always in the theories and models set forth to explain the subject. This book has sought to establish a different *imago Dei* model, a model which, while not myopically focused on those with severe cognitive disabilities, includes and takes account of such people.

It has been argued here that the image of God is not something *inside* of people, nor is it constituted by a set of criteria (substantive, functional, or relational) that differentiates people from animals or angels. The image of God is simply what God created human beings as and to be. Because man-the-image-of-God is predicated upon the creative purpose and action of God, human beings, regardless of how broken in body or soul, cannot be anything other than *imago Dei*.

At a basic level, this idea runs counter to our classical atomistic understanding not only of human beings, but of the world in which we live. We feel an affinity to analyses that we can reduce, quantify and sum. Living organisms are comprised of organs, which are in turn comprised of cells, which are in turn comprised of organic chemical compounds, which are in turn comprised of atoms. Materialistically speaking, living organisms can be understood as being constituted by their atomic, molecular, and biochemical make-up. But does a materialist approach really tell us anything about human beings, particularly the *worth* of human beings?

Using the going rate for chemicals, the company DataGenetics has calculated that the worth of the human body is about $160.[1] Given the materialistic assumptions of people like Peter Singer and

---

[1] DataGenetics, "What is Your Body Worth?" http://www.datagenetics.com/blog/april12011/ (accessed on September 28, 2013).

Steven Pinker, perhaps this is why they and those who share their presuppositions ascribe such little value to human beings, particularly to "defective" human beings.

But the value of people cannot be determined by the going rate of the chemicals of which they are made up, any more than an image of a duck, exquisitely crafted by a master wood carver, can reasonably be thought to be worth only the price of the wood it is carved from.

Human beings are the image of God regardless of their abilities or lack of them. All human beings are broken in some way. Whatever abilities they retain, the image is not predicated upon these abilities. Rather, all human ability is based upon an ontological antecedent: human beings are made as the image of God. Their worth and value is predicated upon this fact alone, and because of it their worth is inestimable.

If the argument set forth here is compelling, it begs the question, "What are we to do with it?" As noted in Chapter Four, all sound Christian theology is practical, and the way to God's blessing is through becoming effectual doers and not merely forgetful hearers (James 1:25). This final chapter will set forth suggestions for seminary professors, pastors, and parishes to put into action this reconsideration of the *imago Dei* in the light of those with severe cognitive disabilities.

A Word to Seminary Professors

Those who teach at theological seminaries are the well-spring of the ideas that will inform and shape the thought of the rising generations of pastors. Sometimes, however, the demands of an academic career may limit real-life experience in the pulpit and pastoral office. This is not to intimate that seminary professors are not involved in their local churches or denominations, nor that they are "mere academics." But in some cases seminary professors have little pastoral ministry experience and may not have had to face some of the very hard practical questions and issues that are the stock and trade of those who daily and over decades shepherd a portion of Christ's flock.

My understanding of the *imago Dei* as I entered the ministry was shaped by my seminary training. As I look back over syllabi and lecture notes from two decades ago it is evident to me that the *imago* doctrine as taught to me traced the lines of a criteria-based substantivism, functionalism, and relationalism. The responses of the sample of modern Protestant clergy detailed in Appendix 3 suggest that my theological educational experience was not unique. It was not until God sent my daughter into my life that I felt the inadequacy of what I had been taught and the need for an *imago* theology that included people like Rebecca, rather than admitting her as an anomaly.

Unlike most pastors, seminary professors have the privilege of engaging in the theological endeavor. Pastors are much like physicians, the majority of which do not engage in medical research but are busy applying the standard and accepted fruit of medical research. Pastors are often so busy applying accepted soul medicine that they themselves do not have time for original theological research and reflection. Whether this is good or bad, it is a fact.

Theological reflection always has a contextual referent. For many theology professors, the contextual referent is by default the rarified intellectual setting of the theological seminary. Since pastors learn their *imago* theology largely from their seminary professors, is it any wonder so large a number of respondents expressed an *imago* theology that tends toward an intellectual substantivism?

A broadened context for thinking theologically about the *imago Dei* would be very helpful to the church. My exhortation to seminary professors who teach the doctrine of the image of God is simply this: if the church you are a part of does not have within its membership (*de jure* or *de facto*) those with severe cognitive disabilities, become involved with a l'Arche community or a group home near you. You may do something as spiritual as taking up the duties of a chaplain, or as "earthy" as helping out with repairs or doing the dishes, but get to know people with severe intellectual disabilities enough that they become a part of your theoretical paradigm and are thus included in your theological reflection. This will produce more accurate theological models, which will in turn serve the church better in preparing those who will shepherd flocks which will (or should) by all indications include a growing number of those with severe cognitive disabilities.

A Word to Pastors

Modern pastors in the United States live and minister in a complex setting. Diverse issues from mass public shootings at places of worship to child molestation occupy at least some of the thought of every modern pastor. On top of this (or integral to it) pastors are tasked with the care of souls and the proclamation of a gospel which, if set forth accurately, makes them the savor of life to some people and the stench of death to others who will not be shy to let their pastors and others know about what they perceive to be their foul odor. Who is sufficient for these things? (2 Cor. 2:16).

Certainly it would be unreasonable to expect pastors to reconsider their theology in the light of those with severe cognitive disabilities and single-handedly start new ministries to such people. Pastors, however, will be the visionaries for the congregations they shepherd, and those congregations will take their attitudinal cues from them.

There are people in every community, and perhaps even people who were once a part of a congregation, who have a family member with intellectual disabilities and who do not now attend church because they do not believe they will be welcomed there. Pastors can begin to change this situation by thinking intentionally about such families. Through blogs and other internet resources pastors can begin to understand the challenges of those who have family members touched by severe cognitive disability.

As pastors have opportunity to meet such families it is important to refrain from the "theological candy" of repeating such

Implications and Practical Applications

clichés as "God doesn't make mistakes" (in such a way as to intimate that there is nothing "wrong"), or "Your child is just different." This is the approach of much of the Disabilities Rights Movement, and while it may bring some temporary sweetness to the hearts of parents who hear such platitudes, in their heart of hearts they know that something is *wrong*. Candied clichés will not and cannot nourish the hurting soul.

The Bibles that pastors have on their desks tell of a great and good God who because of his greatness and goodness created man as his own image and likeness. That likeness and image is the foundation of human abilities that were given to bring glory to God and good to mankind and the world in which he was placed. Moreover, that image and likeness held out a promise of hope for an even more God-like future.

The Scriptures tell of a God who because of his greatness and goodness pronounced a curse upon mankind and his environment commensurate with man's rebellion; a curse that results ultimately in death, and includes all the harbingers of death such as heart disease, cancer, and cognitive disability, harbingers which remind us that life in a state of being separated from God is not merely a "not good," but a positive "very bad."

Yet for all of mankind's fallenness, and for all of the effects of both moral and surd evil, people do not cease to be the image of God. Contrary to the assertions of people as diverse as Luther, Hitler, and Singer, human beings, no matter how touched by the fall, never become "animal life," "masses of flesh without a soul," "life unworthy of life," or "people unworthy of the status of personhood." Things like these are said because of an acceptance (consciously or otherwise) of a criteria-based hierarchy of value.

The value of such people in society and in the church is suspect when such a hierarchy is assumed, because people with severe cognitive disabilities seem to be superfluous and noncontributing members who take more than they give. Such thinking comes from a hyper-protagorian ethos that would proclaim "*I* am the measure of all things." But when they measure themselves by themselves and compare themselves with themselves, they are without understanding (cf. 2 Cor. 10:12). The goal is not that everyone should be like the "normal people," but that they all together should attain to the measure of the stature of the fullness of Christ (Eph. 4:13), a stature which will become a reality for all of the people of God, however severe the effects of the fall they bear now.

Pastors cannot and should not single-handedly try to shoulder the work that properly is the task of the whole body. But the body will seldom take up any task for which the pastor has not provided vision. Pastors are the bridge between theological knowledge and the faithful practice that is to be carried out by parishes as a whole.

A Word to Parishes

In the spring of 2013 *Leadership Journal* conducted an interview with Jim Martin, Vice President of Church Mobilization for the International Justice Mission. Although he was not addressing the topic considered here, Martin's words are apropos: "It's a natural human tendency to insulate ourselves from risk and suffering. We crave security. But in some ways, we are creating a life for ourselves where we don't need any faith. In the Old Testament, when people repeatedly tried to set up their lives in a way that didn't require faith, this always made God angry. Many of us are in situations that require very little risk of us. The problem is, if we are risk-averse, we will become faith-poor."[2]

If a congregation does not now have in attendance people with severe cognitive disabilities, the thought of welcoming such people can be daunting. "What should I do? How should I behave around them?" Even if people with severe cognitive disabilities attend, the discomfort can be palpable if the congregation has not

---

[2] Jim Martin, "Just Church: An Interview with Jim Martin," *Leadership Journal* (Spring 2013): 17.

been instructed. Not long ago I visited a church in New England which had open space in their sanctuary sufficient to accommodate wheelchairs. On that particular Sunday I noted that caregivers had brought five or six people, the majority in wheel chairs, who had evident cognitive disabilities. I was delighted to see that no one seemed in the least put off because these people were there; but I was disheartened when after the service not a single person greeted them or their care-givers. They were allowed to be there, but not welcomed to be there.

Should all churches have a "cognitive disabilities ministry?" Some very large churches that I know of do indeed have such ministries which provide much appreciated respite to parents of children with intellectual disabilities. But must a church reach a certain size before it can include and minister to those with cognitive disabilities and their families? Is a church of one hundred people precluded from or absolved of the moral responsibility of engaging in such ministry?

While I do not question the benefit or validity of large churches that have such ministries specifically for those with severe cognitive disabilities, there can be an attending danger with such programs. It is possible for a church to create a "cognitive disabilities leper colony" to which people with such disabilities are shunted off and isolated, rather than including them in the life of the church.

I would argue that *any* and *every* congregation can and should be a place to *potentially* welcome and embrace families which include members who have severe cognitive disabilities. The hypothetical nature of the statement is due to the fact that some church architecture may not be able to accommodate the specific needs of all such people, particularly if the structure was built prior to the 1990s. It would be unreasonable to expect (and in many cases impossible for) a congregation of one hundred to make the modifications that may be necessary in a particular instance; nor would a congregation be able to anticipate all of the modifications which may be needed in every possible case.

Implications and Practical Applications

Is it possible for a church that presently does not have anyone among its congregation with severe cognitive disabilities to prepare for the reception of such people? Kenneth Campbell has noted, "Faith communities that only deal with those impacted by disability on an *ad hoc* basis admit they do not know many people with disabling conditions."[3] Yet Campbell's statement is focused on those with *physical* disabilities. While it is possible to plan for accessibility for those with physical handicaps, anticipating the needs for those with cognitive handicaps is much more difficult.

When considering a ministry that is inclusive of those with severe cognitive disabilities, a parish must be proactive in its attitude, but of necessity must be reactive to the real and particular instances that it encounters. It would simply be impossible for most churches to proactively put in place all that could be necessary for those with cognitive disabilities due to the varied complexity of such disabilities.

Consider, for example, Autism Spectrum Disorder (ASD), the diagnosis of which requires two criteria: 1) Social communication and interaction difficulty manifested in problems associated with reciprocating social or emotional interaction, severe problems in maintaining relationships, and inability to appropriately exhibit or understand non-verbal communication cues; and 2) restricted and repetitive behavior, to include at least two of the four: stereotyped or repetitive speech, excessive adherence to routines and resistance to change, highly restricted interests that are abnormally intense or focused, and hyper or hypo reaction to sensory input.[4]

Such a description for diagnosis does not convey anything about the people who have such a diagnosis, nor the level of severity

---

[3] Kenneth J. Campbell, "That My House May be Full: Implementing a Church Ministry With People Impacted by Disabilities" (D.Min. Thesis, Gordon-Conwell Theological Seminary, 2010), 71.

[4] Susan L. Hyman, "New DSM-5 Includes Changes to Autism Criteria," *American Academy of Pediatrics News* (June 4, 2013), http://aapnews.aappublications.org/content/early/2013/06/04/aapnews.20130604-1 (accessed September 28, 2013).

of the impairment, nor their ability to actively participate, nor what adjustments if any may need to be made. To say "Robert has autism" tells us very little about Robert, and, until we meet him, we little know how to include him in the ministry of the church.

Two boys who are members of the same local church both have an ASD diagnosis. At age ten, one boy (who was diagnosed by age three) is able to participate in Sunday school, Vacation Bible School, and children's choir with a designated "shadow" to help him follow directions and cope with unexpected changes. Without such a "shadow" this boy would be unable to cope with the social interactions that take place at the church. The other boy, who was not diagnosed until he was fifteen, grew up in the church, participating in all of its activities, and although he has had some social difficulty that at times has caused friction with his peers, no extraordinary intervention took place or was needed. Yet both boys are diagnosed as being on the Autism spectrum.

Because of the variation in actual conditions of those with cognitive disabilities diagnoses, it is simply not possible in the abstract to establish a "ministry to autistic people," nor to those with Down syndrome, or to any condition that qualifies as a cognitive disability. Nor should the church try to do so. "The church must be careful in making any modification to cultic activities when considering persons impacted by disabilities.... Such an approach begins with the assumption that the person impacted by a disability is a stranger rather than a friend."[5]

Rather than a ministry *to* such people, the church should foster within itself an attitude of ministry *with* such people, that is, a ministry which is inclusive of such people. This will certainly include ministry to such people, just as all members of the body need ministering to (cf. 1 Cor. 12:25–26). As much as possible, however, those with cognitive disabilities should be included in the overall life of the church.

[5] Campbell, 74.

Implications and Practical Applications

It is important to understand that people with cognitive disabilities (or any disability) may not be able to participate in everything that takes place. If a church youth group has planned a retreat that includes a team-building ropes course, obviously someone in a wheelchair would not be able to participate in the ropes segment of the retreat.

While we must be careful not to become "worshipers of our worshipful atmosphere,"[6] a cognitively disabled worshiper who becomes disruptive for an extended period of time may need to be removed from the service. However, it is important that it be conveyed by word and especially (re)action that it is perfectly acceptable to leave the sanctuary with a disruptive child (or adult) in the middle of worship.

Churches in the U.S. have a tendency toward triumphalism, a tendency displayed and underscored by nearly every televised broadcast of Sunday services. Cameras pan and zoom in a way to convey a picture of sanctuaries full of impeccably dressed "normal" people. It is a picture many, if not most churches, would want to present. But does it match Paul's description of the church in the first letter to the Corinthians?

> God has chosen the foolish things of the world to shame the wise, and God has chosen the weak things of the world to shame the things which are strong, and the base things of the world, and the despised. God has chosen the things that are not, that He might nullify the things that are, that no man should boast before God. But by His doing you are in Christ Jesus, who became to us wisdom from God, and righteousness and sanctification, and redemption, that, just as it is written, "Let him who boasts, boast in the Lord." (1Cor 1:27–31 NASB)

---

[6] See Scott Brown, "Children Destroy Worshipful Atmospheres," http://hopebaptistchurch.info/wp-content/uploads/2013/01/Brown-Children-Destroy-Worshipful-Atmospheres.pdf (accessed on October 3, 2013).

The fact is that the church needs those with severe cognitive disabilities. They remind us that we live in a world that is fallen, something that we try very hard to forget and hide. As Jean Vanier has noted, they remind us that the goal in life is not always to "be productive," but sometimes it is just to "be together." It is not enough for the church to tolerate such people in their midst. The church must welcome such people, for they are, according to the Scriptures, indispensable:

> Just as a body, though one, has many parts, but all its many parts form one body, so it is with Christ. For we were all baptized by one Spirit so as to form one body—whether Jews or Gentiles, slave or free—and we were all given the one Spirit to drink. Even so the body is not made up of one part but of many. Now if the foot should say, "Because I am not a hand, I do not belong to the body," it would not for that reason stop being part of the body. And if the ear should say, "Because I am not an eye, I do not belong to the body," it would not for that reason stop being part of the body. If the whole body were an eye, where would the sense of hearing be? If the whole body were an ear, where would the sense of smell be? But in fact God has placed the parts in the body, every one of them, just as he wanted them to be. If they were all one part, where would the body be? As it is, there are many parts, but one body. The eye cannot say to the hand, "I don't need you!" And the head cannot say to the feet, "I don't need you!" On the contrary, those parts of the body that seem to be weaker are indispensable, and the parts that we think are less honorable we treat with special honor. And the parts that are unpresentable are treated with special modesty, while our presentable parts need no special treatment. But God has put the body together, giving greater honor to the parts that lacked it, so that there should be no division in the body, but that its parts should have equal

concern for each other. If one part suffers, every part suffers with it; if one part is honored, every part rejoices with it. Now you are the body of Christ, and each one of you is a part of it (1 Cor. 12:12–27 NIV).

The members that appear to be weaker (ἀσθενής, suffering from a disabling illness, experiencing some incapacity or limitation[7]) are in fact "indispensable." The word (ἀναγκαῖος) means, "necessary, as meeting a need."[8] Although many of his statements have been criticized by more historically orthodox Christians, Leslie Newbigin notes correctly, "The poor, the deprived, the handicapped are not primarily a problem to be solved by the rich, the comfortable, and the strong. They are the bearers of a witness without which the strong are lost in their illusions."[9]

In Paul's letter, those with incapacity, limitation, and disabling illness whom society generally regards as "without honor" (ἄτιμος; unimportant and insignificant at best, despised and dishonored at worst[10]) are to be regarded with profuse, abundant, extraordinary honor (τιμὴ περισσή). Those whom societies which value strength, physical beauty, and intellect would hide away and who would be deemed "inappropriate for public display" (ἀσχήμων) are to be esteemed in the church as being "abundantly appropriate for display" (εὐσχημοσύνη περισσή). Among the members of the church, including those who have incapacity, limitation, and disabling conditions there is to be no division—no schism (σχίσμα).

Such people are necessary members of the body of Christ. They remind us of our own brokenness and weakness, and the fact that the church is not the society of the mighty, but the society of

---

[7] BDAG, 1, 2.

[8] See BDAG 1.

[9] Leslie Newbigin, "Not Whole Without the Handicapped," *Partners in Life, The Handicapped and the Church*, ed. G. Muller-Fahrenholz (Geneva: World Council of Churches, 1979), 25.

[10] BDAG 1, 2.

damaged sinners who are being redeemed. Partakers of Christ all, we are "new creation" (2 Cor. 5:17), and yet we are in progress, being transformed, for none of us has yet become what we shall be. Those with severe cognitive disabilities were not long ago referred to as "retarded," slowed. In the church the term is not inaccurate. They are, as it were, still *in utero*, not yet born from the groaning creation (Rom. 8:22). They remind us that we too are still *in utero*, still waiting to be born, waiting for the redemption of our bodies, our adoption as sons (Rom. 8:23).

All of humanity, every single person, is the image of God. Broken, distorted, and denied as it may be by materialists, humanity is no less the *imago Dei*. And it was into *this* creation, broken and distorted due to mankind's sin, that the Son of God came, and by his incarnation he became *the* image of God.

He was not recognized as such. "He had no form or majesty that we should look at him, and no beauty that we should desire him. He was despised and rejected by men; a man of sorrows, and acquainted with grief; and as one from whom men hide their faces he was despised, and we esteemed him not" (Isa. 53:2–3 ESV). "Vivid imagery is provided ... in the suffering servant figure who is without beauty, disfigured, and mutilated. ... [The] incarnation replaces the triumphant, impregnable, and all powerful God image with a vulnerable, suffering God image characterized by persons in marginalized conditions: 'This fellow welcomes sinners and eats with them.'"[11]

Christ has entered into our condition and suffering, and thus those who suffer and are his are participants in his sufferings. The hope that Christ brings in our suffering, however, is no misery-loves-company consolation. The resurrection of Jesus is the hope for the healing of all maladies of body and soul, and the banishment of all evil, surd and moral. The sufferings of this present time are

---

[11] John Foster Doud, "Church Accessibility for Person with Disabilities: A Religious Imperative" (D.Min. Thesis, McCormick Theological Seminary, 1993), 18–19.

not worthy to be compared with the glory that will be revealed in us (Rom. 8:18). The church that would truly welcome those with severe cognitive disabilities must have and hold out this hope, and not resign itself to accepting that the "very bad" of severe cognitive disability is normal and "just different," a "view which might not hold much solace for the parents of a profoundly retarded child."[12]

A church that would be truly welcoming to those with severe cognitive disabilities must hold out the hope of the gospel. It must be a church that prays for one another's healing now, and reminds one another that healing of disabilities in the eschaton is a certainty for all the members of Christ's body. The lives of all people are a declension from the normal, from what we were created to be and to become. The pattern for the change that the church eagerly hopes for and confidently awaits is the resurrected Christ himself. "We will all be changed" (1 Cor. 15:5), "conformed to the image of his Son" (Rom. 8:29); specifically the resurrected and glorified Son so that "just as we have borne the image of the dusty man, so we shall bear the image of the man from heaven" (1 Cor. 15:49).

As the race is run, it must be run according to the rules, for "No one competing as an athlete receives the victor's crown unless he competes according to the rules" (2 Tim. 2:5). The rules of the race remind us that we run as a body, and not as individual limbs. The story told by Vanier of the young man with Down syndrome who had trained intensely to win the hundred-meter race and was winning, only to go back and help a fallen fellow-competitor limp across the finish line dead last shows the true nature of winning.[13]

If the goal of glorification is being conformed to the image of the glorified Christ, the church in contemplating how it will receive the severely cognitively disabled does well to consider the words of John Murray:

---

[12] Campbell, 76.
[13] Jean Vanier, *Encountering the Other* (Mahwah, NJ: Paulist Press, 2005), 18.

[Glorification] is the complete and final redemption of the whole person when in the integrity of body and spirit the people of God will be conformed to the image of the risen, exalted, and glorified Redeemer, when the very body of their humiliation will be conformed to the body of Christ's glory.... The truth that glorification must wait for the resurrection of the body advises us that glorification is something upon which all the people of God will enter *together* at the same identical point in time. There is no priority for one above the other.... One will not have any advantage over another—all together will be glorified with Christ.... It is as a body that the whole company of the redeemed will be glorified

It is not the vague sentimentality of those whose interest is merely the immortality of the soul. Here we have the concreteness and realism of the Christian hope epitomized in the resurrection to life everlasting and signalized by the descent of Christ from heaven with the voice of the archangel and the trumpet of God.[14]

A myopic preoccupation with "my spiritual growth" is at least in part at the root of impatience and intolerance with those in the church that have severe cognitive disabilities. Such a myopic preoccupation, however, is completely at odds with a sound understanding of the Scriptures, and what constitutes real spiritual growth. There are no redeemed, justified, holy individuals apart from the redeemed, justified, holy community. The apocalyptic vision that the apostle John had of the redeemed may be a multitude of individuals, but it is a multitude nonetheless (Rev. 7). The very definition of the church (ἐκκλησία) is of an assemblage, a gathering, a body made up of many parts.[15]

---

[14] John Murray, *Redemption Accomplished and Applied* (Grand Rapids, MI: Eerdmans, 1955), 175–80.
[15] See BDAG 1, 2, 3. cf. 1 Cor. 12:20.

Implications and Practical Applications

The teaching of the New Testament is that every member of the church is given gifts (Eph. 4:4–16) which come from the Holy Spirit and are given to be used for the common good of the church (1 Cor. 12:4–8). These gifts are divided into the two sub-categories of speaking and serving gifts: "Whoever speaks, as the utterances of God; whoever serves, as by the strength which God supplies; so that in all things God may be glorified through Jesus Christ" (1 Peter 4:11).

Into which category fit the gifts of those with cognitive disabilities? The immediate response may be that their gifts would naturally tend toward those of serving, and this may be so when considering people who have high functioning forms of trisomy 21 (Down) or ASD, but what of people like Oliver de Vinck and Kelly? Not being ambulatory nor able to follow instruction, they are unable serve.

I would argue that their gift may well fall under the speaking rubric. This may seem a strange suggestion since they are non-verbal as well as non-ambulatory. But if it is true that "the heavens declare the glory of God; the skies proclaim the work of his hands; day after day they pour forth speech; night after night they reveal knowledge; they have no speech, they use no words; no sound is heard from them, yet their voice goes out into all the earth, their words to the ends of the world" (Ps. 19:1–4), may it not be that such people, made as the image of God and providentially brought into the life of the church also declare the glory of God? If the inanimate creation pours forth speech without words or sound, is it not feasible that those who are constituted living images of the living God may do the same without speech, words, or sound?

People with severe cognitive disabilities display to us Christ in the disabling weakness of his crucifixion and death. They witness to us that while our disabilities may differ, we all bear the effects of the fall, surd and moral. In showing abundant honor to the least of these (Matt. 25:34–40), we show abundant honor to Christ.

If the Creed is taken seriously as the church confesses "We look for the resurrection of the dead and the life of the world to come," people with severe cognitive disabilities witness to us yet more. People of dust will put on immortality and will be changed (cf. 1 Cor. 15:53–54). Mankind as *imago Dei* may be marred and broken, but the *imago* cannot be obliterated because the *imago* is not something *in* them or added *to* them. It simply *is* them.

For all who are in Christ, the *imago Dei* will be restored as all the redeemed are conformed to the image of Christ; the image of Christ, not in his humiliation, disabled, dysmorphic, and weakened by scourging, crucifixion, and death. The redeemed will be conformed to the image of Christ in his exaltation, in his permanent transfiguration, in his glorification. "Beloved, now we are children of God, and it has not appeared as yet what we shall be; we know that when he appears we shall be like him, for we shall behold him just as he is" (1 John 3:2).

United to Christ, redeemed humanity is now for a little while lower than the angels, as Christ himself was made for a little while lower than the angels (see Heb. 2:5–14). As Christ in his humanity is now exalted above the angels (cf. Heb. 1), so his redeemed people united to him are to judge angels (cf. 1 Cor. 6:3; Heb. 2:6–11).

It is not merely out of kind-hearted mercy that the church is called to esteem with special honor those who would be deemed unpresentable, those who society (inexplicably) tolerates and may even care for once they are here, but encourages the abortion of if their disabling condition is discovered *in utero*. Those whom the world casts off, whom it regards as insignificant, unimportant, and unnecessary will, if they are redeemed by Christ, one day judge angels (cf. 1 Cor. 6:3). Many who are now regarded as least and last will be esteemed as first (cf. Matt. 20:16). A church that gains such a vision will not view a ministry that includes those with severe cognitive disabilities as remarkable. It will view such a ministry as complete, normal, and essential.

Epilogue

"Come here, Rebecca."

She was oblivious to my voice. She was lost, deep in thought. In her right hand was a book which she was looking at intently.

"Come here, Rebecca."

She turned toward me and smiled. She reached for my face and kissed me. She looked different than when she was a child. The large spaces between her teeth and the facial dysmorphisms of the condition she was born with were gone.

We walked along in the warmth, holding hands. The sun shone brightly, but the light that enveloped us did not come from it. And we talked. To hear her voice brought the satisfaction of a joy that only derives from a long-awaited outcome at the end of a lengthy and hard road.

I wake up. It is not an unusual night.

I strain to remember what her voice sounded like, but it's gone. I cannot recall it. But the dream gives me hope, a hope that the busyness of life does not often afford me time to reflect on in my waking hours. It is a hope based upon the Christ, upon his gospel, and upon the Scriptures.

When I look at Rebecca, I see past the disabilities, past the dysmorphisms. My daughter does not bear the image of God. She is the image of God, as am I. Her brokenness now reminds me that I am broken. It has not yet appeared what we shall be.

I can only love Rebecca, and I do not do that as well as I should. I cannot do anything to change her, to stop her seizures, to eliminate the frustration she so evidently feels at times. The pain of my

Epilogue

impotence has faded now into acceptance. But it is an acceptance of my impotence, not an acceptance of her condition.

My helplessness in being able to make her better reminds me of my helplessness to make myself better. Rebecca has preached to me, but not with words. My Augustinianism was for so many years merely theoretical. In my heart of hearts I was an arrogant Pelagian. I know better now how hopelessly broken I am apart from God's grace, a grace which I cannot conjure, command, or appropriate, yet a grace that God so freely and undeservedly gives.

I reflect on my dreams and anticipate that they will never become a reality. My vision is too small. God will do beyond what I could ask or imagine; no eye has seen nor ear has heard, nor, I suspect, has any mind dreamed the things he has prepared for those who love him. I know only that I will be saved through the grace of the Lord Jesus in the same way that Rebecca will be.

I can hardly conceive what it will be like to be wholly conformed to the image of the risen and glorified Christ. I can hardly conceive of what it will be like for my daughter to be wholly conformed to his image as well.

Sometimes when we are out people will momentarily stare at Rebecca and then look away. I don't blame them. She is abnormal even in this abnormal world. What are they thinking? Do they feel embarrassed for her? I cannot say.

But perhaps in the regeneration of all things, when heaven and earth occupy the same space and time, angels will stop and stare at Rebecca and then avert their eyes in embarrassment of themselves; and in reverent wonder will worship the God who, having created her as his own image, who made her for a little while lower than the angels, who suffered the rebellion of mankind and then entered into mankind's suffering; who rose not only from the grave, but far above the heavens, has by his grace conformed Rebecca to the fullness of his image, and has at the last crowned her with an honor and glory that far surpasses theirs.

Appendix 1

Survey

1. Which of these best describes your position in the church?

- ○ Pastor
- ○ Senior Pastor
- ○ Executive Pastor
- ○ Associate/Assistant Pastor
- ○ Youth Pastor
- ○ Evangelist
- ○ Staff specialist (e.g., missions, discipleship, family, etc.)

2. Which TRADITION (not necessarily denomination) best describes you?

- ○ Anglican/Episcopal
- ○ Baptist
- ○ Evangelical
- ○ Lutheran
- ○ Pentecostal
- ○ Presbyterian/Reformed
- ○ Non-denominational/inter-denominational
- ○ Wesleyan
- ○ Other

3. In what state do you minister? _____

Appendix 1

4. What is your highest level of theological education and earned theological degree?

- O No formal theological education
- O Bachelor's degree in ministry, Bible, theology, etc.
- O Master of Theological Studies (MTS)
- O Master of Arts (MA, MAR, MRE, etc.)
- O Master of Divinity (M.Div.)
- O Master of Theology (Th.M. or STM)
- O Doctoral degree (Ph.D., Th.D., D.Min.)

5. At which school or seminary did you receive your primary formal theological education (leave blank if no formal theological education)?

_____

6. What year did you graduate from that institution (leave blank if no formal theological education)? _____

7. Would you please write a paragraph (as brief or detailed as you would like up to 300 characters) on what it means for man to be made in the image of God? _____

_____
_____
_____
_____

8. This survey is anonymous except for the location (state) that you have provided. May I have your permission to quote from your paragraph in my thesis? Please note that the purpose of this study is not to evaluate "right" or "wrong" answers, but to explore how ministers in the U.S. understand the biblical concept of the image of God.

- O Yes
- O No

Appendix 2

Raw Data

RESP. NUM.	POSITION	TRADITION	STATE	EDU.	PRIMARY THEO. ED.	GRAD YEAR	IMAGO CATEGORY	INTELLECT
1	Pastor	Baptist	NC	Dr	Christian Bible College	2005	Functional	Explicit
2	Pastor	Wesleyan	KS	None			Physical	Implicit
3	Senior Pastor	Baptist	TX	MDiv	Southwestern Baptist Theological Seminary	1996	Substantive	Explicit
4	Senior Pastor	Baptist	FL	Dr	New Orleans Baptist Theological Seminary	1989	Physical	No mention
5	Pastor	Baptist	GA	MDiv	New Orleans Baptist Theological Seminary	1954	Substantive	Explicit
6	Pastor	Wesleyan	TX	MDiv	Brite Divinity School	2010	Substantive	Explicit
7	Pastor	Presbyterian/Reformed	NY	BA	Aberystwyth Theological College	1984	Substantive	No mention
8	Pastor	Presbyterian/Reformed	WI	MDiv	Fuller Theological Seminary	2000	Relational	No mention
9	Senior Pastor	Baptist	KY	Dr	New Orleans Baptist Theological Seminary	1976	Functional	No mention
10	Senior Pastor	Pentecostal	OR	None			Substantive	No mention
11	Pastor	Wesleyan	NJ	MDiv	Methodist Theological School	1981	Christological	No mention
12	Pastor	Wesleyan	RI	MDiv	Brite Divinity School	1989	Substantive	No mention
13	Associate/Assistant Pastor	Other	SD	MDiv	Sioux Falls Seminary	2013	Representative	Explicit

APPENDIX 2

RESP. NUM.	POSITION	TRADITION	STATE	EDU.	PRIMARY THEO. ED.	GRAD YEAR	IMAGO CATEGORY	INTELLECT
14	Pastor	Other	ID	MA	Andrews University	1980	Functional	Implicit
15	Pastor	Baptist	IL	MA	Maranatha Bible College	1999	Functional	Explicit
16	Senior Pastor	Baptist	AL	MDiv	New Orleans Baptist Theological Seminary	2002	Substantive	No mention
17	Senior Pastor	Baptist	CA	None			Functional	Implicit
18	Pastor	Baptist	MO	None			Functional	Implicit
19	Pastor	Wesleyan	OH	MDiv	Ashland Theological Seminary	2012	Substantive	Explicit
20	Pastor	Anglican	WA	Dr	Princeton Theological Seminary	1983	Substantive	No mention
21	Associate/Assistant Pastor	Non-denom	OR	MA	Pugett Sound Christian College	1976	Substantive	No mention
22	Pastor	Presbyterian/Reformed	TX	None			Substantive	No mention
23	Pastor	Evangelical	MO	MA	Multnomah Biblical Seminary	1992	Substantive	No mention
24	Senior Pastor	Evangelical	MN	MDiv	Crown College	1973	Substantive	Explicit
25	Pastor	Presbyterian/Reformed	OR	MDiv	San Francisco Theological Seminary	1997	Substantive	Explicit
26	Pastor	Baptist	OK	None			Substantive	No mention
27	Pastor	Wesleyan	MO	MDiv	St. Paul School of Theology	1990	Functional	Implicit
28	Pastor	Wesleyan	IA	MDiv	University of Dubuque Theological Seminary	1990	Representative	Implicit
29	Senior Pastor	Non-denom	NJ	MA	Abilene Christian University	1978	Representative	No mention
30	Pastor	Presbyterian/Reformed	VA	Dr	Union Theological Seminary, VA	1981	Representative	Implicit
31	Pastor	Wesleyan	PA	MDiv	Asbury Seminary	2001	Functional	Implicit
32	Pastor	Other	WI	MDiv	Eden Theological Seminary	1993	Relational	Implicit
33	Pastor	Wesleyan	RI	MDiv	Boston University School of Theology	2003	Functional	Implicit
34	Senior Pastor	Evangelical	KS	MDiv	The Iliff School of Theology	1972	Christological	No mention
35	Pastor	Baptist	OH	Dr	Golden Gate Seminary	2013	Substantive	No mention

Appendix 2

RESP. NUM.	POSITION	TRADITION	STATE	EDU.	PRIMARY THEO. ED.	GRAD YEAR	IMAGO CATEGORY	INTELLECT
36	Senior Pastor	Other	OH	MDiv	United Theological Seminary	1975	Relational	No mention
37	Senior Pastor	Pentecostal	AL	BA	Southeastern University	1991	Ontological	No mention
38	Pastor	Lutheran	KS	MDiv	Concordia Seminary	1979	Relational	Implicit
39	Pastor	Wesleyan	MN	MDiv	Duke Divinity School	2001	Relational	No mention
40	Pastor	Other	PA	MTS	Alliance Theological Seminary	2006	Substantive	Explicit
41	Senior Pastor	Baptist	TX	None			Relational	No mention
42	Pastor	Lutheran	ND	MDiv	Concordia Seminary	1987	Representative	No mention
43	Senior Pastor	Baptist	AL	MA	Southwestern Baptist Theological Seminary	1993	Functional	Explicit
44	Senior Pastor	Evangelical	MN	Dr	Trinity International University	2012	Substantive	Explicit
45	Pastor	Presbyterian/ Reformed	DC	MDiv	Union Theological Seminary, NY	1982	Substantive	No mention
46	Pastor	Lutheran	IA	MDiv	Wartburg Theological Seminary	1988	Functional	Implicit
47	Pastor	Evangelical	NY	MDiv	Princeton Theological Seminary	2012	Redemptive	No mention
48	Executive Pastor	Baptist	MN	MA	Wheaton College	2007	Christological	No mention
49	Senior Pastor	Other	CT	MDiv	Andover Newton Theological School	1976	Functional	Implicit
50	Senior Pastor	Wesleyan	OH	MDiv	Asbury Seminary	1997	Functional	Implicit
51	Pastor	Presbyterian/ Reformed	MI	Dr	Princeton Theological Seminary	1995	Substantive	No mention
52	Pastor	Other	ME	MDiv	Yale Divinity School	1975	Functional	Implicit
53	Senior Pastor	Presbyterian/ Reformed	IL	Dr	McCormick Theological Seminary	1965	Functional	Implicit
54	Pastor	Baptist	AL	MDiv	New Orleans Baptist Theological Seminary	1991	Substantive	No mention
55	Senior Pastor	Lutheran	OR	Dr	Lutheran Theological Southern Seminary	1987	Substantive	Implicit
56	Senior Pastor	Baptist	TX	MDiv	Southwestern Baptist Theological Seminary	2002	Functional	Implicit

Appendix 2

RESP. NUM.	POSITION	TRADITION	STATE	EDU.	PRIMARY THEO. ED.	GRAD YEAR	IMAGO CATEGORY	INTELLECT
57	Senior Pastor	Evangelical	CA	MDiv	Trinity Evangelical Divinity School	1998	Representative	No mention
58	Staff Specialist	Presbyterian/ Reformed	OR	MDiv	Western Seminary	2009	Representative	Denied
59	Pastor	Presbyterian/ Reformed	OH	MDiv	Andover Newton Theological School	1984	Relational	No mention
60	Staff Specialist	Anglican	WA	MDiv	Loyola University	2012	Substantive	No mention
61	Associate/ Assistant Pastor	Presbyterian/ Reformed	AZ	MDiv	Fuller Theological Seminary	2006	Functional	No mention
62	Senior Pastor	Presbyterian/ Reformed	WA	Dr	Trinity Evangelical Divinity School	2001	Substantive	No mention
63	Pastor	Baptist	TX	Dr	Hardin-Simmons University	1966	Substantive	No mention
64	Pastor	Wesleyan	DE	MDiv	Gordon-Conwell Theological Seminary	1971	Ontological	No mention
65	Pastor	Other	IN	MDiv	Erlham School of Religion	1984	Ontological	Implicit
66	Pastor	Presbyterian/ Reformed	NY	MDiv	Union Theological Seminary/VA	1999	Substantive	No mention
67	Senior Pastor	Presbyterian/ Reformed	OH	MDiv	Princeton Theological Seminary	1974	Functional	Implicit
68	Pastor	Wesleyan	KS	MA	St. Paul School of Theology	2005	Substantive	No mention
69	Pastor	Non-denom	MA	None			Functional	Explicit
70	Senior Pastor	Wesleyan	MI	MDiv	Candler School of Theology	1987	Relational	No mention
71	Senior Pastor	Lutheran	WI	MDiv	Concordia Seminary	1973	Substantive	No mention
72	Associate/ Assistant Pastor	Baptist	NC	MA	Southwestern Baptist Theological Seminary	1998	Substantive	No mention
73	Senior Pastor	Evangelical	GA	MDiv	Southern Baptist Theological Seminary	1966	Redemptive	Implicit
74	Senior Pastor	Presbyterian/ Reformed	WA	MDiv	Austin Presbyterian Theological Seminary	1995	Relational	No mention
75	Pastor	Baptist	AL	MDiv	Beeson Divinity School	1996	Relational	No mention
76	Pastor	Other	MN	MDiv	Claremont School of Theology	2003	Relational	No mention

Appendix 2

RESP. NUM.	POSITION	TRADITION	STATE	EDU.	PRIMARY THEO. ED.	GRAD YEAR	IMAGO CATEGORY	INTELLECT
77	Associate/Assistant Pastor	Presbyterian/Reformed	OH	MDiv	Louisville Presbyterian Theological Seminary	1997	Relational	No mention
78	Senior Pastor	Baptist	OH	BA	Liberty University	2011	Representative	Explicit
79	Senior Pastor	Baptist	LA	Dr	New Orleans Baptist Theological Seminary	1993	Relational	Explicit
80	Evangelist	Other	MN				Substantive	No mention
81	Pastor	Other	VA	BA	Bethany Thelogical Seminary		Redemptive	Implicit
82	Youth Pastor	Evangelical	CO	MDiv	Southern Baptist Theological Seminary	2010	Representative	No mention
83	Senior Pastor	Evangelical	CO	MDiv	Master's Seminary	1994	Representative	No mention
84	Executive Pastor	Non-denom	OR	MA	Multnomah University	1986	Substantive	No mention
85	Senior Pastor	Presbyterian/Reformed	AZ	Dr	Princeton Theological Seminary	1990	Substantive	No mention
86	Senior Pastor	Baptist	IN	Dr	Northeastern Baptist Theological Seminary	1989	Relational	Implicit
87	Pastor	Lutheran	MT	MDiv	Trinity Seminary, OH	1968	Ontological	No mention
88	Senior Pastor	Non-denom	GA	BA	Atlantic Christian College	1976	Functional	Implicit
89	Pastor	Baptist	KY	Dr	Southern Baptist Theological Seminary	1996	Relational	No mention
90	Pastor	Wesleyan	VA	Dr	Northwest Christian University	1991	Substantive	No mention
91	Pastor	Wesleyan	CO	None			Substantive	Implicit
92	Pastor	Anglican	WA	MDiv	Church Divinity School of the Pacific	2002	Relational	Explicit
93	Associate/Assistant Pastor	Non-denom	TX	BA	Columbia International University	2008	Representative	No mention
94	Pastor	Lutheran	TX	Dr	Trinity Seminary	1979	Functional	No mention
95	Pastor	Wesleyan	OH	None	Ashland Theological Seminary		Substantive	Explicit

Appendix 3

Survey Analysis

In order to better understand how Protestant ministers in the United States understand the doctrine of the *imago Dei*, the author conducted a study between June 22 and July 6, 2013 which looked specifically at the understanding of pastors working in a church context, rather than seminary professors or other academics, due to the fact that pastors generally have a wider audience than do professors, and thus the potential to more directly and broadly shape ideas and attitudes.

The study investigated three questions: 1) is there a monolithic or diverse understanding of the *imago* doctrine among Protestant ministers? 2) Is there any discernible pattern with regard to ministers' understanding of the *imago* doctrine based on theological tradition or level of theological education? 3) Does the understanding of the *imago Dei* on the part of all or any of the ministers surveyed show any tendency toward being inclusive of or exclusive of those with cognitive disabilities?

Survey Methodology

A survey was designed using Survey Monkey, a link to which was sent to a random sample of Protestant clergy serving in churches in various pastoral capacities in the United States. The survey collected basic demographic information regarding position in the church, theological tradition, state in which the respondents

Appendix 3

minister, level of theological education, institution of primary theological education, and year of graduation from that institution. Each respondent was then asked to write a paragraph, as brief or detailed as each desired, about what it means for man to be made in the image of God.

A list of contacts for emailing the link to the survey was purchased from Williams Direct,[1] a company that specializes in providing daily-updated lists of churches to vendors and others for the purpose of marketing and sales. The Williams Direct lists are "opt in" lists, that is, they are comprised of addresses of those who have confirmed their willingness to be contacted by vendors.

The obtained list was a randomly generated list of 2,000 church email addresses filtered for Protestant traditions. Excluded were addresses for Roman Catholic, Eastern Orthodox, Mormon, and Jewish clergy. In total, 1190 emails were sent, randomized from the provided (and already randomized) list. The subsequent randomization was done by first sorting the provided list by email address in order to avoid nominal, geographic, or denominational skewing. Emails were then sent in batches on June 22 and 24, 2013 using the following sequencing: Emails were sent to the first 250 on the list, the next 250 were skipped; sent to the next 150 on the list, skip the next 150; sent to the next 100 on the list, skip the next 100; sent to the next 50 on the list, skip the next 50; sent to the next 250 on the list, skip the next 250; sent to the next 150 on the list, skip the next 150; sent to the next 100 on the list.

Of this original mailing of 1,050, 110 emails were returned as undeliverable, leaving a total of 940 delivered emails. In order to achieve a number of delivered emails of at least 1,000, an additional 140 emails were sent on June 29, 2013, randomized in the following manner: the middle 50 of the first 250 skipped on the list; the middle 40 of the first 150 skipped on the list; the middle 30 of

---

[1] Williams Direct, Lawrence, KS, http://churchladies.com/default.aspx (accessed July 8, 2013).

Appendix 3

the first 100 skipped on the list; the middle 20 of the first 50 skipped on the list. Of these additional 140 emails sent, 8 were returned as undeliverable. In total, 1,072 emails were successfully delivered inviting recipients to participate in the survey.

Of the 1,072 delivered emails asking recipients to take the survey, 97 surveys were returned between June 22 and July 6, 2013. Two of the surveys were discarded because the participants appeared to provide a narrative answer to a different question than the one that was asked, leaving a total of 95 usable surveys.

Demographics of the Sample

Location

The 95 respondents were from a diversity of geographical locations, indicating an absence of skewing with regard to location. The sample represented 35 states and the District of Columbia. States not represented were Alaska, Arkansas, Hawaii, Maryland, Mississippi, Nebraska, Nevada, New Hampshire, New Mexico, South Carolina, Tennessee, Utah, Vermont, West Virginia, and Wyoming.

Ohio had the greatest representation (9), followed by Texas (8), Oregon (7), Minnesota (6), Alabama and Washington (5 each), and Kansas (4). Colorado, Georgia Missouri, New York, Virginia and Wisconsin each had three (3) respondents. Arizona, California, Iowa, Illinois, Indiana, Kentucky, Michigan, North Carolina, New Jersey, and Pennsylvania each had two (2) respondents. Connecticut, Delaware, Florida, Idaho, Louisiana, Massachusetts, Maine, Montana, North Dakota, Oklahoma, Rhode Island, and South Dakota each had one (1) respondent.

Among the states that had the greatest representation there was still a diversity of ecclesiastical traditions represented. For example, of Ohio's nine (9) respondents, two (2) indicated Baptist, three (3) indicated Wesleyan, three (3) indicated Presbyterian/Reformed, and one (1) indicated Other.

Appendix 3

Ecclesiastical Tradition

The largest tradition indicated was Baptist (23), followed by Presbyterian/Reformed (17), Wesleyan (17), Evangelical (9), Lutheran (7), Non-denominational or inter-denominational (6), Anglican/Episcopal (3), and Pentecostal (2). A total of 11 respondents indicated Other for theological tradition (see fig. 1).

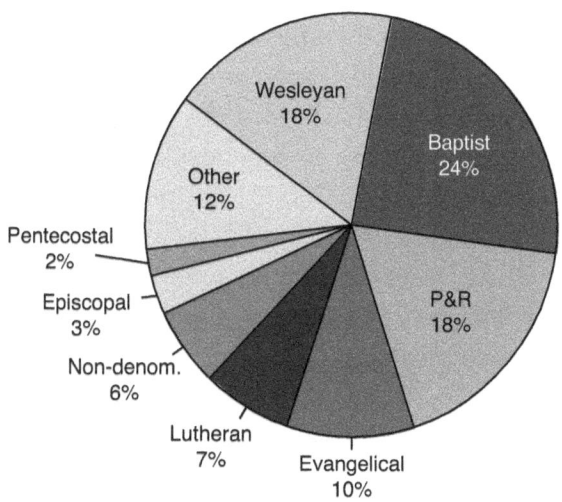

Fig. 1: Ecclesiastical Tradition

Institutions of Primary Theological Education

A diversity of institutions for respondents' primary theological education was also in evidence. Of the 86 respondents that had formal theological education, a total of 62 institutions were indicated from a variety of confessional traditions, and across the spectrum of more liberal to more conservative. The modal number for those attending a particular theological institution was 1 (49). The institution represented by the greatest number of graduates was New Orleans Baptist Theological Seminary (6), followed by Princeton Theological Seminary (5), Southwestern Baptist Theological Seminary (4), and Concordia Theological Seminary (3). Andover Newton Theological School, Asbury Theological

Appendix 3

Seminary, Ashland Theological Seminary, Brite School of Theology, Fuller Theological Seminary, St. Paul School of Theology, Trinity Evangelical Divinity School, Trinity Theological Seminary, and Union Theological Seminary (VA) were each represented by 2 respondents. There was no skewing in the overall responses due to theological institution of primary education.

Decade of Completion of Primary Theological Education

Respondents indicated a range of years for completion of their primary theological education from 1954 to 2013. The decade that produced the largest number of respondents to this survey was the 1990s (23), followed by the 2000s (18), the 1980s (16), and the 1970s (14). The 1950s, 1960s, and 2010s were represented in the single digits. There was broad diversification of theological tradition and educational institution across these decades, indicating a lack of bias with regard to theological education or tradition in any decade of graduation (see fig. 2).

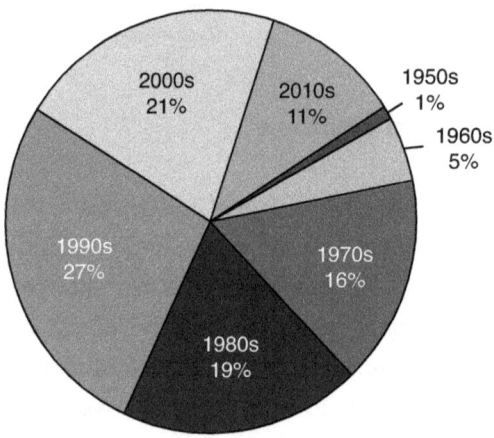

Fig. 2: Decade of Completion of Primary Theological Education

Position in the Church

With regard to position in the church, 51 (the largest number of respondents and more than half) indicated they served as Pastors;

Appendix 3

32 indicated that they served as Senior Pastors; 6 indicated that they served as Associate/Assistant Pastors; 2 each indicated that they served as Staff Specialists and Executive Pastors, and 1 each served as Youth Pastor and Evangelist. It was noted that there was a diversity of tradition, theological education, and location of the 83 serving as Pastors or Senior Pastors. Since those serving in these capacities are likely to preach regularly, their understanding of any given doctrine is likely to have significant influence over the congregations they serve (see fig. 3).

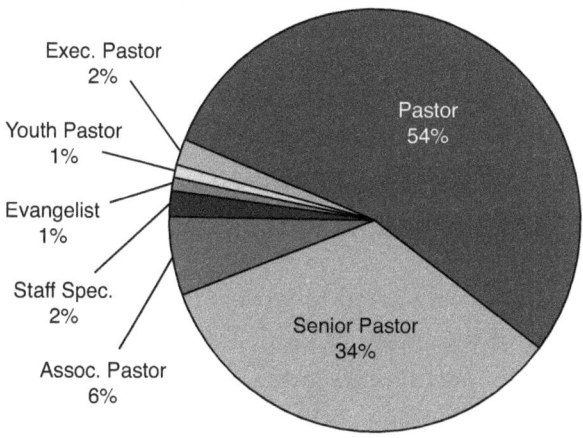

Fig. 3: Position in the Church

Level of Education

The largest number of respondents (49) indicated that they had an M.Div. degree; 18 indicated that they had an earned theological doctoral degree; 10 indicated that they had a theological master's degree (e.g., M.A., M.A.R, etc.); 1 indicated an M.T.S.; 6 indicated that they had a theological bachelor's degree; and 8 indicated that they had no formal theological education. No respondent indicated a Th.M. as their highest level of theological education (see fig. 4). Respondents' level of education was similarly distributed over location and tradition.

APPENDIX 3

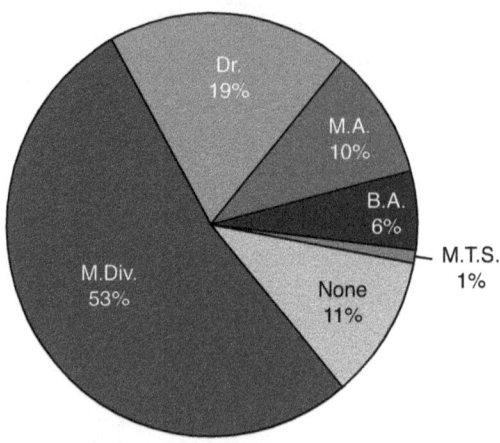

Fig. 4: Level of Theological Education

Analysis of Respondents' Understanding of the Image of God

Respondents were asked to write a paragraph regarding their understanding of the image of God. The original intention was to divide the essays into the categories of the substantive, functional, or relational understandings of the image of God. However, upon examination it became evident that although many of the essays fit neatly into these categories, a number of them did not, and additional categories were needed.

The essays were read multiple times, and descriptive criteria were developed which led to the formation of eight categories. Each essay was then read and placed in one of the categories, then read again several days later to verify that each was categorized the same both times. This led to the following criteria and categorizations:

1. Substantive: Respondents were placed in this category if language was used which indicated that the image of God was a constituent part or component of or within human beings (e.g., the soul, the intellect, emotions, etc.).

Appendix 3

2. Functional: Respondents were placed in this category if language was used which indicated that the image of God was to be identified with things human beings actively do, such as exercise dominion, create, till the ground, etc.
3. Relational: Respondents were placed in this category if language was used which indicated that the image of God was to be found in the relationships that human beings have with God, with one another, with the rest of creation, or with any combination of the three.
4. Ontological: Respondents were placed in this category if language was used which indicated that the image of God was without reference to constituent parts, was not specified as functional or relational, and if it was in some way indicated that the image of God is simply what human beings are.
5. Representative: Respondents were placed in this category if the language used specified that mankind was God's representation to the rest of creation passively or without specification as to whether that representation is passive or active (responses that indicated activity were placed in the functional category).
6. Physical: Respondents were placed in this category if the image of God was viewed solely or primarily in terms of human beings' bodily existence.
7. Redemptive: Respondents were placed in this category if the image of God was understood as something that only Christians are, possess, or reflect.
8. Christological: Respondents were placed in this category if the image of God was understood primarily in terms of human beings conforming to the incarnate Son of God before and after the fall of mankind.

In addition to the above categories, the responses were arranged into four groups: 1) Those responses which made no mention of intellect with regard to the image of God, 2) those responses which

Appendix 3

explicitly indicated in some way that intellect is necessary to the image of God, 3) those responses which strongly implied that intellect is constitutive of, or integral to the image of God, and 4) those responses which specifically denied that intellect (i.e., a certain level) was necessary to the image of God.

Results

Overall, 37% of all respondents' essays indicated a substantive understanding of the image of God. Those indicating a functional understanding made up 22%. A relational understanding was indicated by 17%. The representative view accounted for 12%. An ontological understanding accounted for 4%, the christological and redemptive understandings were represented by 3% each, and a physical understanding accounted for 2% (see fig. 5).

Similar responses were found in each sub-group. Among Baptists, 36% indicated a substantive understanding, 30% a functional understanding, and 22% a relational understanding. The representative, christological, and physical understandings were represented by 4% each. None of the Baptists in the sample indicated an ontological or redemptive understanding of the image of God (see fig. 6).

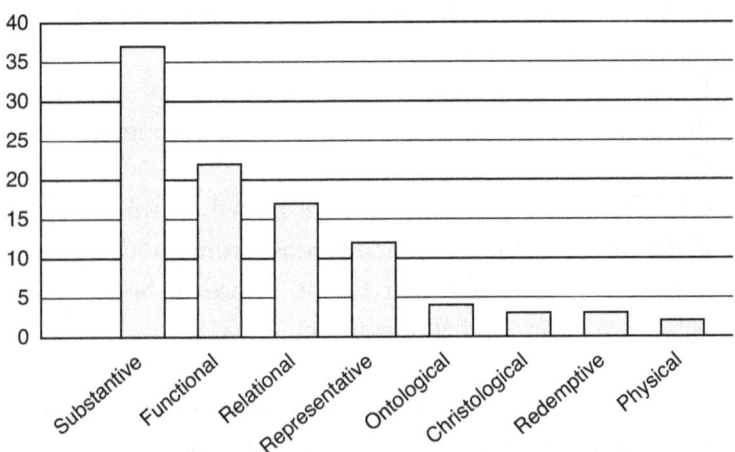

Fig. 5: Entire Sample Understanding of *Imago* by Percentage

APPENDIX 3

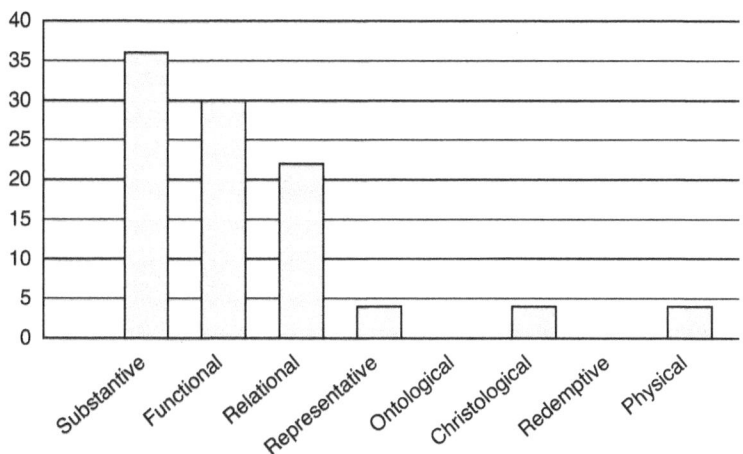

Fig. 6: Baptist Understanding of *Imago* by Percentage

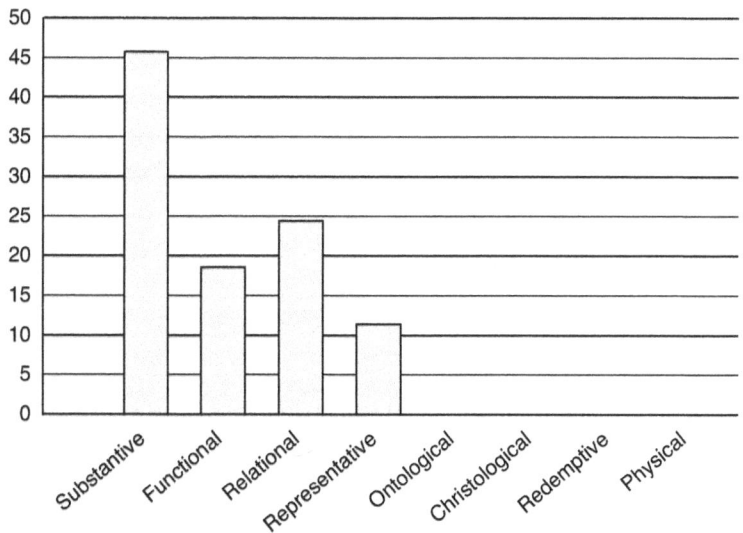

Fig. 7: Presbyterian Understanding of *Imago* by Percentage

APPENDIX 3

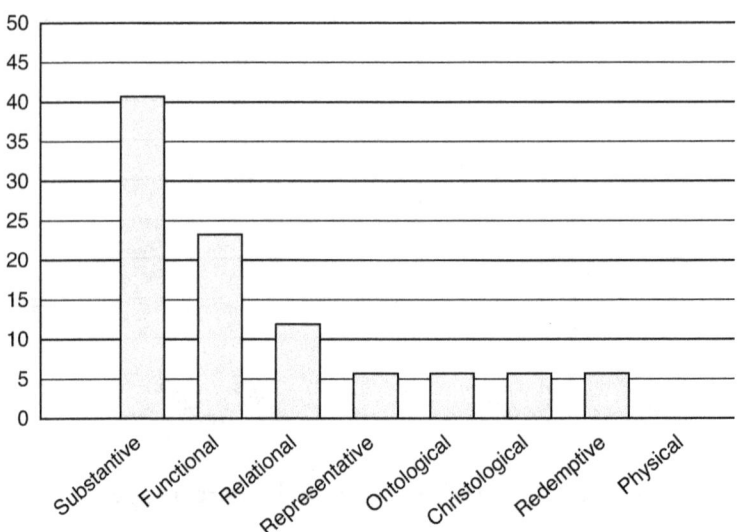

Fig. 8: Wesleyan Understanding of *Imago* by Percentage

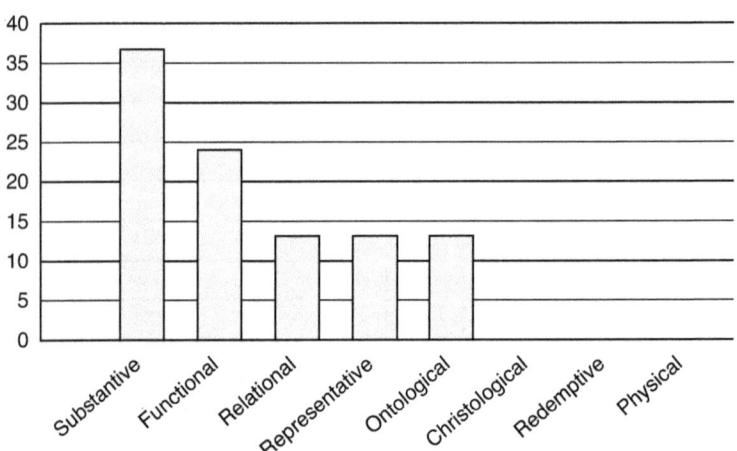

Fig. 9: Lutheran Understanding of *Imago* by Percentage

Appendix 3

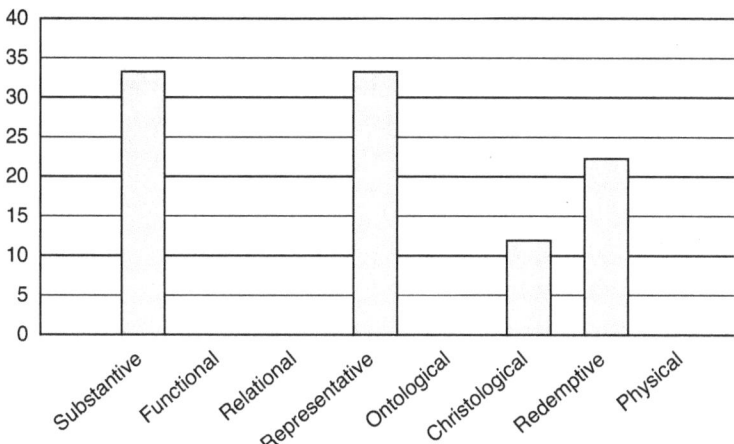

Fig. 10: Evangelical Understanding of *Imago* by Percentage

The majority of those indicating they belonged to a Presbyterian/Reformed tradition also indicated conceptions of the *imago Dei* that were weighted toward the categories of substantive, functional, and relational. The substantive understanding of the image of God accounted for 46%. The relational view was represented by 23%, the functional view by 18%, and the representative view by 12%. The christological, ontological, physical, redemptive, and relational views of the *imago Dei* had no representation among this segment of the sample (see fig. 7).

Likewise among those indicating a Wesleyan tradition, 41% indicated a substantive understanding; 24% indicated a functional understanding; and 12% indicated a relational understanding. The christological, ontological, physical and representative understandings represented 6% each. A redemptive understanding was not represented in this group (see fig. 8).

The pattern was also evident among those from a Lutheran tradition: 37% had a substantive view of the image of God, 24% had a functional understanding, and 13% had a relational understanding. The representative and ontological views each also got 13% representation by the group. The christological, physical, and redemptive

Appendix 3

views were not represented as a primary understanding of the *imago Dei* by this segment the sample (see fig. 9).

Evangelicals deviated somewhat from the pattern. Although 33% expressed a substantive understanding of the image of God, an equal number expressed a representative view. A redemptive understanding accounted for 22%, and a christological understanding for 12%. The functional, relational, physical and ontological views were not represented (see fig. 10).

Although those indicating their tradition as Other were used for calculating data for the group as a whole, the potential diversity of traditions represented within that set militated against calculating them as a stand-alone group. For the Anglican/Episcopal and the Pentecostal groups, the respective samples were too small to draw any conclusions about them, and they were not calculated.

With regard to the effect of level of education on the understanding of the *imago Dei*: the pattern held with those who indicated that they had no formal theological education. A substantive understanding was held by 50%, a functional by 30%, and a relational by 10%. Ten percent of the sample group also indicated a physical understanding. The christological, ontological, redemptive, and representative views were not indicated (see fig. 11).

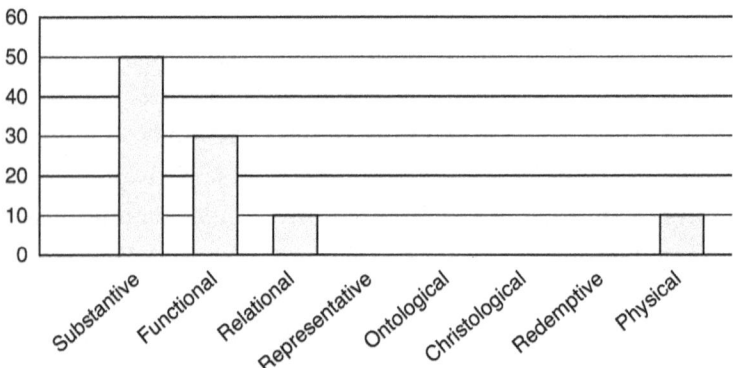

Fig. 11: Understanding of *Imago* by Those with no Formal Theological Education by Percentage

Appendix 3

Among those with Master's degrees in some theological discipline (other than M.T.S or M.Div.), 50% indicated a substantive understanding of the image of God, 30% a functional understanding, 10% a representative understanding, and 10% a christological understanding. The relational view was not in evidence, nor were the ontological, physical, or redemptive views (see fig. 12).

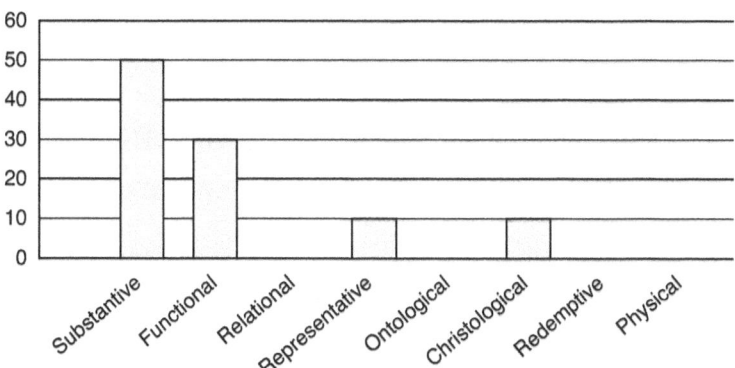

Fig. 12: Understanding of *Imago* by Those with Master's Degrees (MA, MAR, MRE, etc) by Percentage

Of those who held a Master of Divinity degree as their highest level of theological education, 27% had a substantive understanding of the image of God, 24% a relational understanding, and 20% a functional understanding. A representative view was held by 15%, an ontological view by 6%, and the christological and redemptive views by 4% each. A physical understanding was not in evidence (see fig. 13).

Among those with an earned doctorate in some theological discipline, 49% had a substantive view of the image of God, 22% a functional view, and 17% a relational view. The physical and representative views accounted for 6% each. The christological, ontological, and redemptive views were not in evidence (see fig. 14).

Those indicating that they had Bachelor's degrees in biblical studies or theology and the single M.T.S. were not calculated due to small sample size.

Appendix 3

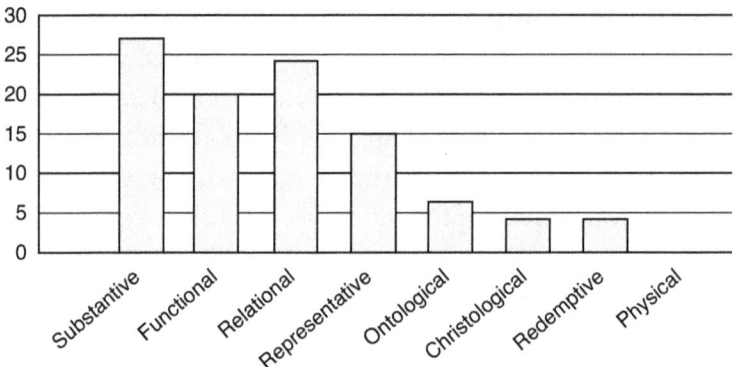

Fig. 13: Understanding of *Imago* by Those with M.Div. by Percentage

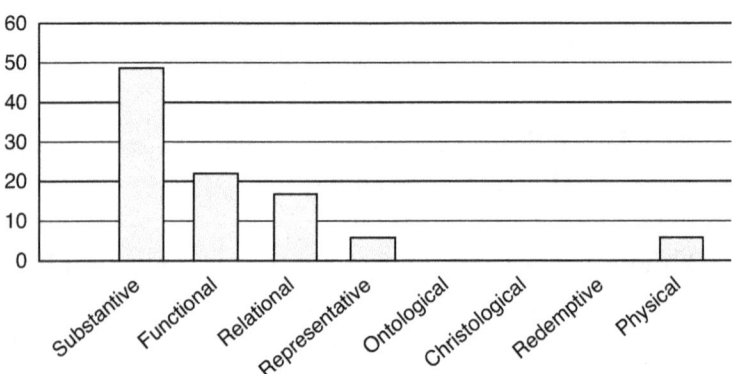

Fig. 14: Understanding of *Imago* by Those with Theological Doctorates by Percentage

With regard to those who understood intellect as being in some way constitutive of the image of God, the greatest number of the overall sample (54%) gave no indication of a connection; 27% were judged to have made an implicit connection; and 18% made an explicit connection of the intellect to the image of God. Only one respondent (1%) specifically made a point of denying that the image of God was associated with a certain level of intellect (see fig. 15).

Appendix 3

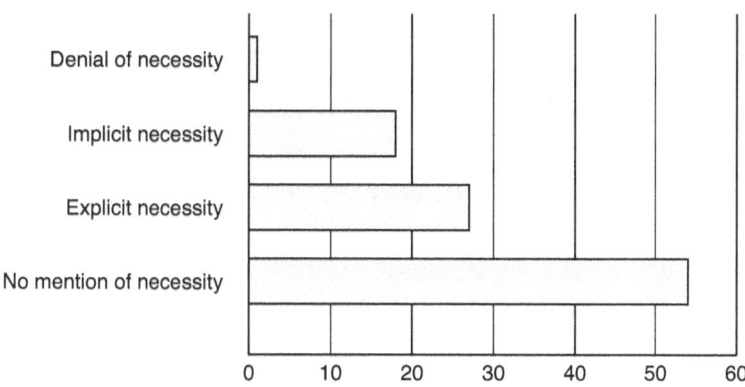

Fig. 15: Percentage of Responses Indicating the Necessity of Intellect as Constitutive of the Image of God

Among the traditions that had adequately sized samples, Baptists had the largest percentage of respondents that understood the image of God in terms that were explicitly intellectual (30%), followed by Evangelicals (22%), Wesleyans (18%), and Presbyterian/Reformed (6%).

Selection of Respondents' Narratives

The respondents' paragraphs delineating their understanding of the image of God were read and classified by the aforementioned criteria in order to stratify the responses into groups. While several of these responses were classic exemplars of a particular theory of the *imago Dei*, some of them were more difficult to classify because they indicated the influence of more than one understanding. Some of the essays were particularly detailed, insightful, and thought provoking.

Substantive Understanding

Many of the narrative answers expressed a classic substantive understanding of the *imago Dei*. "There is in us that which reflects the very nature and being of God," a statement which indicates that the image is something within human beings. Some answers specified that the image of God was to be found in those qualities which make

Appendix 3

human beings differ from the animals: "Man has attributes not found in animals, such as knowledge and intellect, feeling of guilt, remembrance, love, planning for future, etc." "In the creation narrative, it is this eternal soul that sets us apart from the other animals that were created." "We bear this image ... in our unique qualities as human beings."

A number of respondents showed an Augustinian influence in which the imago was understood not only substantively, but in terms of imago trinitatis reflected in the three attributes (alluded to often by synonyms) of mind, will, and emotion. One respondent explicitly mentioned a reflection of the Persons of the Trinity.

> The image of God is best viewed in the Great Commandment and in light of the Trinity. The greatest commandment is to love God with all your heart, soul, mind, and strength. The Trinity represents this makeup. The Heart—God is Love, the Mind—Jesus the divine Logos, and the Spirit—soul, together makes up the Godhead and is the source of all the Godhead's strength. Unlike the Trinity, because of sin, we as humans are not unified. Thus salvation and the call to be unified in love towards God in heart, mind, soul and strength is a call to be transformed into the image of Christ who is the very likeness and image of God.

Several respondents who held the substantive view explicitly denied that the *imago Dei* was to be associated with the body. "... The image has nothing to do with the physical, but has to do with the spirit ..." "... My *imago Dei* is in no way physical ..." "To me 'the image of God' is not to be taken in a literal, visible form—God is a spirit ..." "Being made in God's image does not refer to the physical structure of our bodies or our gender. Rather, it refers to the soul, the eternal part of our being that will live forever, either with Christ in heaven, or apart from Christ in hell ..."

Several respondents who indicated a substantive understanding of the *imago Dei* believed the image of God to be in some way lost in fallen man. "When sin entered man the image we were created in was distorted.... We were no longer capable of reflecting the image of God." One respondent indicated that to be made in the image of God was to be without sin. To the question of what it means for man to be made in the image of God, (s)he wrote "Adam was made without sin like God."

A few respondents whose answers were categorized as being primarily substantive gave full, thoughtful answers and could have been multiply categorized. One such respondent noted, "...It probably means that there is in us infinitely more possibility than we can imagine...." Another responded:

> Genesis 1:26 states: "Then God said, 'Let us make mankind in our image, in our likeness...'" (NIV) Everything about mankind that is uniquely human—conscience, reasoning, language, desire to know God, emotions, knowledge of right and wrong, spiritual character as expressed in the Fruit of the Spirit—are all reflections of God's image in a person's life. It is not evident in every life because the curse of sin has warped, blurred, and often obscured the image of God in a person's life. The spiritual rebirth of that person by the death and resurrection of Jesus Christ through the Holy Spirit marks a defining change in the person's life. The image of God begins to be reflected more clearly and more fully as the Holy Spirit takes control and aligns the person's character with the image of God already within. The evidence of the work of the Holy Spirit in a believer's life is the Fruit of the Spirit blossoming in their character and the clear reflection of God's image in their life.

Functional Understanding

The second largest grouping showed a functional understanding of the image of God. The primary criterion for recognizing this category was language indicating abilities, activities, or specific functions to be constitutive of the image of God.

Appendix 3

One respondent's answer displayed a text-book functionalism: "The image of God is tied to mankind's calling and purpose for being created, which is to '... rule over the fish of the sea and the birds of the air and over every living creature that moves on the ground' Gen. 1:27. The image of God therefore is those qualities that allow humankind to reflect God's sovereign rule specifically over the earth as God rules all things...."

Not all paragraphs categorized as functional tracked so closely with the Genesis text. One respondent indicated that the *imago Dei* was to be found in humankind's ability to love God and his fellow man: "To have the capacity to dedicate mind, soul and spirit to the service of God.... His image can be translated into our ability to reflect his love for fellow man...."

One very intriguing paragraph was categorized in the functional category, but was multifaceted in its allusions and included relational and representative aspects:

> Luke 2:52 tells how Jesus grew intellectually (wisdom), physically (stature), spiritually (favor with God), and socially (favor with man). I think this verse reveals much about how we are made in the image of God. Like God we are volitional beings able to make intelligent, rational decisions; we are able to reason and make wise or right choices, displaying the image of God. Certainly God is Spirit, so physically we [are] not able to draw such a direct correlation but even our bodies are an illustration of the Godhead. The submissiveness of the body to the head is a continual picture of the submission of the Son to the Father. I do believe that the special design of man, as it is so different from animals, is God's best choice to display His own glory. Spiritually we are in His likeness morally. Man was created in righteousness and perfect innocence, a reflection of God's holiness. Sin disfigured the perfect reflection but God provided the sacrifice that would begin our restoration back to righteousness and true

holiness (Eph. 4:24). Only man is capable of knowing God and having a spiritual relationship with Him through prayer, meditation on His word, and worship. Then socially, God created man to have fellowship; fellowship with Him and with one another. Adam initially had communion with God and then God gave him the gift of Eve to love. Though sin led them to be removed from the garden, the two of them continued to enjoy fellowship with God and each other as we do today. Again sin has marred the image, but we know the day is coming, when he shall appear, we shall be like him; for we shall see him as he is.

Relational Understanding

The third most represented category was made up of those whose understanding of the image of God was relational. One respondent showed the clear influence of Barth on his concept of the image: "... God exists to live in loving, righteous community first within the Trinity and then with his creation. For us to be made in his image means that we are called to live in righteous, loving relationship with God and with each other . . . ." One respondent, reflecting on passages from the Book of Common Prayer, wrote, "... When I've taught about this [the image of God], I share how because our Triune God is a God of relationship, that we are created to be in relationship—with God, one another and all of creation ..."

Other Categories

While the remainder of the categories were not greatly represented, some of the paragraph answers were interesting. Although several of those taking the survey specifically denied man's physical frame as in any way being a part of the image of God, two featured the somatic aspect of the image of God prominently. "Physically God made us based on God's own image, thus we are children of God. We are unlike any other living being that God Created . . ." "The Hebrew word for image means 'to carve.' We were carved into the shape of God. This puts man in a more lofty position that anything else God created..."

Although none of the answers spoke in direct ontological terms ("man *is* the image of God"), those which were placed in this category indicated that man is simply like God in characteristic ways: "'We are made in God's image' to me means we share in some of God's characteristics..." "It means to share the same basic personality traits such as mercy, compassion, sense of justice and the others that we most readily identify as existing in God." In the same way that personality traits (attributes) do not constitute the divine nature but are co-substantial with it, these answers seemed to indicate that human traits (attributes) do not constitute the *imago Dei* but are con-substantial with the image of God.

The Image of God and Intellect

A number of respondents made an explicit connection between the image of God and intellect. "... God created us male and female a humanity that is marked by—diversity, creativity, intellect, compassion, and capacity for beauty, mercy, and expression and embodiment of love to be a blessing like God is a blessing in relation to all creation." "We are stamped with God's likeness upon each of us, male and female. We have intellect, emotions, and a will just as our Creator God does..."

Referring specifically to what constitutes the image of God, one respondent wrote, "To spread the Gospel message to a lost and dying world requires man to be able to think and reason about abstract information and transfer this to a tangible, realistic conclusion." Another wrote, "*Imago Dei* means that we are given freedom, rationality, and volition, as no other member of the animal kingdom was given. We can reason...." Still another saw the *imago* in that "We are given the capacity to love, and to reason, and thus make choices freely...." "The *imago Dei*... gives us the gift of reason...." "An animal has instinct, but doesn't reason and relate as man does. We have an eternal composition that is like God so that we relate to

Him . . . ." Another wrote that to be made in the image of God ". . . means that we are free to make choices: to love, to create, to reason, and to live in harmony with creation and with God. . . ."

Only one respondent of the 95 specifically addressed the issue of incapacities and indicated that disability did not diminish the image of God:

> All human beings have been created with the unique capacity, awesome responsibility and privilege of making visible the communicable attributes of the invisible God. This is irrespective of age, gender, and even disabilities (mental and physical). Because all human beings are made in God's image, every human being has intrinsic value and worth. Although the image of God has been fractured by sin, the image is being renewed in those who belong to Jesus Christ by grace through faith. (Gen. 1:26–27; 9:6; James 3:9; Col. 3:9–10)

Conclusions

This study provides an initial investigation and analysis of the understanding of the *imago Dei* doctrine among Protestant ministers in the U.S. In order to determine the statistical significance of these findings and broadly generalize them, one or more similar randomized emailing lists would need to be obtained, a request for the completion of the same survey sent, the paragraph answers categorized by the same criteria, and the results obtained statistically compared with the results of this study. To enable such a study in the future, the questionnaire used for this study, as well as a table of the raw data obtained by this study, is included in Appendixes 1 and 2.

Indicative patterns were revealed in this study which are useful for gaining an understanding of how Protestant ministers in the U.S. comprehend the doctrine of the *imago Dei*. The patterns indicate unambiguous answers to the questions posed at the start of this chapter.

Appendix 3

The results of the study suggest that while there is a diversity of understanding of the *imago Dei* among ministers, there were also clear patterns of influence. Overall and in most traditions, the substantive, functional, and relational understandings of the image of God (most often in that order) together accounted for greater than 75% of the responses. The other five categories of classification were unevenly distributed and represented in small percentages (often single digits).

The sample as an aggregate and each group within it striated by level of theological education and ecclesiastical tradition preponderantly favored a substantive understanding of the *imago Dei*. This is due likely to the fact that the substantive view is the oldest and most prevalent theory of the *imago* doctrine, appearing consistently in the well-known patristic, medieval, and Reformation writers.

The aggregate sample secondarily favored a functional understanding of the image of God. Many of the answers show the influence of more modern writers such as von Rad, Clines, Hall, and Sherlock. This pattern was evidenced in all subgroups filtered by education, with the exception of the M.Div, group, which, while still indicating the same "top three" as the other groups, had a slight preference for the relational understanding over the functional understanding (using language that suggested Barth's influence).

The pattern also was evident in all ecclesiastic traditions, except for those who identified themselves as Evangelicals, none of whom indicated a functional or relational understanding of the image of God. The reasons for this are not clear, but perhaps since Evangelicals tend not to be self-consciously connected to long theological traditions (in comparison to e.g., Lutherans, Anglicans, and Presbyterians), they may be influenced less by the oldest theory of the *imago Dei* (substantive) and more by contemporary writers. Those who indicated a Presbyterian/Reformed tradition showed a preference for the relational understanding over the functional, which is likely due to the influence of Barth, who is from that tradition and has influenced much of the scholarship in that tradition.

Appendix 3

A large percentage (but not the majority) indicated that the *imago Dei* was identified with intellect either explicitly (by mention) or implicitly (by describing activities or relational skills in a way that would require a certain level of intellect). Taken at face value and to its logical conclusions, this might suggest (at least to those who hear statements indicating that intellect is constitutive of the image of God) that participation in the *imago Dei* requires a certain level of intellect, and would thus tend to raise questions about the status of those with cognitive disabilities *vis-à-vis* the image of God. The narrative paragraphs would suggest that when considering the doctrine of the *imago Dei* ministers in the U.S. are inclined to view the doctrine through the lens of typical human beings, rather than through a lens that would be consciously inclusive of those with intellectual disabilities.

The substantive understanding of the *imago Dei* has been historically understood in terms which, if not making intellect the sole identifying characteristic, at least includes it, and many of the paragraph responses categorized as being substantive specifically mentioned intellect or cognitive ability.

The functional understanding, which also had a strong representation, was almost always conceived of in terms that require a certain level of cognition. Exercising dominion, creating, tilling the ground—all of these things would be impossible for people like Oliver de Vinck and Kelly.

While it is not necessary to conceive of the relational understanding in such a way as to require a certain level of intellect (viz. Reinders), in application it most often and most naturally is conceived of in just that way. Barth understood the quintessence of the *imago Dei* to be found in the relationship of husband and wife. Marriage, by definition, requires a certain level of intellectual ability in order to be able to responsibly enter into such a covenant, a level of ability that not all those with cognitive disabilities possess. In addition, friendship is most naturally understood as a "two-way street," a reciprocal relationship which by definition requires a certain minimal level of cognitive ability.

Appendix 3

The patterns revealed by this study are significant. Although categorization of respondents who saw intellect as explicitly or implicitly necessary to the *imago Dei* was approached conservatively, 45% gave answers that indicated such an understanding. The majority of the entire sample and each subgroup understood the *imago* in substantive terms, that is, in terms of some criteria or criterion that establishes the image of God. To the degree that the *imago Dei* is conceived of as consisting in observable criteria, or in paradigms that require intellectual ability, those with the most severe cognitive disabilities may not be understood to participate in the image of God, or may be understood to participate only by way of exception. The results of this study provide impetus for a reconsideration of the doctrine of the *imago Dei* with respect to those who have severe cognitive disabilities.

Appendix 4

Herman Bavinck's Reformed Dogmatics

The literary treatment of the phrase "image of God" or "likeness of God" as it is found in the Scriptures of the Old and New Testaments is out of all proportion to the mere number of passages containing these words or their correlatives. An exhaustive study of the doctrine and interaction with the theological literature would require several volumes. Because the literature review proceeds in chronological order, it was necessary to set a temporal *terminus a quo* for the modern theologians that would be considered here. Owing to the universal impact of his work, in reviewing the systematic and historical theology related to this doctrine, Karl Barth's work was chosen as the temporal starting point in dealing with modern theologians.

Herman Bavinck's *Gereformeerde Dogmatiek* was published several years before Barth's work, and for that reason was not treated in the body of this book. Yet Bavinck has been enormously influential in orthodox Reformed theology, and the more so since his work has been translated into English. He deserves to be treated in this study of the image of God in light of those with severe cognitive disabilities.

This is so, not only because of the extent of his influence in the orthodox Reformed community, but because while not consciously interacting with the theological referent of those who are severely cognitively disabled, Bavinck's careful thinking on the doctrine anticipates a corrective to formulations of the doctrine that are technically exclusive of those with severe cognitive disabilities.

Appendix 4

Bavinck begins his treatment of the doctrine by noting the distinction between human beings and animals. "At God's command the animals were brought forth by the earth (Gen. 1:24); man, however, was created, after divine deliberation, in the image of God, to be master over all things."[1] Following the pattern set by Augustine, he writes "The entire world is a revelation of God, a mirror of his attributes and perfections. . . . But among creatures, only man is the image of God."[2]

However, Bavinck rejects the idea of locating the *imago* in the differences between human beings and animals. He makes no attempt to find the image substantively: "It is not stated that man was created only in terms of some attributes, or in terms of only one person of the divine being [*cf.* Augustine], nor that man bears God's image and likeness only in part, say, only in the soul, or the intellect, or in holiness. The case is rather that the whole human person is the image of the whole Deity."[3] "The whole being, therefore, and not *something in man*, but *man himself* is the image of God."[4] Thus, even "The human body belongs integrally to the image of God."[5] For Bavinck there can be no isolation of certain qualities, attributes, or aspects of human beings in which resides the *imago Dei*. It is rather the human being in his or her totality that is the image of God: "The whole human being is the image and likeness of God, in soul and body, in all human faculties, powers and gifts. Nothing in humanity is excluded from God's image; it stretches as far as our humanity does and constitutes our humanness."[6]

Although Bavinck at times speaks of the image in functional terms, he is careful to speak of it as *evidenced* in the functions, rather

---

[1] Herman Bavinck, *Reformed Dogmatics*, vol. 2, *God and Creation* (Grand Rapids, MI: Baker Academic, 2004), 511.
[2] Ibid., 530–31.
[3] Ibid., 533.
[4] Ibid., 554.
[5] Ibid., 559.
[6] Ibid., 561.

Appendix 4

than *consisting in* the carrying out of these functions. "But Genesis 1:26 clearly indicates that the image of God *manifests itself* in man's dominion over all the created world"[7] [italics added]. Likewise, "the image of God manifests itself in the virtues of knowledge, righteousness, and holiness with which humanity was created from the start."[8] The image does not *consist* in knowledge, righteousness, and holiness but is rather seen *through* these virtues. Presciently anticipating the exegetical work of biblical scholars incorporating Ancient Near Eastern studies a century later, Bavinck states, "In our treatment of the doctrine of the image of God, then, we must high light . . . the idea that a human being does not *bear* or *have* the image of God, but that he or she *is* the image of God."[9]

The fact that for Bavinck the human being is the image of God, and that the image is manifest by certain qualities expressed through behaviors, rather than the image consisting in or being constituted by those qualities or behaviors, would allow for a consideration of the image vis-à-vis those with cognitive disabilities.

For Bavinck, there is an eschatological orientation to the image of God. "The ultimate destiny of humanity . . . was Adam's goal and not yet a given of his creation."[10] "Although Adam was created in God's image, he was not that image immediately in the full sense . . . the first man, however highly placed, did not yet possess the highest humanity."[11] Although he barely develops it, Bavinck's concept of the destiny of man at his creation is seen in his use of the term *mikrotheos* applied to Adam (and by implication to human beings in general).[12]

Treating the fall of mankind, Bavinck draws sharp lines between the Lutheran and Reformed formulations of the doctrine.

---

[7] Ibid., 533.
[8] Ibid., 557.
[9] Ibid., 554.
[10] Ibid., 563.
[11] Ibid., 564.
[12] Ibid., 531.

Appendix 4

He maintains that in the Reformed understanding, Adam's "condition was provisional and temporary, and could not remain as it was. It either had to pass to higher glory, or to sin and death."[13] In his creation, Adam anticipated a more God-like state. Even in his state of innocence, it had not yet appeared what Adam may be.

Bavinck avers that for Lutherans, however, "Adam did not have to become anything; he only had to remain what he was . . . ." Thus after the fall, "the state to which believers in Christ are elevated is essentially equated with that of Adam before the fall."[14] He states, "Lutheran theology does not trouble itself much about human destiny. Adam had everything he needed; he only had to remain as he was. . . . Adam did not have to gain anything higher for his descendants"[15] Bavinck is critical of this view. He says, "if human beings have the image of God [sic] . . . if they lose it they do not become animals. Always and forever they remain human and to that extent are always and forever the image of God."[16] His analysis of the Lutheran understanding of the image of God makes Luther's unsettling statements that those with severe intellectual disabilities are mere "animal life" and "lumps of flesh without souls" predictable.

In reflecting on the Reformed tradition, Bavinck sees the image of God as something essential to man rather than as an addition to an already-complete nature. He distinguishes between the image of God in a narrower sense (which has been lost) and a broader sense (which cannot be lost). The image of God thus can be wrecked, but it cannot in an ultimate sense be annihilated. Adam's state of original righteousness included as a normal (essential) state

---

[13] Ibid., 564.
[14] Ibid., 572.
[15] Ibid., 586.
[16] Ibid., 585. Bavinck uncharacteristically speaks of the image here as a possession. This is not a denial of his clear statements that the human being *is* the image of God rather than *has* the image of God. The undertow of two millennia of theological phrasing is difficult to consistently resist.

Appendix 4

the health of a human being; that without it a human cannot be true, complete, or normal. When man loses that [aspect of the] image of God he does not simply lose a substance while still remaining fully human. Rather, he becomes an abnormal . . . human being. . . . He then lacks something that belonged to his nature, just as a blind man loses his sight, a deaf man his hearing, and a sick man his health.[17]

Although Bavinck never considers those with cognitive disabilities, statements like these allow for an easy inclusion of those with disabilities (including intellectual disability) into the corpus of fallen humanity, and enable those who are able-minded to see the essential solidarity in their fallenness with those who are intellectually disabled.

Finally, Bavinck deals with the eschatological destiny of mankind. As has already been indicated, he saw that in his creation and even before the fall, Adam did not express and reflect the image to the fullest extent for which God had designed humanity. While in man's creation human beings are *mikrotheos*, Bavinck avoids mention of the word *theosis* with regard to man's telos. This is not because he denies that the destiny of human beings in Christ is "a higher state of blessedness than that which prevailed in paradise on earth."[18] Rather, his avoidance of discussing in what exactly this "higher state of blessedness" consists and of the word *theosis* appears to be due to concern over extravagant formulations of the doctrine which taught an absorption into the divine: "In Christological disputes after the fourth century . . . the deity of Christ and of the Spirit was affirmed particularly that they were the author of deification for humans. The essence of the state of glory increasingly came to be . . . deification, a participation in the divine nature that was not only moral, but corporeal, a 'melting union' with God."[19]

---

[17] Ibid., 551.
[18] Ibid., 572.
[19] Ibid., 539.

Appendix 4

Bavinck anticipates Barth's relational understanding of the *imago Dei*, yet in a much more sophisticated and covenantal way. Bavinck maintains that it is humanity-in-community that shows forth the image of God in its fullness. He states, "Full and complete humanity is found in community; humanity as a whole is the image of God—in creation and redemption."[20] "The image of God is much too rich to be realized in a single human being, however richly gifted that human being may be."[21]

While Adam himself was made in the image of God, "male and female he created *them*." (Gen. 1:26, ESV). For Barth the *imago* was to be found in the relationship of a man to his wife, specifically in the distinction of their respective genders. For Bavinck, the *imago* is found in not only that relationship, but in a broader community. "It is not good that the man should be alone (Gen. 2:18). Nor is it good that the man and woman should be alone. Upon the two of them God immediately pronounced the blessing of multiplication (Gen. 1:26)." Bavinck thus sees humanity itself as an organism "that is finally the only fully developed image of God. . . . humanity is the image and likeness of God."[22]

This kind of language may lead one to believe that Bavinck denied that individual human beings are each the image of God. This, however, is not the case.

> Every human person is an organic member of humanity as a whole, and at the same time, in that whole, he or she occupies an independent place of his or her own. . . . Every human being, while a member of the body of humanity as a whole is, at the same time, a unique idea of God, with a significance and a destiny that is eternal.[23]

---

[20] Ibid., 563.
[21] Ibid., 577.
[22] Ibid.
[23] Ibid., 587.

Appendix 4

The notion that humankind only jointly and not severally is the image of God would be disastrous to perceiving value in the most physically and intellectually damaged human beings. Such a collectivistic understanding of the *imago Dei* might even form the basis for a justification of "removing" such people from the collective, so that the image might be improved. Yet an *imago* concept isolated to the collective is hardly what Bavinck had in mind. On the contrary, Bavinck affirms "Every human being is himself or herself an image of God."[24]

There is nothing in Bavinck's treatment of the image of God to indicate that those with severe cognitive disabilities were a part of his theological referent. Yet his broad learning and deep and sophisticated thought lead him to an *imago* doctrine that contains little if anything that would be exclusive of those with severe cognitive disabilities. His covenantal understanding of the *imago*, in fact, binds the destinies of all of God's redeemed people together, making them inseparable from one another: "Every human being is himself or herself an image of God, yet that image is only fully unfolded in humanity as a whole."[25]

While the able-minded might be inclined to think that such a statement means that those with intellectually disabilities will be perfected in the image of God along with them, there is nothing in Bavinck's statement or his theology that would be preclusive of understanding it the other way: apart from them—those with severe cognitive disabilities—we shall not be made perfect.

---

[24] Ibid.
[25] Ibid.

Bibliography

Adamson, James. *The Epistle of James*. Grand Rapids. MI: Eerdmans, 1976.

Alcorn, Randy. *Heaven*. Wheaton, IL: Tyndale House, 2004.

Archdiocese of Baltimore. "Sacramental Preparations for Persons with Disabilities." http://www.archbalt.org/evangelization/disabilities-ministry/sacramental-preparation.cfm (accessed September 26, 2013).

Aristotle. *Nicomachean Ethics*. Translated by Terence Irwin. Indianapolis, IN: Hackett Publishing, 1985.

Augustine. *The Trinity*. Translated by Edmund Hill. Hyde Park, NY: New City Press, 1991.

Barnes, M.P. *Life Expectancy for Those with Disabilities* revised 9th version. Newcastle upon Tyne: International Centre for Neurorehabilitation and Neuropsychiatry, May 2007.

Barth, Karl. *Church Dogmatics*, 3.1–4, "The Doctrine of Creation." Translated by J. W. Edwards, O. Bussey, and H. Knight. Edited by G. W. Bromily and T. F. Torrance. Peabody, MA: Henrickson, 2010 (reprinted).

Basil the Great. *On the Human Condition*. Translated by Nonna Verna Harrison. Crestwood, NY: St. Vladimir's Press, 2005.

Bauckham, Richard J. *Jude, 2 Peter*, Word Biblical Commentary. Waco, TX: Word, 1983.

Bavinck, Herman. *Reformed Dogmatics*, vol. 2, *God and Creation*. Translated by John Vriend. Grand Rapids: Baker Academic, 2006.

Beates, Michael S. *Disability & the Gospel*. Wheaton, IL: Crossway, 2012.

Beckerleg, Catherine Leigh. "The 'Image of God' in Eden: The Creation of Mankind in Genesis 2:5–3:24 in Light of the *mīs pî pīt pî* and *wpt-r* Rituals in Mesopotamia and Ancient Egypt." Ph.D. diss., Harvard University, 2009.

Bekins, Peter. "Non-prototypical Uses of the Definite Article in Biblical Hebrew." *Journal of Semitic Studies* 58, 2 (Autumn 2013): 225–40.

Berinyuu, Abraham. "Healing and Disability." *International Journal of Practical Theology* 8 (2004): 202–11.

Berkhof, Louis. *Principles of Biblical Interpretation*. Grand Rapids, MI: Eerdmans, 1988.

———. *Systematic Theology*. Grand Rapids, MI: Eerdmans, 1982 (reprinted).

Berkman, John. "Are Persons with Profound Intellectual Disabilities Sacramental Icons of Heavenly Life? Aquinas on Impairment." *Studies in Christian Ethics* 26(1) (2013): 83–96.

Berkouwer, G. C. *Man: The Image of God*. Translated by Dirk W. Jellema. Grand Rapids, MI: Eerdmans, 1962.

Berlinski, David. *The Devil's Delusion: Atheism and Its Scientific Pretensions*. New York: Crown Forum, 2008.

Betenbaugh, Helen. *A Theology of Disability*. Dallas, TX: Perkins School of Theology, 1992.

Bishop, Marilyn E., ed. *Religion and Disability: Essays in Scripture, Theology and Ethics*. Kansas City, KS: Sheed & Ward, 1995.

Black, Edwin. *War Against the Weak: Eugenics and America's Campaign to Create a Master Race*. Washington, DC: Dialog Press, 2012.

Blass, F. and A. DeBrunner. *A Greek Grammar of the New Testament and Other Early Christian Literature*. Translated by Robert W. Funk. Chicago: University of Chicago Press, 1961.

Bonaventura. *The Mind's Road to God*. Translated by George Boas. Indianapolis, IN: Bobbs-Merril, 1981.

Bonhoeffer, Dietrich. *Life Together*. Translated by John W. Doberstein. San Francisco: Harper & Row, 1954.

Bibliography

The Book of Church Order of the Orthodox Presbyterian Church. Willow Grove, PA: The Orthodox Presbyterian Church, 2011.

Bourke, Vernon J. ed., *The Essential Augustine.* Indianapolis, IN: Hackett Publishing, 1985.

Botterweck, G. Johannes & Helmer Gringgren, eds. *Theological Dictionary of the Old Testament.* Grand Rapids, MI: Eerdmans, 1974.

Brock, Brian & John Swinton. *Disability in the Christian Tradition: A Reader.* Grand Rapids, MI: Eerdmans, 2012.

Brown, Scott. "Children Destroy Worshipful Atmospheres," http://hopebaptistchurch.info/wp-content/uploads/2013/01/Brown-Children-Destroy-Worshipful-Atmospheres.pdf (accessed on October 3, 2013).

Bruce, F. F. *The Epistles to the Colossians, to Philemon, and to the Ephesians.* Grand Rapids, MI: Eerdmans, 1984.

Bullinger, E. W. *Figures of Speech Used in the Bible.* Grand Rapids, MI: Baker, 1968.

Calvin, John. *Commentary on Genesis 1–31*, vol. 1. Grand Rapids, MI: Christian Classics Ethereal Library, 2005. http://www.ccel.org/ccel/calvin/calcom01.vii.i.html (accessed February 16, 2013).

_____. *Institutes of the Christian Religion.* Translated by Ford Lewis Battles. Edited by John T. McNeill. Philadelphia: Westminster Press, 1960.

Campbell, Kenneth J. "That My House May be Filled: Implementing a Church Ministry with People Impacted by Disabilities." D.Min. thesis, Gordon-Conwell Theological Seminary, 2010.

Cantor, Norman L. *Making Medical Decisions for the Profoundly Mentally Disabled.* Cambridge, MA: MIT Press, 2005.

Cairns, David. *The Image of God in Man.* New York: Philosophical Library, 1953.

Centers for Disease Control. "Autism Spectrum Disorders, Data and Statistics." http://www.cdc.gov/ncbddd/autism/data.html (accessed February 15, 2013).

Churchland, Paul M. *Matter and Consciousness*. Cambridge, MA: MIT Press, 1984.

Clines, D. J. A. "The Image of God in Man." *Tyndale Bulletin* 19 (1968): 53–103.

Clowney, Edmund. *The Church*. Downers Grove, IL: InterVarsity Press, 1995.

Collins, C. John. *Did Adam and Eve Really Exist? Who They Were and Why You Should Care*. Wheaton, IL: Crossway Books, 2011.

Collins, Francis S. *The Language of God*. New York: Free Press, 2006.

Coniaris, Anthony M. *Achieving Your Potential in Christ: Theosis*. Minneapolis, MN: Light and Life Publishing, 1993.

Conn, Harvie M., ed. *Inerrancy and Hermeneutic*. Grand Rapids, MI: Baker, 1988.

Cotter, David W. *Berit Olam Studies in Hebrew Narrative & Poetry in Genesis*. Collegeville, MN: The Liturgical Press, 2003.

Creamer, Deborah. "Finding God in Our Bodies: Theology from the Perspective of People with Disabilities," *Journal of Religion in Disability & Rehabilitation* 2, 1 (1995): 27–42 (part 1); 2, 2 (1995): 67–87 (part 2).

Cross, F. L. & E. A. Livingston, eds. *The Oxford Dictionary of the Christian Church*. Oxford: Oxford University Press, 1983.

Dagg, John L. *Manuel of Theology and Church Order*. Harrisonburg, VA: Gano Books, 1982 (reprinted).

Darwin, Charles. *The Origin of Species*. New York: Signet Classics, 2010 (reprinted). de Vinck, Christopher, *The Power of the Powerless*. New York: Doubleday, 1988.

Doud, John Foster. "Church Accessibility for Person with Disabilities: A Religious Imperative." D.Min. thesis, McCormick Theological Seminary, 1993.

Douma, J. *The Ten Commandments Manual for the Christian Life*. Translated by Nelson D. Kloosterman. Phillipsburg, NJ: P&R Publishing, 1992.

Dumbrell, William J. *Covenant and Creation A Theology of Old Testament Covenants*. New York: Thomas Nelson, 1984.

Ecumenical Disability Advocates Network. "A Church of All and For All: An Interim Statement." *International Review Mission* 93, 370–71 (July—October 2004): 505–25.

Edwards, Paul, ed. *The Encyclopedia of Philosophy*. New York: MacMillan, 1972 (reprinted).

Ehrman, Bart D. *Lost Christianities: Christian Scriptures and the Battles over Authentication*. Chantilly, VA: The Teaching Company, 2002.

Eiesland, Nancy L. *The Disabled God: Toward a Liberation Theology of Disability*. Nashville, TN: Abingdon Press, 1994.

Enns, Peter. *Inspiration and Incarnation: Evangelicals and the Problem of the Old Testament*. Grand Rapids, MI: Baker, 2005.

———. *The Evolution of Adam*. Grand Rapids, MI: Brazos Press, 2012. Ewell, Walter A., ed. *Evangelical Dictionary of Theology*. Grand Rapids, MI: Baker Book House, 1984.

Finlan, Stephen and Vladimir Kharlamov, eds. *Theosis Deification in Christian Theology*, vols. 1 and 2. Eugene, OR: Pickwick Publications, 2006.

Fisher, H. M. *et. al.*, eds. *Doctrinal Treatise, Old German Baptist Brethren*, 3rd ed. Covington, OH: The Vindicator, January 1970.

Fieseler, Nick. *Imago Dei*. Enumclaw, WA: Wine Press, 2012.

Fleischer, Doris Zames & Frieda Zames. *The Disability Rights Movement*. Philadelphia: Temple University Press, 2011.

Frame, John. *Systematic Theology; An Introduction to Christian Belief*. Phillipsburg, NJ: P&R Publishing, 2013.

Friedlander, Henry. *Origins of Nazi Genocide from Euthanasia to the Final Solution*. n.l.: Henry Friedlander, 1995.

Furnham, A., C. Thomas, and K. V. Petrides. "Patient Characteristics and the Allocation of Scarce Medical Resources." *Psychology, Health & Medicine* 7, 1 (2002): 99–106.

Garr, W. Randall. *In His Own Image and Likeness Humanity, Divinity, and Monotheism*. Boston: Brill, 2003.

Gauger, Ann, Douglas Axe, and Casey Luskin. *Science & Human Origins*. Seattle: Discovery Institute, 2012.

Gill, John. *A Body of Doctrinal and Practical Divinity*. London: Whittingham & Rowland, 1815.
Govig, Steward D. *Strong at the Broken Places: Persons with Disabilities and the Church*. Louisville, KY: John Knox Press, 1989.
Glerup, Michael, ed. *The Ancient Christian Texts Commentaries on Genesis 1–3 Severian of Gabala and Bede the Venerable*. Downers Grove, IL: InterVarsity Press, 2008.
Graham, Billy. *How to Be Born Again*. Nashville, TN: Thomas Nelson, 1989.
Guthrie, Donald. *New Testament Theology*. Downers Grove, IL: InterVarsity Press, 1981.
Hall, Douglas J. *Imaging God: Dominion as Stewardship*. Grand Rapids, MI: Eerdmans, 1986.
Haller, Beth A. *Representing Disabilities in an Ableist World*. Louisville, KY: Advocado Press, 2010.
Harrison, Nonna Verna. *God's Many-splendored Image: Theological Anthropology for Christian Formation*. Grand Rapids, MI: Baker Academic, 2010.
Hauerwas, Stanley M. "Christian Care of the Retarded." *Theology Today* 30, 2 (1998): 104–15.
_____. "Community and Diversity: The Tyranny of Normality" in *Journal of Religion Disability & Health* 8, 3/4 (2004): 37–43.
_____. *Suffering Presence: Theology Reflections on Medicine, the Mentally Handicapped, and the Church*. n.l., n.p.: 1986, 159–82.
_____. "Suffering the Retarded: Should We Prevent Retardation?" *Journal of Religion, Disability, and Health* 8, 3/4 (2004): 87–106.
_____. "The Church and the Mentally Handicapped: A Continuing Challenge to the Imagination" in *Journal of Religion, Disability & Health* 8, 3/4 (2004): 53–62.
_____. "The Gesture of a Truthful Story" in *Theology Today* 42, 2 (July 1985): 181–89.
_____. "Timeful Friends: Living with the Handicapped" in *Journal of Religion, Disability & Health*. 8, 3–4 (2004): 11–25.

Hawking, Stephen and Leonard Mladinow. *The Grand Design*. New York: Random House, 2010.

Hendrickson, Laura. *Finding Your Child's Way on the Autism Spectrum*. Chicago: Moody Press, 2009.

Hodge, Charles. *Systematic Theology*. Grand Rapids, MI: Eerdmans, 1982 (reprinted).

Hoekema, Anthony A. *Created in God's Image*. Grand Rapids, MI: Eerdmans, 1986.

Hollinger, Dennis P. *Choosing the Good: Christian Ethics in a Complex World*. Grand Rapids, MI: Baker Academic, 2002.

_____. *The Meaning of Sex: Christian Ethics and the Moral Life*. Grand Rapids, MI: Baker Academic, 2009.

Howard, Thomas Albert, ed. *Imago Dei: Human Dignity in Ecumenical Perspective*. Washington, DC: The Catholic University Press, 2013.

Hubach, Stephanie O. *Same Lake Different Boat: Coming Alongside People Touched by Disability*. Phillipsburg, NJ: P&R Publishing, 2006.

Hughes, Philip Edgcumbe. *The True Image*. Grand Rapids, MI: Eerdmans, 1989.

Hull, John M. "A Spirituality of Disability: The Christian Heritage as Both Problem and Potential." *Studies in Christian Ethics* 16, 2 (2003): 21–35.

Hyman, Susan L. "New DSM-5 Includes Changes to Autism Criteria." *American Academy of Pediatrics News* (June 4, 2013), http://aapnews.aappublications.org/content/early/2013/06/04/aapnews.20130604-1 (accessed September 28, 2013).

Jacobs, Jonathan D. "An Eastern Orthodox Conception of Theosis and Human Nature" *Faith and Philosophy* 26, 5 (2009): 615–27.

Kellicott, William E. *The Social Direction of Human Evolution: An Outline of the Science of Eugenics*. New York: D. Appleton & Company, 1919.

Kiel, C. F. & F. Delitzsch. *Commentary on the Old Testament*, vol. 1, *The Pentateuch*. Grand Rapids, MI: Eerdmans, 1986 (reprinted).

Kipling, Rudyard. *The Works of Rudyard Kipling, Complete & Unabridged.* London: Octopus Books, 1984.

Kline, Meredith G. *Images of the Spirit.* Eugene, OR: Wipf & Stock, 1999 (reprinted).

_____. *Kingdom Prologue.* Overland Park, KS: Two Age Press, 2000.

_____. *The Structure of Biblical Authority,* 2nd ed. South Hamilton, MA: Gordon-Conwell Theological Seminary, 1989.

Kreeft, Peter. *Making Sense of Suffering.* Ann Arbor, MI: Servant Books, 1986.

Kuitert, H. M. *Do You Understand What You Read?* Translated by Lewis B. Smedes. Grand Rapids, MI: Eerdmans, 1970.

Kuhn, Thomas S. *The Structure of Scientific Revolutions.* Chicago: University of Chicago Press, 1962.

Ladd, George Eldon. *A Theology of the New Testament.* Grand Rapids, MI: Eerdmans, 1974.

L'Arche Internationale. "Charter of the Communities of L'Arche." Quebec: General Assembly of the Federation, May 1993, 2, http://www.larcheusa.org//wpcontent/uploads/2011/03/Charter-of-LArche.pdf, 1 (accessed February 2, 2013).

L'Arche USA. "Identity and Mission." http://www.larcheusa.org/who-we-are/identity-and-mission/ (accessed February 2, 2013).

_____. "Who We Are," http://www.larcheusa.org/who-we-are/larche-international-2/ (accessed February 2, 2013).

Lee, Philip J. *Against the Protestant Gnostics.* New York: Oxford University Press, 1987.

Lewis, C. S. *Mere Christianity.* New York: Harper One, 1980 (reprinted).

_____. *The Problem of Pain.* New York: Macmillan, 1962.

_____. *The Weight of Glory.* New York: Harper One, 1980 (reprinted).

Lillback, Peter A. *The Binding of God: Calvin's Role in the Development of Covenant Theology.* Grand Rapids, MI: Baker Academic, 2001.

Louth, Andrew, ed. Ancient Christian Commentary on the Scripture Genesis 1–11, vol. 1, *Old Testament.* Downers Grove, IL: InterVarsity Press, 2008.

Lucas, Greg. *Wrestling with an Angel: A Story of Love, Disability, and the Lessons of Grace.* n.l.: Cruciform Press, 2010.

Lucas, R. C. *The Message of Colossians & Philemon.* Downers Grove, IL: InterVarsity Press, 1980.

Luther, Martin. *A Critical and Devotional Commentary on Genesis.* Translated by John Nicholas Lenker. Minneapolis, MN: Lutherans in All Lands, 1904.

Machen, J. Gresham. *The Christian View of Man.* Carlisle, PA: Banner of Truth, 1984 (reprinted).

Marsh, Michael N. "On Being Disabled." *Modern Believing* 53, 3 (2012): 295–310.

Martin, Jim. "Just Church, An Interview with Jim Martin." *Leadership Journal* (Spring 2013): 17.

Martin, Ralph P. *Ephesians, Colossians, and Philemon.* Atlanta, GA: John Knox Press, 1973.

_____. *James.* Waco, TX: Word Books, 1988.

Mattlin, Ben. *Miracle Boy Grows Up: How the Disabilities Rights Revolution Saved my Sanity.* New York: Sky Horse Publishing, 2012.

Maulik, Pallab K. and Catherine K. Harbour. "Epidemiology of Intellectual Disability." *International Encyclopedia of Rehabilitation,* under "Severity of Disorder," http://cirrie.buffalo.edu/encyclopedia/en/article/144/ (accessed March 8, 2013).

Meilander, Gilbert. *Bioethics, A Primer for Christians*, 2nd ed. Grand Rapids, MI: Eerdmans, 2005.

Messer, Neil. "Healthcare Resource Allocation and the 'Recovery of Virtue.'" *Studies in Christian Ethics* 18.1 (2005): 89–108.

Metaxas, Eric. *Bonhoeffer: Pastor, Martyr, Prophet, Spy.* Nashville, TN: Thomas Nelson, 2010.

Meyer, Stephen C. *Signature in the Cell: DNA and the Evidence for Intelligent Design.* New York: Harper Collins, 2009.

Middleton, Richard J. *The Liberating Image: The* Imago Dei *in Genesis 1.* Grand Rapids, MI: Brazos, 2005.

Moltmann, Jürgen. *God in Creation: A New Theology of Creation and the Spirit of God.* San Francisco: Harper & Row, 1985.

Muller-Fahrenholz, G., ed. *Partners in Life, The Handicapped and the Church*. Geneva: World Council of Churches, 1979.

Murray, John. *Christian Baptism*. Phillipsburg, NJ: Presbyterian & Reformed, 1980.

_____. *Collected Writings of John Murray*, vol. 2, *Systematic Theology*. Carlisle, PA: Banner of Truth, 1977.

_____. *The Imputation of Adam's Sin*. Phillipsburg, NJ: Presbyterian & Reformed, 1959.

_____. *Redemption Accomplished and Applied*. Grand Rapids, MI: Eerdmans, 1982 (reprinted).

Niebuhr, Reinold. *The Nature and Destiny of Man*. New York: Charles Scribner's Sons, 1948.

Nicoll, W. Robertson, ed. *The Expositor's Greek New Testament*. Grand Rapids, MI: Eerdmans, 1988 (reprinted).

Nielson, Kim E. *A Disability History of the United States*. Boston: Beacon Press, 2012.

Nouwen, Henri J. M. *Adam God's Beloved*. Maryknoll, New York: Orbis Books, 1997.

Orr, James. *God's Image in Man*. New York: A.C. Armstrong & Son, 1905.

Palin, David A. *A Gentle Touch: A Theology of Being Human*. London: SPCK, 1992.

Pannenberg, Wolfhart. *Anthropology in Theological Perspective*. Edinburgh: T&T Clark, 1985.

Pelikan, Jeroslav. *The Christian Tradition: A History of the Development of Doctrine*. Chicago: University of Chicago, 1971.

Pinker, Steven. "The Stupidity of Dignity." *The New Republic* (May 28, 2008): 28–31.

Pollock, Horatio. "Eugenics as a Factor in the Prevention of Mental Disease." *Mental Hygiene* 4, 4 (October 1921): 807–12.

Poythress, Vern S. *Symphonic Theology*. Phillipsburg, NN: P&R Publishing, 2001.

Primack, Joel and Nancy Ellen Abrams. *The View from the Center of the Universe*. New York: Riverhead Books, 2006.

Rana, Fazale and Hugh Ross. *Who Was Adam?* Colorado Springs, CO: NavPress, 2005.
Rawls, John. *A Theory of Justice*. Cambridge: President & Fellows of Harvard College, 1971.
Reinders, Hans S. *The Future of the Disabled in Liberal Society: An Analysis*. Notre Dame: University of Notre Dame, 2000.
_____. "Introduction to Intellectual Disability, Genetics and Ethics." *Journal of Intellectual Disability Research* 47, 7 (October 2003): 501–4.
_____, ed. *The Paradox of Disability Responses to Jean Vanier and L'Arche Communities from Theology and the Sciences*. Grand Rapids, MI: Eerdmans, 2010.
_____. *Receiving the Gift of Friendship Profound Disability, Theological Anthropology and Ethics*. Grand Rapids, MI: Eerdmans, 2008.
Richards, Lawrence O., ed. *The Revell Bible Dictionary*. Old Tappan, NJ: Fleming H. Revell, 1990.
Richardson, Alan. *An Introduction to the Theology of the New Testament*. Norwich, England: SCM Press, 2012 (reprinted).
Ridderbos, Herman N. *The Coming of the Kingdom*. Philadelphia: Presbyterian & Reformed, 1962.
_____. *Paul An Outline of His Theology*. Grand Rapids, MI: Eerdmans, 1975.
_____. *When the Time Had Fully Come: Studies in New Testament Theology*. Grand Rapids, MI: Eerdmans, 1957.
Robinson, Dominic. *Understanding the* Imago Dei: *The Thought of Barth, von Balthasar and Moltmann*. Burlington, England: Ashgate Publishing, 2011.
Robinson, James M., ed. *The Nag Hammadi Library*. San Francisco: Harper Collins, 1990.
Romero, Miguel J. "St. Thomas Aquinas on Disability and Profound Cognitive Impairment." Th.D. diss., Duke University, 2012.
Rosen, Christine. *Preaching Eugenics: Religious Leaders and the American Eugenics Movement*. New York: Oxford University Press, 2004.

Routledge, Robin. *Old Testament Theology: A Thematic Approach.* Downers Grove, IL: InterVarsity Press, 2008.

Schaff, Philip, ed. *The Creeds of Christendom.* Grand Rapids, MI: Baker, 1983 (reprinted).

Scougal, Henry. *The Life of God in the Soul of Man.* Harrisonburg, VA: Sprinkle Publications, n.d.

Shedd, William G. T. *Dogmatic Theology.* Nashville, TN: Thomas Nelson, 1980 (reprinted).

Sherlock, Charles. *The Doctrine of Humanity.* Downers Grove, IL: Interarsity Press, 1996.

Singer, Peter. *How Are We to Live?* Amherst, NY: Prometheus Books, 1995.

_____. *Practical Ethics*, 3rd ed. Cambridge: Cambridge University Press, 2011.

_____. *Rethinking Life and Death: The Collapse of Our Traditional Ethics.* New York: St. Martin's Press, 1994.

Smail, Thomas A. "In the Image of the Triune God." *International Journal of Systematic Theology* 5, 1 (March 2003): 22–32.

Smalley, Stephen S. *1, 2, 3 John.* Waco, TX: Word Books, 1984.

Soto, Carlos. "The Veil of Ignorance and Health Resource Allocation." *Journal of Medicine and Philosophy* 37 (2012): 387–404.

Soulen, Kendall R. and Linda Woodhead, eds. *God and Human Dignity.* Grand Rapids, MI: Eerdmans, 2006.

Sproul, R. C. "Galileo Redux." *Tabletalk* (July 2001): 60–61.

Stavropolous, Christoforos. *Partakers of the Divine Nature.* Translated by Stanley Harakas. Minneapolis, MN: Light and Life Publishing, 1976.

Steere, Cathy. *Too Wise to be Mistaken, Too Good to be Unkind.* Sandy Spring, OK: Grace & Truth Books, 2005.

Strange, Alan D. "Understanding the Federal Vision." *New Horizons of the Orthodox Presbyterian Church*, February 2007. http://www.opc.org/nh.html?article_id=478 (accessed September 26, 2013).

Strech, Daniel, Matthis Synofzik, and Georg Marckmann. "How

Physicians Allocate Scarce Resources at the Bedside: A Systematic Review of Qualitative Studies." *Journal of Medicine and Philosophy* 33 (2008): 80–99.

Strong, Augustus H. *Systematic Theology*. Old Tappan, NJ Fleming H. Revell, 1979 (reprinted).

Swinton, John. "The Body of Christ Has Down's Syndrome: Theological Reflections on Vulnerability, Disability, and Graceful Communities." *International Journal of Practical Theology* 13, 2 (2003): 66–78.

_____, and Esther McIntosh. "Persons in Relation: The Care of Persons with Learning Disabilities." *Theology Today* 57, 2 (2001): 175–84.

_____. , ed. *Critical Reflections on Stanley Hauerwas' Theology of Disability*. New York: Routledge, 2004.

_____. "Who is the God We Worship? Theologies of Disability; Challenges and New Possibilities." *International Journal of Practical Theology* 14 (2011): 273–307.

Tada, Joni Eareckson. *Joni*. Grand Rapids, MI: Zondervan, 2001 (reprinted).

Taube, Friedel. "'Not Stupid Just Different': Raising Awareness of Down Syndrome." Deutsche Welle. http://www.dw.de/not-stupid-just-different-raising-awareness-of-down-syndrome/a-16825825 (accessed September 7, 2013).

Temple University. "Disability History Timeline." http://isc.temple.edu/neighbor/ds/disabilityrightstimeline.htm (accessed February 25, 2013).

Thompson, J. A. ed. *Handbook of Life in Bible Times*. Downers Grove, IL: InterVarsity Press, 1986.

Thompson, John L., ed. *Reformation Commentary on the Scriptures of the Old Testament*, vol. 1, *Genesis 1–11*. Downers Grove, IL: InterVarsity Press, 2012.

Tripp, Paul David. *Dangerous Calling: Confronting the Unique Challenges of the Pastoral Ministry*. Wheaton, IL: Crossway Books, 2012.

_____. *Instruments in the Redeemer's Hands.* Phillipsburg, NJ: P&R Publishing, 2002. Van Drunen. *Natural Law and the Two Kingdoms: A Study in the Development of Reformed Social Thought.* Grand Rapids, MI: Eerdmans, 2010.

Van Gemeren. *The Progress of Redemption.* Grand Rapids, MI: Zondervan, 1988.

Van Til, Cornelius. *Christianity and Barthianism.* Philadelphia: Presbyterian & Reformed, 1962.

_____. *The Defense of the Faith*, 3rd ed. Philadelphia: Presbyterian & Reformed, 1967.

Vanier, Jean. *Becoming Human.* Toronto: Anansi Press, 1998.

_____. *The Challenge of L'Arche.* London: Darton, Longman & Todd, 1989.

_____. *Encountering the Other.* Mahwah, NJ: Paulist Press, 2005.

_____. *The Heart of L'Arche.* Toronto: Novalis Publishing, 2012.

Versteeg, J. P. *Adam in the New Testament: Mere Teaching Model or Historical Man?* Translated by Richard B. Gaffin Jr. Phillipsburg, NJ: P&R Publishing, 2012.

Visser, Sandra and Thomas Williams. *Anselm.* New York: Oxford University Press, 2009.

Vlachos, Hierotheos. *Orthodox Spirituality, A Brief Introduction.* Translated by Effie Mavromichali. Levadia, Greece: Birth of the Theotokos Monastery, 1994.

Volpe, Medi Ann. "Irresponsible Love: Rethinking Intellectual Disability, Humanity, and the Church." *Modern Theology* 25:3 (July 2009), 491–501.

von Rad, Gerhard. *Genesis, A Commentary* revised ed. Philadelphia: Westminster Press, 1973.

_____. *Old Testament Theology.* Translated by D. G. M. Stalker. San Francisco: Harper and Row, 1962.

Vos, Geerhardus. *Biblical Theology Old and New Testaments.* Carlisle, PA: Banner of Truth, 1975 (reprinted).

_____. *The Pauline Eschatology.* Phillipsburg, NJ: Presbyterian & Reformed, 1986 (reprinted).

Waldron, Samuel E. *A Modern Exposition of the 1689 Baptist Confession of Faith*. Durham, England: Evangelical Press, 1989.

Waltke, Bruce K. and M. O'Connor. *An Introduction to Biblical Hebrew Syntax*. Winona Lake, IN: Eisenbrauns, 1990.

Ware, Kallistos. *The Orthodox Way*. Crestwood, NY: St. Vladimir's Seminary Press, 1979.

Ware, Timothy, *The Orthodox Church*. New York: Penguin Books, 1993.

Weikart, Richard. *From Darwin to Hitler: Evolutionary Ethics, Eugenics, and Racism in Germany*. New York: Palgrave Macmillan, 2004.

Welch, Edward T. *Shame Interrupted*. Greensboro, NC: New Growth Press, 2012.

_____. *What Do You Think of Me? Why Do I Care?* Greensboro, NC: New Growth Press, 2011.

Wenham, Gordon J. *Genesis 1–15*, Word Biblical Commentary. Waco, TX: Word, 1987.

Williams, Ronald J. *Williams' Hebrew Syntax*, 3rd ed. Toronto: University of Toronto Press, 2007.

_____. *Hebrew Syntax: An Outline*, 2nd ed. Toronto: University of Toronto Press, 1986.

Index of Scripture

Genesis
1—93, 138, 141, 156, 158–59, 163, 165, 177n27
1:1—164n3
1–2—78, 126
1–3—90
1:1–2:3—93
1:11–12—80
1:20—150, 164
1:21—1, 150, 164
1:22—164, 167
1:24—150, 164, 266
1:25—150
1:26—53, 76, 81, 91, 143, 145n20, 146n22, 168, 168n3, 169n8, 172n18, 198, 257, 270
1:26–27—21, 53, 59, 76, 77, 78, 80, 84, 90, 126, 137–39, 141–42, 145n20, 146, 148, 172n18, 261
1:26–28—87
1:26–31—125
1:27—258
1:27—53, 141, 143, 146, 146n22, 159, 165, 168, 172, 172n18
1:28—164, 166–67
1:31—44, 56, 164, 173
2—165, 177
2–3—77, 146n22
2:5–3:24—77
2:7—125, 150, 164–65, 187
2:9—178
2:17—177–78
2:18—270
2:19–20—168
2:20—168
2:22—125
3—44, 122, 144, 159
3:1—165
3:1–5—144, 174
3:5—81, 144–45
3:7—180
3:8–11—180
3:12—180
3:15—178
3:17–19—180
3:18—178, 186
3:18–19—179
3:19—179, 180
3:23–24—178
4:10—112
5—159
5:1—90, 141–43, 149
5:1–2—87
5:3—79, 81, 138, 148–49, 151, 160, 198
8:21—185
9—157, 160
9:6—4, 30, 59n, 90, 138, 145–47, 159, 191, 197, 261
9:6–7—87

Exodus
3:14—10, 166
4:11—112
6:3—142

Index of Scripture

25:18—145n20
26:1—145n20

Leviticus
19:14—202
21:16-23—190

Deuteronomy
4:15-19—138
5:8—145n20
10:18—47
27:18—202

1 Samuel
6:5, 11—138

1 Kings
6:20—191
12:28—145n20

2 Kings
10:29—145n20
11:18—138
16:10—141

2 Chronicles
23:17—138

Nehemiah
8:1-3—190

Job
1:6—165
29:15—203
38:1-7—165

Psalms
8—143
19:1-4—229
38:12—13n32
39:7—138
73:20—138
115—139
115:4-8—139
123:2—199
135:18—157
146:4—188

Proverbs
6:6-11—179

Isaiah
40:25—161
46:5—161
53—86
53:2-3—226
53:10—150

Ezekiel
7:20—138
16:17—138
23:14—138

Daniel
2-3—138
12:3—149

Amos
5:26—138

Matthew
3:7—165
4—186
4:17—189
4:23—189
4:23-24—203
4:24—204
8:5-16—204
10:8—209n85
12:34—165
14:2—209n85
14:14—204
15:22—204
15:30—204
16:21—210n85
17:9—209n85
17:15—7
17:23—210n85
20:16—230
20:28—91
21:14—204
23:33—165
25:34-40—47, 229
25:40-45—203
26:32—210n85
26:34—210n85
26:48—186
27:52—209n85
27:64—210n85
28:7—210n85

Mark
2:1-12—204
3:10—204

5:25–30—204
5:38–43—208
6:14—209n85
6:13—208
12:26—209n85
14:28—210n85
15:17—186
16:6—210n85

Luke
2:8–11—44
3:38—126n, 197
5:15—204
5:32—258
6:17–19—204
7:22—209n85
8:47—204
9:7—209n85
9:41—186
10:33–34—208
14:1–4—204
16:30—209n85
16:31—209n85
17:11–14—204
20:34–36—176
20:37—209n85
22:51—204
23:46—186
24:4—185
24:6—210n85
24:14—210n85
24:25–27—188
24:44–47—188

John
1:12–13—81, 197
2:22—210n85
3:2—189
3:16—93
4:46–54—208
4:47—204
5:1–15—203n70
5:21—209n85
5:6—184, 204
5:29—149
7:39—150n27
8:44—165
8:46—186
9:1–2—182
9:3—182
11:12—209n85
11:43–44—201
12:1—209n85
12:9—209n85
12:17—209n85
14:18—150n27
20:12—185
21:14—210n85

Acts
3:15—209n85
4:10—209n85
5:30—209n85
8:9–24—203
10:40—209n85
13:30—209n85
13:37—209n85

15:11—212
17:26—155
17:28–29—191, 197
17:29—155
26:8—209n85

Romans
1:18–25—181
1:18–32—157
1:23—139
3:23—185, 198
3:28—198
4:24—209n85
4:25—210n85
5—185
5:1—199
5:12—177, 180, 185, 198
5:12–14—179
5:13—198
6—152
6:4—210n85
6:9—210n85
6:10—151
6:13–19—199
7:4—210n85
8—113
8:3—151
8:11—209n85
8:18—227
8:20–21—44
8:22—226

Index of Scripture

8:23—195, 226
8:29—148, 192, 227
8:29–30—187
8:30—198–99
8:34—210n85
9:11–20—202
9:18—204
10:9—209n85
13:14—152

1 Corinthians
1:27–31—223
2:26—209n85
2:27—209n85
5:25–26—222
6:3—144, 157, 230
6:14—209n85
10:18—154
10:20—154
11:7—90, 144, 172
12:4–8—229
12:10—155
12:12–27—225
12:18–24—96
12:22–23—114
15—174, 178, 185
15:5—227
15:12—2015n85
15:15—209n85
15:20—210n85
15:29—209n85
15:32—209n85
15:35—209n85
15:49—227
15:52—209n85
15:53–54—230
15:13—210n85
15:16—149, 210n85
15:17—149
15:22—149
15:28—194
15:37—209n85
15:42—209n85
15:44—209n85
15:45—150
15:45–49—149, 160
15:48–49—160
15:49—148, 151, 160, 187, 212

2 Corinthians
1:7—154
1:9—209n85
2:16—217
3:13, 18—193
3:17—150
3:17–18—148
3:18—151, 187
4:4—148, 186
4:14—209n85
4:16—212
5:15—210n85
5:17—188, 226
5:21—186
5:27—153
10:12—219
11:3—165

Galatians
1:1—209n85
3:22—198

Ephesians
1:4—201
1:20—209n85
2—86
2:1—201
2:1–3—185
2:3—198
2:3–7—81
4:4–16—229
4:13—219
4:24—259

Philippians
2—95
2:6—81
2:7—151
3:10–11—192
3:10–12—188
3:21—192, 194, 212

Colossians
1:13—152
1:15—148, 150, 152, 161, 174, 186
1:18—174
1:27—152
2:9—151–52
2:12—209n85
3:4—152

3:9—161
3:9–10—151–52, 261
3:10—57, 161, 212

1 Thessalonians
1:10—209n85

1 Timothy
1:3–6—134
5:21—185

2 Timothy
2:5—227
2:8—210n85

Titus
1:2—161
3:5—151, 199

Hebrews
1—230
1:2—148n25
1:3—148n25
1:4—144
1:14—144
2:5–14—230
2:6–11—230
2:6–15—138
2:7–9—157
2:13—150
2:16—144, 185
2:17—188
4:15—131n281, 186
5:7—186
6:18—161
7:26—186
10:5—161
11:9—209n85
12:14—198

James
1:25—215
3:9—59n33, 90, 144–47, 160, 191, 197, 261
5:14–15—207, 209

1 Peter
1:1–2—185
1:3—151, 199
1:10–12—144
1:21—209n85
1:23—151, 199
4:11—229
5:1—154

2 Peter
1:3–4—154
1:4—81, 153, 157, 161, 191, 193n52, 198

1 John
3:1—153
3:2—212, 230

Jude
1:5—155
1:14—126n265

Revelation
1—189
1:13—150
1:14–26—193
7—228
20—165
20:1—165
21:1–5—44
21:1–7—190
21:4—113
21:5—191
21:16—191

4 Maccabees
15:2—148n25

Index of Subjects and Names

abortion, 110, 230
Adam, 9, 12, 15, 56, 67, 74, 80–81, 89, 97–99, 116, 121, 123–30, 132, 138, 147–52, 168, 172, 174–76, 178–80, 184, 186–87, 191–92, 197–98, 211, 257, 259, 267–70
age of accountability, 116
Americans with Disabilities Act, 32–35
analogia entis, xiii, 1, 21, 51–52, 170
analogia relationis, xiii, 2, 21, 43, 51, 62, 170
ancient Near East, 22, 50, 62, 73–78, 91–93, 131, 208
Angelman syndrome, 173, 200
Anselm of Canterbury, 13
Athanasius, 153
Augustine of Hippo, xii, 10–11, 13, 55, 67, 118, 166, 171, 266
Autism Spectrum Disorder, 6, 221–22, 229

baptism, 86, 116, 203–7, 210
Barmen Declaration, 29

Barth, Karl, xiii, xvii, 2, 21–23, 44, 49, 50–54, 56, 59, 62, 64–65, 69, 71, 81, 105, 111, 131, 163, 170–71, 173, 259, 262–63, 265, 270
Basil, 9, 168, 213
Bauckham Richard, 157
Beates, Michael, 112–14, 118
Beckerleg, Catherine, 22, 77–81, 156, 191
Bede, 10, 12–13
Behr, John, 4, 192
Berkouwer, G.C., 22, 56–58, 64, 75, 85, 171
body of Christ, 89–90, 101, 114, 127, 194, 225, 228
Bonaventure, 13, 67, 95
Buck, Carrie, 27

Calvin, John, 16–17, 57, 184, 193, 204, 212
Cantor, Norman, 33, 34
Carnegie Institute, 27–28
church, xi, xiv–xv, xxi, 7, 12, 14, 19, 21–22, 26, 28–30, 34–35, 39, 43, 46, 48, 50, 62, 88–89,

Index of Subjects and Names

93–94, 96, 100–4, 106, 108–9, 118, 123, 132, 134–35, 149, 151, 166, 170, 178, 183, 189, 192–94, 204–9, 211–13, 216–30, 240–41, 244
Chytraeus, David, 18
Clark, Gordon, 175
Clines, D. J. A., 22, 73–76, 79, 142, 262
Collins, C. John, 128
Collins, Francis, 123, 129–30, 132
crucifixion, 107, 188–89, 229–30

Darwin, Charles, 24–26, 123, 125, 130
Davenport, Charles, 26–28
death, xi, 4, 19–20, 42–43, 50, 89–90, 97, 107, 113, 117, 120, 127–29, 174, 176, 179–80, 186–88, 190, 193, 206, 209, 217–18, 229–30, 257, 268
Deutsche Christens movement, 28–31
Diadochus, 9
Disabilities Rights Movement, 29, 32–36, 39, 44, 183, 218
disability theologians, xxi, 44, 49, 56, 58, 94, 106, 109–10, 112, 134, 163
divine nature, 81, 91, 153, 191, 198, 260, 269
Douma, Jochem, 180
Down syndrome, 53, 118–19, 174, 180, 200, 207, 222, 227

Eden, 77–78, 156, 186, 191
Eisland, Nancy, 106–8, 113, 123, 183–84, 187, 189–190
Enns, Peter, 125–28, 130, 132
Epicurus, 178
eschaton, 75, 107, 113, 131, 176, 189, 191, 227
eugenics, xi, 26, 28, 30–31
Eugenics Record Office, 27

faith, 1, 44, 83, 101, 115–16, 127, 134, 149, 167, 198–200, 204–8, 210, 219, 261
firstborn, 148, 150, 152, 174
Fletcher, Joseph, 100
fragile X syndrome, 111
Frame, John, 290

Gaffin, Richard, 127–28
Galton, Francis, 24, 26, 31
Garr, Randall, 50, 140–43, 145
Gauger, Ann, 130–31
God, xi–xv, xvii–xix, xxi, xxvi–xxvii, 1–5, 7–24, 29–30, 36–37, 42, 44, 46–93, 95–96, 98–99, 101–3, 105–16, 118–26, 128–31, 133–34, 137–53, 156, 163–78, 180–82, 184–95, 197–7, 209–16, 218–19, 223–24, 226, 228–32, 241, 246–48, 251–71

Hall, Douglas, 22, 81–83, 85–86, 169, 262

Index of Subjects and Names

Hauerwas, Stanley, 21, 26, 99–106, 199
Hawking, Stephen, 180–81
Hinter, Russell, 171
historical Adam debate, 45, 49, 132
Hitler, Adolph, 26, 28–29, 40, 218
Hodge, Charles, 19, 175, 201
Hoekema, Anthony, 8, 14, 16, 22, 59, 60–61, 122, 170, 211
Hollinger, Dennis, 176
Holmes, Oliver Wendell, 27
Holy Spirit, 69, 75, 86, 89, 137, 145, 150, 193, 196, 199, 203, 224, 229, 256–58, 269
Hubach, Stephanie, 118–22, 183
Hughes, Philip, ix, 22, 64–66, 141, 148

image of God
imago Dei, xii–xiv, xxi, 1–7, 9–22, 29–31, 33, 43–46, 48–50, 52–56, 58–70, 72, 74–76, 81–94, 97, 100, 105, 109, 113–14, 118, 122–23, 127, 130–33, 135, 137, 140, 143–44, 149, 151–52, 163–66, 168–74, 177, 180–83, 185–89, 192, 195, 197, 211–16, 226, 230, 240, 251–52, 255–56, 258, 260–64, 266, 270–71
imago Dei, functional view, xiii–xiv, 10–12, 21–22, 44, 59, 68, 70–71, 76, 81, 87, 163, 166, 168–69, 173, 187, 213–14, 246–48, 251–53, 257–58, 262–63, 266
imago Dei, relational view, xiv, 4, 21–23, 71, 81, 105, 131, 163, 171, 173, 187, 213–14, 246–48, 251–53, 258–59, 262–63, 270
imago Dei, substantive view, xiii–xiv, 1, 7, 15, 18–19, 21–22, 29, 44, 67, 70, 83, 123, 133, 140, 152, 163, 166, 173, 187, 213–14, 246, 248, 251–53, 255–57, 262–64
imago Trinitatis, 67
intellect, xii–xiv, 2, 8–9, 11–15, 17–22, 29, 38, 43, 45–46, 49, 53–54, 58, 65, 67, 75, 84, 109, 123, 130, 132, 167–68, 173, 178, 180, 200, 202, 211, 213, 225, 246–47, 254, 256, 260, 263–64, 266
Intelligent Design Movement, 129
Irenaeus, 8

Jesus Christ, xi, xiii–xv, 6, 8, 16–18, 31, 34, 44, 57–61, 63–69, 74–76, 81, 85–86, 89–90, 95–96, 98, 101–3, 105–8, 113–14, 117, 120, 127, 131, 135, 138, 142, 148–54, 174, 176–77, 182, 184–95, 197–200, 203–6, 208–10, 212, 216, 219, 223–24, 226–32, 256–58, 261, 268–69

Kellicot, William E., 25
kingdom of God, 103, 120, 152–53, 189–90, 203, 260

Index of Subjects and Names

Kline, Meredith, 22, 75–76, 80, 137, 143, 145, 148, 171, 196–97
Kuhn, Thomas, 162
Kuitert, H. M., 122, 125

language, xvii, 2, 49, 6–67, 71–72, 74, 85, 95, 104, 119, 130–31, 136–37, 149–50, 152, 167, 172, 174, 180, 183, 193, 200, 208, 246–47, 257, 262, 270
Laughlin, Harry H., 28
Lewis, C. S., 16, 122, 124, 181, 184, 196
Liberation Theology, 106, 189
Lucas, Greg, 114–16, 118, 122, 205
Luther, Martin, xi, 15–18, 29–30, 77, 134, 146, 197, 212, 218, 268

Machen, J. Gresham, 20
Meillaender, Gilbert, 171
Middleton, J. Richard, 6–7, 22, 90–93, 136, 177
Moltmann, Jürgen, 22–23, 61–64
Müller, Ludwig, 28

Nazi, 26, 30, 35
Neibuhr, Reinhold, 53–54, 56
Nouwen, Henri, 58, 97–100

Origen, 8–9
Orr, James, 19–20

palatoschisis, 111, 173
Pinker, Steven, 5, 192, 215

Pollock, Horatio, 26
Poythress, Vern, 290
Prader-Willi syndrome, 16
Primack, Joel, 162
Princeton Seminary, 19–20

Rana, Fazale, 130–31
Rauschenbusch, Walter, 30
Rawls, John, 41
reason, xxv, xxvii, 2, 4, 9–10, 12–14, 16, 26, 30–31, 42, 44, 54, 57, 71–72, 81, 84–85, 90, 110, 120, 128, 130, 147, 177, 213, 224, 258, 260, 265
regeneration, 61, 151, 199–200, 232
Reinders, Hans, 3, 14, 21, 23–24, 34–35, 39, 53, 70, 106, 109–12, 134, 183, 214, 263
resource allocation, 39–43
resurrection, xiii, 14, 44, 89–90, 99, 107–8, 127, 148–51, 153, 174, 186–88, 192, 199, 209, 226, 228–29, 257
revelation, 290
Richardson, Alan, 125

sacraments, 205–7
Septuagint, xxiii, 59, 142
Sherlock, Charles, 22, 87–90, 129–30, 172–73, 262
similitudo, 8, 10, 12, 16
sin, xiv, 10, 44, 55, 57, 59, 63, 69, 82, 85, 88–89, 95, 98, 103, 106–8, 110, 112–18, 121–22, 127–32,

138, 145–48, 151, 153, 173, 179, 182, 184–86, 195, 197–99, 201, 205–6, 208, 211–12, 226, 256–57, 259, 261, 268
Singer, Peter, xi, xxvi, 4–5, 42–43, 48, 100, 132, 192, 214, 218
Social Gospel, 30–31
Soto, Carlos, 41–42
surd evil, 44, 98, 179–80, 182, 184–87, 218
Swinton, John, 11, 16–17, 21, 34, 99–100, 104–6, 109, 146

Tada, Joni Eareckson, xi, 35–36
temptation, 78, 144–45, 174
theodicy, 178–79

theosis, 7, 64, 153–54, 191–95, 269
Thomas Aquinas, 4, 13–15, 28, 41, 53, 67, 162, 168, 171–72, 192, 200
transvaluation, 106
Trinity, 290

Vanier, Jean, 37, 49, 53, 94–100, 109, 224, 227
Van Til, Cornelius, 175
virtue ethics, 48, 99
Vos, Geerhardus, 20, 149
Vulgate, xxiii, 13, 59, 142

Westminster Standards, 153, 206

Zwingli, Ulrich, 17–18

George C. Hammond is the pastor of Bethel Presbyterian Church in Leesburg, Virginia and a Teaching Fellow for the C. S. Lewis Institute's Fellows Program, Loudoun campus. A graduate of Westminster (M.Div., 1992) and Gordon-Conwell (D.Min., 2014) theological seminaries, he has served his Presbytery as chairman of the Committee on Candidates and Credentials, and as a member of the Committee on Home Missions and Church Extension, and his community as former Senior Police Chaplain of the Leesburg Police Department. He resides in a suburb of Washington, DC, with his wife, Donna, and their four children, of which Rebecca is the youngest.

Available in the Reformed Academic Dissertation Series

◆

How Should We Treat Detainees? An Examination of "Enhanced Interrogation Techniques" under the Light of Scripture and the Just War Tradition,
by J. Porter Harlow

From Inscrutability to Concursus: Benjamin B. Warfield's Theological Construction of Revelation's Mode from 1880 to 1915,
by Jeffrey A. Stivason

Marks of Saving Grace: Theological Method and the Doctrine of Assurance in Jonathan Edwards's A Treatise Concerning Religious Affections,
by Eric J. Lehner

The Triune God of Unity in Diversity: An Analysis of Perspectivalism, the Trinitarian Theological Method of John Frame and Vern Poythress,
by Timothy E. Miller

It Has Not Yet Appeared What We Shall Be: A Reconsideration of the Imago Dei *in Light of Those with Severe Cognitive Disabilities,*
by George C. Hammond

Forthcoming

Preaching with Biblical Motivation: How to Incorporate the Motivation Found in the Inspired Preaching of the Apostles into Your Sermons,
by Ray E. Heiple Jr.

The Doctrine of the Spirituality of the Church in the Ecclesiology of Charles Hodge,
by Alan D. Strange

Forthcoming (cont.)

The Trinity, Language, and Human Behavior:
A Reformed Exposition of the Language Theory of Kenneth L. Pike,
by Pierce Taylor Hibbs

"King of Israel" and "Do Not Fear, Daughter of Zion":
The Use of Zephaniah 3 in John 12,
by Christopher S. Tachick

A Development Not a Departure: The Lacunae in the
Debate of the Doctrine of the Trinity and Gender Roles,
by Hongyi Yang

Free to Be Sons of God
by Geoffrey M. Ziegler

www.ingramcontent.com/pod-product-compliance
Lightning Source LLC
LaVergne TN
LVHW040612250326
834688LV00035B/524